This book is a must read for all health care professionals and students who wish to touch again the reasons they went into the healing profession in the first place. It will make you cry, it will make you laugh and throughout, in deeply human terms, it will let you know again the true meaning of caring. Thank you, Sue Hassmiller, for this vivid and compelling reminder that in medical care, there should be nothing about us without us!
—Donald Berwick, MD, MPP, Lecturer of Health Care Policy,
Department of Health Care Policy, Harvard Medical School;
President Emeritus and Senior Fellow,Institute for Healthcare Improvement;
Former Administrator of the Centers for Medicare & Medicaid Services

A poignant, raw, vitally true portrait of what grief and loss really feel like. I know—I lost my wife suddenly. Sue Hassmiller's journey of tragic loss and finding the path again can help you understand what you're going through and help point you toward hope in the midst of tragedy.
—Lewis G. Sandy, MD, Executive Vice President,
Clinical Advancement, UnitedHealth Group

Through all the stages of our life, there may be a time when loss, sudden or expected, happens. This book is a riveting account of loss but also gives us a refreshing account of hope that we will be able to come through the experience with new perspectives.
—Alicia Georges, RN, EdD, FAAN, National Volunteer President, AARP;
Chair, Department of Nursing, Lehman College/ City University of New York

It took the tragic loss of Sue's husband and best friend, Bob, and the care of two extraordinary nurses, to reveal to her something that was missing in her deep understanding of patient care—the imperative of the human connection, of how compassion bolsters providers' clinical skills. This book eloquently describes why, as Bob's legacy, she has turned her brainpower and her heart to the mission of keeping compassion in healthcare front and center.
—Bonnie Barnes, FAAN, Co-founder and Chief Executive Officer,
The DAISY Foundation

A must-read book about love and heartbreaking loss with action steps that bridge pain to a future of hope, second chances, and the "gift" of re-settled happiness. Sue's story with Bob is a gift of endless love, unfreezing fear, and grief to forward actions and new opportunities.

—Bethany Hall-Long PhD, RNC, FAAN, Delaware Lt. Governor
and Professor of Nursing, University of Delaware

I followed Sue's blog in its entirety. It made such an impact on me as a nurse leader. Last October. she presented, along with two of Bob's nurses, at a major nursing conference about the experience. She said the U.S. has many good clinically competent nurses, but we are lacking great clinically competent caring nurses who most importantly, also have great compassion. Since becoming president of Chamberlain University I have told Sue's story at each of our twenty-one campuses during our town halls, emphasizing the importance of a culture of care. It resonates with every single nurse and nursing student I share this with!

—Karen Cox PhD, RN, FACHE, FAAN,
President, Chamberlain University

Sue unexpectedly found herself in the valley and found a way where there seemed to be no way. Her vulnerable and honest perspective is a gift to anyone journeying through their own suffering.

—Dan Greco, Pastor,
Lifetree Community Church, Robbinsville, New Jersey

Resetting

Resetting

An Unplanned Journey of Love, Loss, and Living Again

SUSAN B. HASSMILLER

NEW YORK

LONDON • NASHVILLE • MELBOURNE • VANCOUVER

Resetting

An Unplanned Journey of Love, Loss, and Living Again

Published in New York, New York, by Morgan James Publishing. Morgan James is a trademark of Morgan James, LLC. www.MorganJamesPublishing.com

ISBN 9781642796346 paperback
ISBN 9781642796353 eBook
Library of Congress Control Number: 2019943530

Cover Design by:
Chris Treccani
www.3dogcreative.net

Interior Design by:
Christopher Kirk
www.GFSstudio.com

Unless otherwise noted, Scripture is taken from the Holy Bible, New International Version®, NIV® copyright ©1973, 1978, 1984, 2011 by Biblica, Inc.® Used by permission. All rights reserved worldwide.

Morgan James is a proud partner of Habitat for Humanity Peninsula and Greater Williamsburg. Partners in building since 2006.

Get involved today! Visit
MorganJamesPublishing.com/giving-back

To all who came to my rescue, may you receive back all the love
and compassion you so generously bestowed on me.

To John Robert and Abigail Grace, never forget that your Pops loved you both
like no other and he will watch over you in your darkest days
as well as through all your triumphs and celebrations

CONTENTS

FOREWORD

*W*hen Sue Hassmiller approached me about writing the foreword for her book, a compilation of the blog entries she wrote during her husband's tragic accident, his death, and the subsequent years of grief and healing that followed, I was both honored and intimidated.

In addition to being a dear friend, Sue is one of the most compassionate and committed leaders I've had the privilege of working with in over eleven years of service with the American Red Cross. From my perspective, it always seemed that the Red Cross mission—to prevent and alleviate human suffering—was fundamental to the identities of both Sue and her beloved late-husband, Bob. I was humbled that someone I admired so dearly had asked me to contribute to her book, because the personal and emotionally powerful words Sue shared in her blog had affected me deeply. It seemed a daunting task to give her writings the proper introduction her words deserved.

So with that in mind, perhaps the best way I can begin is to explain that to fully understand the depth of emotion in Sue's writings, you need to first understand a bit more about the relationship that existed between Sue and Bob.

Everyone at the Red Cross who knew Bob knew two things: Bob had an unbelievable sense of dedication to our organization's humanitarian mission, and he was absolute and unwavering in his love and commitment to Sue. One of my favorite Red Cross stories deals with the role our storied institution played in helping to bring these two soul mates together.

As Sue describes in this book, she first started volunteering with the Red Cross when she was in college, after the organization helped her locate her parents in the aftermath of a terrible earthquake in Mexico. Sue soon fell deeply in love with our mission. In fact, she was so committed to the Red Cross that when Bob asked her out for the very first date, Sue told him she wouldn't go out with anyone unless he was involved with the American Red Cross. Bob was so smitten he quickly went to his local Red Cross and signed up for sailing lessons. He proudly showed his certificate to Sue, and thus began their incredible relationship.

As the couple progressed through their professional years and began a family together, they both become increasingly involved with the Red Cross. Sue's incredible commitment to and advocacy for nursing led her to become one of our most respected and highly-regarded leaders. Similarly, Bob was also recognized and loved throughout our organization for his wonderful spirit of volunteerism.

Bob served as the Chair of the Charlottesville Virginia Board of the Red Cross, where he was a regular blood donor and a member of our local Disaster Action Team. These volunteers are the lifeblood of the American Red Cross. They are deployed within minutes of a local disaster, often waking up in the middle of the night to respond to home fires and other tragedies. They provide food, shelter, comfort, and hope to people facing some of the most difficult situations imaginable.

After Bob retired, he became very engaged with the Red Cross in New Jersey. He was the volunteer partner for the local Disaster Services team and the lead for all the faith-based partnerships for the region. Of course, Bob also continued to work tirelessly as a Disaster Action Team volunteer, helping to respond to hundreds of events in Camden and other communities.

Bob's compassion, quick-thinking, and beautiful sense of humor were such tremendous gifts to everyone at the Red Cross, and his loss was felt deeply within our organization. In the days after his passing, our team in New Jersey held a smoke alarm installation event in Camden in Bob's honor. They went door-to-door, installing free smoke alarms in homes located in many of the same neighborhoods Bob had personally touched as a disaster volunteer. So many of the residents whom the Red Cross helped that day spoke of how they remembered Bob as a caring and compassionate man, and as a seemingly constant presence in their neighborhood during times of emergency. I can think of no greater testament to his character.

When I learned Bob had died, I was heartbroken. I experienced such incredible sadness, because I had not only lost a friend, but also, the Red Cross (and the world at large) had lost one of the most service-oriented people I had ever met. Most of all, I was heartbroken for Sue, because I know she and Bob were each other's everything.

When Sue first started writing her blog, it was an incredibly difficult experience to read her updates. She didn't pull any punches, and it was painful to know the excruciating hurt and loss my friend was facing. At various times while reading her blog, it seemed to me that Sue was truly broken, and there were those of us who knew her well who thought she might never recover.

But day-by-day, and word-by-word, Sue's writings became less a journey of despair and instead, one of hope and resilience. The experiences she so honestly describes in this book serve as an important example in learning how to carry on through the grief, both big and small, we each face. While reading Sue's words of pain, perseverance, faith, and love, I've found myself reexamining the blessings in my own life with a renewed sense of gratitude, mindfulness, and hope for the future.

While I am certain Sue will never stop grieving the loss of her husband and best friend, I know she faces each day with a thankful heart for the life they shared together. And for my own part, I remain filled with admiration for Bob's remarkable legacy of compassion and caring, which continues to live on in all those he touched.

For those who have experienced love and loss, this book is a must-read. You'll find that it gives you the courage and strength to go on. The setbacks, the tears, the determination, and eventual journey of healing Sue experienced hold lessons for us all.

Gail McGovern
President and CEO
American Red Cross

Left to right: Matt Oley, Kimberly Hassmiller Oley, Susan Hassmiller, Gail McGovern, Mark Robert Hassmiller

INTRODUCTION

*T*his is a journal of grief—the deepest, most painful and honest kind. It is also a love story. The kind of story everyone hopes to live (with the exception of its ending). For thirty-seven years, I lived with my best friend and greatest love, Bob. He loved, cherished and protected me just as he promised he would on our wedding day, but he also taught me deep lessons about life and always made me laugh until he lost his life as a result of a bicycle accident.

Neither of us was perfect, but we somehow found each other—a perfect union of two imperfect beings. No one should ever have to lose a love so great, but I have learned that we all ultimately experience loss. You don't really think about it so much until it happens to you. I find myself saying, "Now that I know people REALLY die, I pay more attention"—an odd statement coming from a nurse.

I kept this journal initially to get information out to our friends and family after the accident occurred, so that I could prioritize being at my husband's side 24/7. I found that journaling about the accident and my feelings surrounding it helped me to grieve.

After I was home and it was all over, I continued to pour out my feelings and profound grief to more than one thousand people who signed up to receive my blog. Little by little, I began to hear from people who read my blog about how much my words were helping them. Some told me they could not start their work day until they read my blog. My words contained lessons for their own lives, thoughts about how to handle their own or another's grief, and how to pay more attention to loved ones. Many readers told me to keep writing because my words were helping them and their loved ones. Their encouragement sustained me and still does. For over a year, I wrote until I felt it was time to not write publicly anymore.

Now I am heeding what so many encouraged me to do—to publish my account so more people can learn important lessons about grief, love, life and—because I am a nurse—health care. I have spent the past twenty-two years of my career at the Robert Wood Johnson Foundation, the largest health and health care philanthropy in the United States. I direct The Future of Nursing: Campaign for Action, a nationwide initiative to improve health through nursing. My experience of being a family member in the intensive care unit (ICU) has led me to speak and write about the importance of ensuring that all patients and family members receive the best and most compassionate care.

Although I have been consumed with grief for so long, I have come—very slowly I might add—to the Shakespearean-era understanding that "it is better to have loved and lost than never to have loved at all."[1] I still hurt, but I am grateful and honored to have been Bob's wife. I am also grateful and honored that you have found this book and might begin to understand these lessons, too.

What you will read are the daily excerpts from my blog. After each journal entry, I include a paragraph about what I was feeling at the time to provide additional context. I don't know how, looking back, but I ended each blog with gratitude.

Biking with Bob

Sunday, September 25, 2016, was a beautiful, crisp fall morning. I wished I had been home to enjoy it with my husband and BFF Bob, otherwise known as "my Robert Boy." Instead, I was at a work-related meeting in Philadelphia, about fifty miles from my home. He sent me a text early that morning to tell me that I would not have ventured out in the cold. He was right. I was a fair weather biker. I texted back to have fun and be safe. It crossed my mind to tell him to stay home, since we planned to leave two days later for a two-week Red Cross study tour in Washington, D.C., and Geneva, Switzerland. We didn't so much as need a sprained ankle.

But telling Bob not to bike would be like telling a pilot not to fly.

Thirty-seven years of marriage and bike riding. It was our life. At home and no matter where we traveled, we rode our bikes. We rode beat up red bikes when we met, but they got us around college in hilly Tallahassee. Bob could more easily navigate the hills with his ten-speed than I could with my three speed, but it hardly mattered at our age. Youth and strong legs paid no attention to speeds on a bike.

We met at a health fair at a Tallahassee mall, an event that I was in charge of and Bob was participating in. I was not immediately smitten with him, but he was clearly smitten with me—he kept following me around. Sniffing after me, I always said. I was interested in a few other people, so I said no to his request for my phone number. Bob then organized a group dinner with some of the health fair participants. I agreed in an effort to show my appreciation, and Bob arranged to sit next to me. He endeared me with his listening skills and sense of humor. I warmed up to him in no time, but told him he needed to become a Red Cross volunteer if he wanted to seriously date me.

I was extremely devoted to the Red Cross because the organization helped me to reunite with my parents after they were stranded in an earthquake in Mexico City in the mid-1970s. Any man who would seriously date me needed to be involved in this wonderful, mission-oriented organization—it was a must. Bob already had an appreciation for the Red Cross. After he was shot as a soldier in Vietnam, a wonderful Red Cross volunteer stayed with him during his surgery and contacted his mother about his condition. He was grateful as well.

Soon after the group dinner, he greeted me with a Red Cross certificate. He had visited the local Red Cross, inquired about the next possible Red Cross class, and signed up for a Basic Sailing class that afternoon. Once he made up his mind to pursue me, any class would do. I smiled when I saw his certificate and knew that he was a keeper. No one had ever cared so deeply for me, and only time would truly show just how deep his love for me was.

After only four months of dating, Bob asked me to move with him to Nebraska, where he landed his first job after completing his PhD studies. Yes, I had only known him for four months, but to two old souls, we had already known each other a lifetime. I did question the location, however. Nebraska was a very far-off land for someone who was born and raised in Florida.

I immediately stated that I was not so sure Nebraska was such a good idea, due to the tornadoes. He told me emphatically—with just the hint of a grin—that I was thinking of Kansas. So, trusting that his notion of the Midwest was right and that no tornado would ever cross state lines from Kansas into Nebraska, I agreed. By the next July—July 4, 1980 to be exact—the day we married, a small tornado hit Lincoln, our home town. It dawned on me that Bob had promised me no tornadoes, but I was wearing my wedding dress, and the car was waiting. There was no turning back. We were partners for life. We had already agreed on those values—tornadoes or no tornadoes.

No Word

I texted Bob a second time that morning to let him know that the meeting would get out early and that he should be in front of the hotel by 11:00 a.m. instead of noon. He didn't respond, but I knew he would be there. He was dependable and punctual—mostly never wanting to miss one minute without me. He was especially excited at any opportunity to drive his new "retirement" convertible. He loved when I sat next to him in that two-seater, wind blowing through our hair and the Beach Boys blaring on the loudspeakers—nothing could beat this.

I walked out of the hotel at 11:00 expecting to see him there, but there was no sign of him. I called Bob again and reached his voicemail. I noticed two unfamiliar phone numbers and was reminded that these calls had come in about an hour ago. I did not pick them up as I did not recognize them and was busy in my meeting. Now, with a sinking feeling, I wondered if these numbers could explain Bob's absence.

I dialed the number, and a perky voice answered that I had reached the trauma unit of a local hospital. After verifying that Bob was indeed a patient there, I immediately asked to speak to him. Instead, I was transferred to a nurse who asked me to come immediately to the hospital. I again demanded to speak to my husband. I needed to hear his voice. The nurse said that she could not get a phone to Bob and reiterated that I should come. I knew then that she was lying—she could get a phone to a patient if she wanted to. Bob had his cell phone on him. Surely, he could talk to me.

He Cried For Me

A colleague drove me to the hospital, where I saw my tall, strong, physically-fit husband reduced to an immovable mass, naked if not for a sheet, among countless tubes. I looked at him, and when he noticed me, he cried. The tears would not stop flowing. Constricted by a breathing tube, he could not speak, nor would he ever speak again. The tears were his words.

I knew that he was crying for me. He was my biggest cheerleader in life, and he never wanted to let me down. He was always physically, mentally, and spiritually strong for me—other-centered like no one I had ever met. He smiled and chided me through the rough spots of our lives. He could not bear what he had done to me. I told him that nothing mattered but getting him well. Even if he was a quadriplegic who could no longer breathe on his own, we would conquer this—of course we would, as we had already conquered so much in our lives together.

The nurse came in and handed me Bob's wallet. I looked inside and found Bob's Red Cross certificate.

Robin, one of my close friends, joined us at the hospital. She led me to a conference room, where I met Abby, the nurse anesthetist who had sedated Bob for his intubation. She had a concerned look and big eyes. Hugging me, she said she was sorry and wished that there was something more she could do. Abby is the name of my treasured granddaughter. For this reason alone—if not for her kind words and warm touch—I would remember her.

I don't remember anything more about this day or night. My daughter Kim, son-in-law Matt, and grandchildren Abby and John were somehow in the picture that day, but other than my strong husband crying, Robin coming to my side, and the nurse, Abby, hugging me, it was a black box. Kim later said that she was the first on the scene, plucked from a happy day of picking apples in a nearby orchard. She said she brought me home and put me to bed, but I don't remember this. I am not sure if someone gave me medicine to help me forget and put me to sleep.

It Can't Be True...It Just Can't Be

I woke to a nightmare. The accident could not possibly be true, but Matt told me that he would take me to the hospital. How could this be? We're going to the hospital? Not me, not now. I told Matt that I would have to sell my condo in Florida. It was on the second floor. I told Matt that I would find one on the first floor that Bob could more easily navigate. I was confused, in shock, experiencing high emotions, but thinking that Bob and I would conquer this.

When I arrived at the hospital, I received a call from my boss, who is a physician. He advised me to transfer Bob to a hospital in Philadelphia that could better treat his spinal cord injuries. I trusted him and requested a helicopter to transport my husband to another hospital in Philadelphia.

I let my nursing colleague network know of this transport, and immediately, a colleague, Beth Ann Swan, who worked as a dean in the Philadelphia hospital system where Bob was to be transported, sprang into action. She never left my side for the ten days we stayed in the ICU there. She ensured a bed would be available for Bob, made sure the helicopter was on its way, and greeted me at the front door with a warm hug when I arrived. She escorted me to the trauma room where Bob was being assessed.

I stayed by Bob's side as the medical professionals poked and prodded him from head to toe. I cannot remember what the doctor said, but he conveyed how severe the injury was and said that it would be a long journey. Something like that—nothing more, nothing less. I am sure that he realized that I could not absorb information very well.

When Bob finally was admitted to the intensive care unit, it was scary, sterile, and unkind. I remember machines, tubes, procedures, beepers, and alarms. No one really asked anything about me, us, or our lives just thirty-six hours ago. The clinicians were highly functioning individuals doing their jobs. They did their jobs well, or so it seemed, but their focus was on the tasks, numbers, tubes, and medicines. All meant to save a life—a life that ultimately could not be saved.

My blog entries that describe those ten days in the ICU and the aftermath of profound grief, loss, and the beginning of healing, follow.

***

ENTRIES AND REFLECTIONS

It is now two days into this nightmare and I am hoping this site will help keep people informed. I cannot respond to everyone who contacts me. First, let me thank everyone for their prayers. It is truly unbearable to me, but my daughter the optimist says I need to stay positive. Bob was biking early Sunday morning by himself, and no one knows what happened, but someone found him on the side of the road and called an ambulance. He was brought to a trauma center in Trenton. He broke his neck in a few places and is paralyzed from upper chest down. Let me stop and say he is my life, so this is very hard to even write. He has taken care of me for thirty-seven years non-stop. Today he was supposed to have surgery to stabilize his upper cervical spine just so things would not worsen, but he now has a bad infection and probably aspiration pneumonia so is on antibiotics and many, many others meds to try to stabilize him. He is in extremely critical condition, and we appreciate all prayers. Will update as I can.

Just the facts, just give the facts. If I say more, I will fall apart. I have to stay strong for Bob. It is an uphill battle. He is exhausted now from the confusion, the lights, and the constant prodding of the ICU staff. I have received the gift of a wonderful place to stay just blocks from the hospital. A high school hockey family who we were close to so many years ago cropped up in a network, and I immediately made a connection. With everyone wanting to do something, Joanne and Jim Oser feel like this is the one thing they can do. They also welcomed sister-in-law Karen and niece Kristen, who have flown in, to also stay in their home. Words have little use in these situations. Hearts and touch do the talking of the gratitude that is felt from so many coming to our rescue.

Reflection

I was lost and confused, and in disbelief and shock. I was in fight and flight mode. I wanted my husband's life to be saved at all costs—just as the nurses and doctors did. But I also wanted the doctors and nurses to acknowledge us as people. Did they not know how beloved this man was? Did they care that today we were supposed to embark on our bucket-list trip? Did they realize how strong my husband was? Look at the muscles on his legs from all his bike riding. Will his strength not help to save his life? I wanted them to understand what Bob meant to me, but I didn't hear them talking to me. They talked past me.

So today, as I would every day from here on out, I took an 8x10 picture of my husband and me and sat in the middle of the team of doctors, nurses, and pharmacists who discussed Bob's care in the hallway outside of his room without even looking at him to convey that this is who they are talking about—the love of my life. Great clinical care is merely a baseline of my expectations for them. They talked to each other only based on the numbers that jumped up on the screen, letting them know which of my husband's systems were failing. I wanted them to save his life, but I needed them to acknowledge me and my desire to fight for him. Don't talk past me.

***

ENTRY   9/28/2016 at 7:41 a.m.

Not sure where to begin—the bad news or the good news. The good news is that I am so grateful for everyone's help. Robin, one of my dearest friends in the world, embraced me from the beginning. The Osers, who have opened their home to me with an endless invitation, and to Nancy Kaufman who arranged the invite. To my Philly support team: Beth Ann Swan who calls herself my pushy friend, but made it possible for us to get here quickly in the helicopter on Monday, and Julie Fairman, who has taken care of me and my family, and to my amazing and loving neighbors who are taking care of my mother and dog, Jake. Finally, to my niece Kristen and sister-in-law Karen who flew in last night to stay with me as long as I need. And of course, to my daughter Kim and son Mark and son-in-law, Matt. I am grateful and devastated and so sad and weak, but it helps to read your comments. The doctors and nurses do all they can to keep Bob alive.

Now as for Bob—the news is not really good today. Again, it is hard to write, but if people are praying, I might as well be specific. The doctors cannot perform surgery to stabilize Bob's cervical spine because he has a bad blood infection and pneumonia. We have to wear gowns, masks and gloves to see him. The doctor said that the infection has to be completely gone before he can operate, and they need to add days to ensure it is gone. Bob also had heart fibrillation last night from fluid overload. Three specific things to pray for—the fever to break, the antibiotics to work, and wisdom to the many, many doctors who are making constant decisions to keep him alive. Also, I am so worried about Bob because I know him inside out. He is the biggest giver I know, and as he is conscious through all of this, I know he is thinking that he does not want to do this to me, and I am so afraid he is not fighting for me. I told him I can handle anything. I know God's will is at hand, but please let God and Bob know that I can handle this.

Reflection

I don't think I could have survived the brutality of this situation if not for my sister-in-law and niece at my side, as well as Beth Ann, who put her life on hold to run interference for me. Kim came as she could, but she was the mother of a two-year-old and four-month-old who never slept. It was surreal, and I was losing my sanity, but Karen, Kristen and Beth Ann never let me out of their sight and arms. They held me when I could not walk, cried with me when I was inconsolable, and they never let me give up hope. Because of them, I did not. I was also grateful to my many neighbors, who cared for my elderly mother, who was staying at home alone.

I was frustrated, confused, and angry with the many setbacks surrounding Bob's failing systems and his infection. I knew so many people were praying, but his condition went from bad to worse. Why?

***

ENTRY   9/29/2016 at 9:52 a.m.

Some of you who have joined this blog know me best, and some of you know my Bob best. For those who don't know me well, all you have to know is that I am blessed to have a wonderful job working with great people, volunteer for an amazing organization (Red Cross), and I live for my grandchildren—but all you really need to know is that I could do NONE OF THIS WITHOUT THE SUPPORT OF BOB. He is the only reason I can do what I do. Please hear this most loudly.

For those who don't know Bob, I can describe him by telling you what I call him and why. I call him my Catholic (which is how he was raised), Midwest, Red Cross guy. So, why do I call him this (always to his face)? It is because this is how he lives his life. He lives by faith, and he gives back to everyone and anyone. I constantly ask him why he keeps giving away our money, and he tells me other people need it more than we do, and I should stop asking him this! I ask him why he has to take so much time to help others, and he tells me because he is able and because that is what brings him joy. He takes the Red Cross part seriously because the Red Cross is about neutrality, impartiality, and helping everyone no matter what their race, religion or creed is, and that is what he believes. He ONLY thinks of others and what their needs might be. Could anyone else live with his mother-in-law for thirty years and still be friends?! More than anything, he has a very difficult time asking for help—I am not sure if that is the Catholic, Midwest, or Red Cross part, but maybe it is also a guy thing. That's why this is killing him.

This is so not fair for someone who lives by faith and by these principles, but going there makes one crazy. But don't think I don't go there—I go there all the time. I spoke with the hospital pastor on call yesterday and asked her why, and she certainly didn't give me any good answers.

Bob's medical condition today has improved slightly. The doctors still cannot perform surgery to stabilize his cervical spine due to his raging infection. The surgery will only prevent further damage. Bob is on antibiotics and a massive dose of Vitamin C, which are working. Two days ago, he had nearly zero white blood cells to fight the infection, but today his numbers have improved. He is paralyzed from the neck and shoulders down, and that will not change with the surgery. That's the hardest sentence to write. I could tell you more medically, but it is all so overwhelming. He is alert today and knows exactly what is happening. He is on a breathing machine and cannot talk to us, but we talk to him, and he acknowledges us with blinks. I know that if he could walk away from all of this he would, but we are asking him to stay with us. Bob is my best friend, and that will never change.

Reflection

When you are in crisis mode, your emotions—both good and bad—are heightened. I never felt so crushed and defeated, yet I never felt so blessed. This is hard to explain. I was not used to having so many people tend to me and my needs, and I felt tremendous gratitude.

There is truth to the saying that you never know how important someone is until you have lost him or come close to losing him. The petty annoyances that fill all marriages went to the wayside and did not surface again. The bags of Doritos that Bob hid under the seat of the car to nourish him when the spirit moved no longer mattered to me. Nor did the times he stopped suddenly at yellow lights to throw all of us thrashing forward to be saved only by our seat belts. Nor how he insisted on taking a nap every single day, no matter the circumstances. I had to plan around his naps! But in the ICU, I could only think of Bob's strengths, wisdom and love. I fretted wildly that I took him for granted. He teased me that his stature dropped a few notches after Abby and John were born. How could I have taken him for granted—a man who almost daily gave his life to me? That's just who he was. I was spoiled, and most assuredly loved.

***

ENTRY   9/29/2016 at 10:12 a.m.

I broke down that day in the ICU waiting room in front of everyone. I screamed at the television droning on with daily side shows of the man who would soon be elected president. I could not stand listening to the lies and disgrace Trump brought to others as he bullied those running against him. Bob, a lifelong Republican, fretted every day that Trump would be elected and bring down Lincoln's people (as he called his compatriots). Bob dreaded that this man would represent him when his moral compass dictated otherwise. Trump was the opposite of everything my husband stood for: truth, courage, leadership, collaboration, and equity. Bob was about building all people up—not just people who looked like him. Yes, we all understood this was a campaign with its expected jabs, but the way that Trump decimated his opponents was more than Bob could bear. He also did not see how a man who had built his reputation on swindling people could possibly be good for the country.

So I swore very loudly at the television, God and everyone in the waiting room about the unfairness that two men so different, yet claiming the same party, should be dealt such different cards—the good one in bed unable to move and the swindler on television belittling everyone with hatred and vengeance.

Someone—Kristen, Karen, or a nurse—threw a wet towel over my head. The shock of it worked, and I began to cry. My niece asked for the name of my primary care physician to order medication; I did not fight it. Being able to sleep at night to fight for my husband's life took precedent.

So, I decided to do two things I thought I would never do. I am accepting meditation therapy from a long-distance friend (Dawn Bazarko put me to sleep last night) and taking anti-anxiety medication (Karen and Kristen insisted). I go in and out, and it is hour by hour. I am being well taken care of by Karen and Kristen. My job is to be an advocate for Bob. I am there at medical rounds, when the medical professionals confer with each other, with a big picture of Bob and me, and make them all look at that first before they speak to me, on the rare occasion they do. Not much else—shock, disbelief, fear, and nervousness.

Blessings for Today: Thankful for Karen and Kristen, who never let me out of their sight or arms. Thankful to the Osers for sharing their home with me. For Robin and Ralph, who brought me a home cooked meal last night; for Dawn who meditated me to bed; for a daughter and son who are pulling together; for neighbors who watch over my mother, take her out and feed her; and who walk my dog, Jake, (more times than he ever has in the last ten years!); Beth Ann Swan, who pulls all the strings for me and always brings me breakfast; for a nursing and physician team second to none for their medical care; for the chief doctor today who, during rounds looked at our picture, and with a tear in his eye asked what I would like the team to know about Bob as a man and as a human being....a very rare show of compassion with this staff. I told them the Catholic, Midwest, Red Cross thing and they all listened patiently; and for all our friends who love us and want to help—your time will come. Although postponing surgery is delaying progress, the care team told me that if they had operated earlier, the infection would have ruined the rods and screws and they would have had to repeat the surgery. For everyone who is praying, and for my husband's love for me—we love each other very much. I wish I could discuss all of this with him and ask him what to do about it all.

Specific Prayer Requests: That the horrible infection will leave his body; that Bob will continue to fight for us; and for strength for Bob and me, my children, and my mother.

Reflection

One of the greatest frustrations was the inability to discuss what was going on with Bob. I needed my best friend to ask his advice about what to do, but he was unable to communicate. In all of our years of married life, we talked about our plans and shared our ideas. We were opposites in many ways: he was an introvert, and I am an extrovert; he was a Republican, and I am a Democrat; he was a rule follower, and I am a rule breaker; and he depended on an afternoon nap, while I plow through the day. In the end, we shared a love and commitment to seeing our problems and our relationship through—and we always relied on humor. I miss the humor most of all.

I whispered in Bob's ear that a clinician finally asked about him as a person. A team that was focused only on organ systems finally asked about him as a person—and not because they wanted to know. It was because of my habit of pulling up a chair in the middle of their medical rounds every morning and listening to them while holding up a picture of Bob and me, or Bob and his grandkids. I suppose they felt forced to acknowledge me and my husband. I was struck with the way they made decisions about Bob's life simply by the lab value that popped up on their screens each morning. As a nurse, I get that they must respond to and fight for him in this way, but they never looked at him or me.

I told Bob that I was somehow relieved and felt acknowledged that they asked about him. I told him that we were Baby Boomers, and Baby Boomers fight hard and never give up and are loyal to the end. I told my dear Robert Boy that I would always love him and never leave his side.

But I remained worried that Bob might not be fighting his infection on purpose. We talked about life and death a lot before this accident, and we both agreed that we did not want to be kept alive if things looked hopeless and we could not communicate. I wondered, with all the regret in me, if Bob wanted to go. I asked Bob and God to fight for me, but it was all falling on deaf ears. The larger plan was unfolding against my will.

***

ENTRY   9/30/2016 at 5:19 p.m.

I could write a book about just what happened since I last posted yesterday morning, which was a fairly positive report (I have a completely new definition of positive now). Since that time, however, we have had some significant setbacks if that is even possible. I am learning that it is all possible. Bob had a cardiac arrest and had to be defibrillated back to life. He had a "do not resuscitate order," but it did not seem to matter. The doctors, the nurses, and I were all in fight mode—the usual fare for ICU staff. I just don't know if Bob and God were. They, better than anyone, felt the situation's brutality—an adverb I would come to adopt to describe these days in the ICU. Yet I was in the ring with them. Couldn't they give me a turn at this fight? Everything was brutal and savagely violent.

I was not in the room with Bob when all this happened, but Kathy, the nurse I considered the most outwardly compassionate of the bunch, came out to the ICU waiting room, shaken to the core. Wasn't she used to these kind of things? Perhaps, the downside of getting to know me and Bob better. Perhaps many health professionals are so good at distancing themselves so they won't have to feel shaken when setbacks happen. But as a health care professional, I know that the adrenaline it takes to pull someone back to life always takes a toll, distance or no distance.

As it turned out, Bob's heart did not give out for good. His biker's heart was strong as an ox, one of his last remaining vital organs to keep him in the game. It was a chance happening that a mucus plug blocked his breathing tube, which shut down his breathing, and then his heart. The cardiac arrest led the doctors to believe that he now needed a tracheotomy—a hole cut in his throat that would allow the breathing tube to work more efficiently.

While this sounds additionally gruesome, it will actually help him to breathe better with the machine and get all the tubes out of his mouth, which he constantly fights. Bob is alert, yet always very groggy. Now that yesterday is over and hopefully we can avert further emergencies, I am hoping to now focus on the main issues, which are the infection and his kidneys.

Enough with the negatives. For the positives, the antibiotics seem to be working, and the surgery has been scheduled for Monday or Tuesday. He must be infection free, however, and there are a lot of hours between now and Tuesday.

Blessings for Today: Small changes that I can hold onto in Bob's condition, like his vital signs are holding; Kristen and Karen who never leave my side. They hold me and make me eat, drink, and walk. For Robin, who stopped at the Red Cross today per my request to pick up a Red Cross notebook for me to write in, a Red Cross blanket to put on Bob, and a Red Cross Pin I put on his gown to help people understand who this man is. (A blanket in spite of his high fever—everything is a trade off!) I cried to see the Red Cross blanket on him, as it is the same one he has given to so many when he volunteered during disasters.

I am grateful to Robin, who comes no matter what. Beth Ann brings me breakfast every day and checks on me several times a day. (I asked her last night if she still had her Dean's job here, and she assured me she did.) I am grateful to the Osers for providing me with a home when others are sleeping in chairs in this waiting room. They also let me be, without asking questions.

For Bob's incredible "main" doctor—he has many—who is proficient and great with explaining everything to me and is so compassionate. He is the only other consistent provider with this kind of compassion, aside from Nurse Abby and Kathy. I call him the "Doctor/Nurse" (I just knew his mother must be a nurse or his wife, and I was right—he just told me his wife is a psychiatric nurse). On another rare occasion, there was a young doctor who cried at the bedside with me as I was telling Bob how much I loved him and that I would never leave his side (and she sees me every morning as I hold up our picture, so all doctors know Bob as a husband, father and grandfather). She hugged me, and with tears in her eyes, told me what a beautiful couple we are and how unique our relationship is. These rare moments of kindness carry me through.

To Kathy, Bob's nurse who offered to drive me home to prevent me from walking in the rain; for Michelle McKay, who works here and watches out for Bob—she is very special; for my wonderful work colleagues and neighborhood friends, who are providing endless support and prayers. For our many friends, who provide food and help with my mother and Jake (Is he still able to walk with all the walks he is being provided?); for Joyce, who tore up my house yesterday looking for important paperwork I needed; for Dawn, my meditation coach who puts me to sleep at night; for Julie, for always stopping by for anything I need; for my incredible daughter, son, and son-in-law, who are a constant source of support; and for Abby, who told me about her day at school, sang to me, and told me she loves me. She said randomly and without knowing a single thing about what is happening except that Pops fell off of his bike that "love will save the day."

Specific Prayer Requests: That Bob can continue to fight this infection; that his kidneys start working better again; that his vital signs hold; and that Bob can feel our love. I woke up this morning realizing that I was asking God for what I wanted, and God somehow reminded me that what I want might not be what He or Bob want. Pray for Bob's and my own capacity and wherewithal to withstand the brutality of this.

Reflection

I am struck that on what was clearly the most brutal and punishing of all days, I found so much to be thankful for. Clearly the practice of being grateful kept my nose above water as much as I needed to keep up the fight for my husband's life. I was holding on by less than a thread, but the power of family and friends gave me the energy I needed to fight. The way people rallied around me and my family was as incredulous to me as the horror of the situation was itself.

My family, friends, and colleagues would seemingly do anything for me. I found that Abby was closest to God and would somehow bring me messages that I needed to hear. I have always held Abby's messages close.

The Red Cross blanket on Bob brought everything together for me—how our relationship began and evolved. The Red Cross was so much a part of our love story—how my Robert Boy raced to get certified when I said I would not date someone who was not a Red Cross volunteer; how volunteering filled our lives with value; and how he used that blanket countless times as a symbol of compassion, hope, and comfort for disaster survivors. Then, when we were the ones who were losing, it was only right for the Red Cross symbol to be present—a symbol that also stands for medical protection in times of war or disaster. I needed, begged, and prayed for medical protection. From that day forward, the blanket never came off.

***

ENTRY   10/1/2016 at 4:59 p.m.

"HIGHS AND LOWS TODAY"

First the low: Bob is not improving and not responding today. His kidneys are not working right, even with a lot of Lasix. Because his kidneys are not working, his body is retaining toxins that are causing him to not respond. The doctors started him on dialysis to get rid of much excess fluid, urine, and toxins. If his mental status does not improve, and he does not wake up with the dialysis, then they will do a brain scan to determine further.

This is too much for me to handle. I can feel my body suffering. I am crumbling inside, but I am going through the motions, nevertheless. I need to, for the sake of my husband and all there was at stake. I am incredibly grief-stricken over the pain and anguish that my Robert Boy is experiencing—the constant assaults to his body. His assaults are my assaults. That happens when two become one. I want to scream, but I can't. I want to throw up, but I can't. I want to run and hide, but I can't. I want to die, but not before taking care of my husband, so I can't. A friend sent me a plaque that said, "Staying strong, when strong is your only option." I am not sure how I feel about that. Yes, I have to stay strong—I have to be there for Bob and speak in coherent sentences to his doctors and nurses, but I resent a plaque telling me to stay strong. How dare it? It did not know that I didn't want to be strong. I want to curl up with my husband and tell everyone to go away and leave us alone and never return.

Now the high: Kim and Matt brought my grandchildren to visit. I met them at the "Please Touch" museum in Philadelphia. We traded places—Kim and Matt stayed at the hospital, while Kristen, Karen, and I played with the kids for hours.

Abby often talks through her stuffed dog, Tessie. She told me that Tessie was on a big bike and fell off and now has so many bumps and bruises that she does not know what to do. Kim and I told her we were sorry about Tessie and hoped she would be okay soon. I picked her up and hugged her, and she noticed Bob's wedding ring around my neck. When she asked me why I am wearing it instead of Pops, I told her it was my way of being close to Pops always because I love him just like she loves him.

I grieved intensely for my granddaughter. She was so close to her Pops—he was her babysitter. I was amazed by how she was trying to process this horrific tragedy. Abby did not know details but made them up as she went along as a means of coping. Kim, upon the advice of a therapist, encouraged us to listen to her and to speak of love and belonging, but to be careful about promising what might or might not happen. Abby gave me the love and hope I needed to carry on—she was my loving distraction for the day and gave me a much needed few hours away from the bedside. Of course, I was torn: I wanted and needed to be with both Abby and my Robert Boy.

Blessings for Today: I feel kind of weak and on empty on this one today to be honest, but it is the same—the love and support of Karen and Kristen, my children, grandchildren, and all of you. I am nervous about losing my favorite doctor (the one I call "Doctor/Nurse") as they rotate every seven days, and clinicians tell me I will have to get used to another style. Haven't I been through enough change? I grieve for my beautiful husband. I am like a breakable twig just waiting to snap and fall at the slightest change in weather.

Specific Prayer Requests: The usual...improvement for my love. Anything please—improved kidney status and to have him wake up and recognize me. Please extra prayers for Mark—he is lost and despondent and has little support, but he is so loving and wants to help me. He has a minimum wage job with long hours. After his shift as a restaurant delivery driver ends, he travels to Philly every night around midnight to see Bob. Please pray for his travel safety and surround him with support and love. Thank you to Amanda, for being his friend and Bethany for talking with him.

Reflection

Looking back, I recall a dearth of consistent compassion from the medical professionals who cared for Bob. The nurses were all competent on the unit. I received compassion in nibbles and bites, but mostly I received competence. It shouldn't have been an either or proposition. I needed both.

As for my son, my prayer requests were desperate pleas for help for him. He, of all family members, had the least amount of resilience and support and was most at risk for emotional assault. But, he didn't want that kind of attention, and he didn't want those kind of prayers—at least that's what he said. He just wanted his father back.

That night, he came to see his father at midnight after his shift ended. He was distraught and disheveled. The nurses told him they would get him after they finished a procedure. He waited for ten minutes, then twenty, then forty, then over an hour, and then he became frantic. I was afraid they did not take him seriously, or for whatever reason, they forget about Bob's only son. I tried to calm Mark down the next morning. He was full of hatred, fear, and grief—for the nurse who did this to him, and to other workers that night who ignored him. Why?

I spoke politely to a nurse to understand what happened. I wanted to give the benefit of doubt. But the casual response that they must have forgotten was so inept and lacking in human compassion. Had she never had a loved one so close to death? How would this lack of compassion make her feel? I asked the nurse if she would mind apologizing to my son, so that he could go on with the simple process of grieving for his father, rather than also be encumbered by this lack of compassion from a nurse. I am not sure an apology was ever made, so I requested that when my son came that night that he be treated with more dignity and consideration. I asked for the name of another nurse he might turn to for explanation other than the one who incited, albeit unintentional, psychological harm.

I was trying to protect my son without angering the staff caring for my husband. I knew better than to make too many waves or requests. It dawned on me, however, that I was so resentful that I had to take up emotional energy on trying to "behave" for the staff. My husband and I always promised to be each other's advocate in the hospital should we not be able to do that for ourselves. That was my job now, and I was trying my best. Why was it so hard? Couldn't everyone understand the dire emotional turmoil we were all under? I needed understanding and compassion. Why was this so hard to come by?

***

ENTRY   10/2/2016 at 9:34 p.m.

"SUNDAY...ONE WEEK ANNIVERSARY OF ACCIDENT"

It's been a week of living with this bad dream, and it feels like a year. This blog has three parts:

Part 1: Last night was one of the worst nights emotionally I have spent. Bob's kidneys failed, and he needed dialysis, and although I signed the consent first thing in the morning, it took the hospital until around midnight to get it up and running. I was frantic all evening, with staff communication issues really upsetting me. I felt that I was being an advocate for my husband, but at least one staff person did not see it that way. I was crushed and hurt by comments made, and it created a situation where I had to call my boss and physician, Risa and Beth Ann to talk me down. It took hours to somewhat resolve my feelings, but when you have a loved one you are watching over, you simply have to do what you have to do and not give a crap in the end. This is my best friend we are talking about here.

Reflection Part 1

As a nurse, I was sensitive about maintaining a positive and appropriate working relationship with the staff. I did not yell at the staff, become gruff with them, cry and moan incessantly, or demand treatments for my husband and me. I knew firsthand that even the best-intentioned nurses shy away from family members who are not nice. I finally asked to speak to a doctor, though, after I waited for over twelve hours for a dialysis treatment to start and watched my husband sink deeper into oblivion. The intern told me it was late, and she did not want to disturb the lead physician, but I insisted. I absolutely insisted. I promised to always be my husband's advocate. Did she not realize this?

After about what seemed like an hour, a nurse handed me a cell phone that I assumed was hers. I saw a text that said something like this: "You know how demanding family members can be. I tried to reason with Mrs. Hassmiller and not disturb you, but she is being unreasonable." I could not believe I had just read that. I was already heartbroken for my husband, family, and me, and now I faced yet another emotional assault from a nurse—one of my own.

I called Beth Ann and Risa crying. They encouraged me to remain focused on the larger issue—my husband and his care. However, this was about my husband and his care. I felt like my heart had been yanked from me and trampled on. I told the nurse manager as calmly as I could the next morning what had transpired, and that I would like an apology and explanation from the nurse, whose phone I assumed it was. I found out later that it was a junior resident physician who had sent the text to the lead physician. She was more concerned with making an excuse to save herself from being chastised by the lead physician. When the lead resident broke this news to me, I asked him to arrange a meeting between us.

The junior resident, the head resident and I met in a private conference room. Beth Ann may have been there as well. I asked the junior resident her name and then asked her to name the person she loved most in the world. When she named her parents, I asked her to choose one. She chose her mother, and I asked her if her mother had ever been ill. No, thank goodness, she said. I asked her to imagine that her mother was near death. I asked her if she would want the best possible care for her mother, and she said nodded. At this point, tears formed in her eyes as she realized where I was going.

I told the junior resident that her mother needed what was described to her as an emergency procedure that might make the difference between life and death, but that procedure—without explanation—was delayed for many, many hours. I asked her how she would feel and what she would do. Then I asked her how she would feel if she read the text that she sent to the lead physician last evening.

Crying openly now, she apologized profusely. I said that I did not want her apology; rather I wanted her to never forget the way that she made a grieving family member feel as she was about to lose the love of her life. I told her that I wanted her to share this story with others, so that all might learn this lesson, so that someday when she might need compassion and understanding, she too might receive it.

The head doctor told me afterwards that I had done her a great favor, and she would be a better doctor because of it. I hope so.

***

Part 2: We had a two-hour family meeting with my favorite Doctor ("Doctor/Nurse") that included my children and son-in-law, a pastor, Kristen, and Karen. It was a meeting about going forward—really? Going Forward? Nothing about the meeting spoke about forward—forward means progress, and it was a meeting about very hard and heart-wrenching decisions that no one should ever have to make. This is between God and Bob—at least I thought we had come to that conclusion the other day, but no. All of a sudden, my children and I are being called to be part of the God/Bob decision-making, and it is not right. I will try to speak for Bob, but God (please hear me on this), you really need to step in here. The worst of it all is that although Bob is so critically ill and just hanging on, his mind is all there. In a cruel sort of twist that part just does not seem right. At least at the moment, my dear love cannot speak but is grappling with all of this privately, but I do know what he is thinking. He is so worried about me and our children, but mostly me. He feels horrible about what happened, but I tell him that I am here and will never leave his side.

Reflection Part 2

That particular morning, I spoke up during the medical rounds. I asked the stethoscope clad doctors with their sterile white coats that seemingly never touch patients—who I privately referred to as the intimidators—if there was a person I could talk to about Bob's situation in regard to the ethics of what was happening. They looked at me like I had three heads. I clarified that I wanted to talk to a medical ethicist who could help me with decisions about what I should do. I informed them that they simply kept adding more and more treatments, and I needed to know what I should do about all of this. The head resident said, "Oh, you mean someone from palliative care." I said, whoever can talk to me about what is being done to my husband and whether he would want all of these continuing insults to his body. Sure, I said, send me someone from palliative care.

***

Part 3: Your prayers have been answered with the fever—it is gone! And all his vital signs are relatively stable, although one plays off the other depending on medications or even a simple turning him on his side. He is in kidney failure from the cardiac arrest the other night. There is no more talk about surgery for the time being, however, due to the cardiac arrest and now kidney failure—he is too fragile. He knows me and my voice and reacts to it. He hears how much we love him and how we are well supported.

Reflection Part 3

I was bereft. My hope was diminishing, and I was unsure of what to pray for anymore. I was done with pleas. There were no good answers. Yes, the fever was gone, but bad things kept happening. The worst of it was kidney failure. I told Bob again and again that I would never leave him, just like we had always promised each other. Love comes and goes in a marriage—at least those passionate feelings of intense intimacy. You work things out. You laugh. You are in it for the long haul and know it is right. This is what matters in life—the sacred vow of marriage and the promise of until death do us part. This is what we meant when we said our vows. And here we were, my love and I, talking about parting. The pain was intense, but the love more so.

***

Blessings for Today: For Karen and Kristen always for never leaving my side: for Beth Ann who anticipates every need I have; for Risa for her clinical expertise and calm wisdom in helping me with medical goals and harsh words from medical staff; for my children for supporting me and helping me with decisions (this is not fair to them); for Matt for giving me ultimate peace of mind in caring for Kim and ensuring that my bills are paid; for Libbie and Paul for making and bringing me the only second home-cooked meal since this ordeal; for Bethany for telling me that I am the strongest person she knows and that I can handle anything that comes my way (I believed her for one fleeting moment); for Dawn for meditating me to sleep.

Specific Prayer Requests: That Bob can have peace in knowing that I am being supported and that I will be able to handle, in time, whatever God's will is. He worries about me most—please pray that he feels peace and can recover and not worry so much about me. And for his kidney failure. And for wisdom to guide the doctors and nurses in their decision-making; for continued support and prayers for my children who are having a very difficult time being without their hero and support system, and especially travel mercies for Mark as he travels late every night to sit with and talk to his Dad. All so hard. Thank you all. Good night.

Reflection

I was bound up in grief—for Bob, me, our children, and grandchildren. The grief was like a noose around my neck. I could hardly breathe and eat. The worst part was putting myself in Bob's place. He did not ask for this. He hated this. And as the ultimate giver, he grieved deeply for me and our family. If he could have talked to me, I was sure he would have told me that he worried most about me. He always said that. I knew deep down that he did not want all this medical treatment. Kim said she would take her Daddy however he came back to us, even if he could just speak and that was all he could do. But the doctors said they could not even guarantee that. He might never come off of a breathing machine. I could not think of anything more painful for a man of such intellect and heart being trapped in a body that could not speak or move.

***

ENTRY   10/3/2016 at 6:29 p.m.

I am not sure how each day can be harder than the day before, but that seems like that's the way this story goes. No major changes today, but Bob is not recovering. I have so many questions about how this can happen to us and why, but it just did. I am so heartbroken, and I will never in my life know another like my best friend. I am clearly uncertain about God's plan for all of this—for now it is the cruelest hoax of all time, and I keep searching for the magic clock to turn this world back eight days.

We had many meetings today about what to do with the palliative care team, who tend more towards caring for you holistically. Just what I needed. I am not sure how they do this line of work, but they are good at it. Answers are not great. The way forward is a hoax—where is that magic clock?

Please read Bob's words about the Clara Barton study tour we were to embark on. It was my dream to pull all this together so that Bob and I could spread the good news of how the Red Cross got started and the good work it does now all over the world. To enable more people to enjoy all the exciting sites and learnings, I arranged to have the American Journal of Nursing post a daily blog of the travels. Today the group started the Geneva leg of the trip, and Bob volunteered to write the first blog. He wrote the blog the night before this nightmare began. These will now remain his last written words. Here are excerpts from the blog:

"For me, interest in this tour and the call to service is personal. My international military experience was bookended by experiences of the Red Cross. In 1969, I landed in Vietnam as a twenty-two-year-old combat platoon sergeant and received what I would later learn was a comfort kit from a Red Cross worker.

By New Year's Eve, I had been shot, operated on in a field hospital in Cu Chi that day, shipped to another hospital in Saigon, and the next day flown to a military hospital in Japan. I was dirty, had broken eardrums, a shattered left wrist, and a right arm largely blown away, and was without glasses so I could barely see.

Out of that blur came a woman whose face I can't remember—but I can remember the Red Cross pin on her lapel. "How can I help you, sergeant?" she offered.

I asked if I could call home, and she found me a phone. Although three days had passed since my battle, my parents had received a telegram that morning from the army saying that I'd been shot, that I was okay, and that more information would come. Two hours later my mother picked up my Red Cross call—a tearful call indeed.

As a Red Cross volunteer now, every time I go to a middle-of-the-night fire call, install a smoke detector, donate blood, pack a Red Cross box for our troops in Afghanistan, deploy to other disasters, or make our Red Cross donation, I understand that without action, these Red Cross ideals cannot be fulfilled. We walk in the footsteps of both Clara Barton and Henri Dunant and many others, and now it's important that we create our own."

Reflection

It pained me enormously to know that Bob and I did not get to take our bucket list Red Cross trip. It would have been a culmination of our lives together. We were both proud of each other for playing our part in the greatest of all humanitarian organizations. Wherever we traveled, we always (usually without an announcement) walked into a local Red Cross building to say we were part of the family. We were always welcomed with open arms. Sometimes language was a barrier, but the mission superseded all language barriers.

We both served together during a disaster in Florida in 2005. Three hurricanes wreaked havoc across the state. At the staging center in Atlanta, where assignments were made, we learned that we would not be together in the same city. That wasn't the idea, and I stated my refusal to go anyplace other than where my husband was going. And that was that. Sensing that I would not budge, the disaster director quickly rearranged to have us placed together.

Bob, who was the chief executive officer of a small non-profit, was content to not be in charge of anything, so he offered to drive the Emergency Response Vehicle (ERV) wherever he might be needed, including delivering meals to those who had no way of eating otherwise. I served as a nurse, and there were plenty of physical and mental health needs to keep me occupied. We both found every excuse to absolutely stay together during our two weeks of service. We felt blessed to be helping others and blessed to be able to help others while staying together.

As for the study tour, I was glad I brought my good friend Jean Johnson in on all the details of our plans. I dubbed her the deputy and asked her early on to take on these responsibilities should I not be able to attend. At the time, I was thinking of my mother. She shrugged off such a notion of my not being able to lead my own tour, but nevertheless, she agreed.

When I called her on the afternoon of the accident to let her know she was in charge, she swung into action. How hard it must have been for her to know of the pain and suffering she was leaving behind, yet thirty eager souls awaited their own bucket list trip. Her job was difficult, but she carried on with it miraculously, with help from others. She delegated responsibilities, and the tour went on without a hitch. I have not been able to—nor have I wanted to think about—what I missed. It was part of the cards that were dealt that I will never understand. To this day, I don't mention the tour to anyone

***

Blessings for Today: Always Kristen and Karen who don't leave my side, make me drink and eat, push pills when necessary, and love me unconditionally. Their husbands, who are providing the space and support at home for them to be here with me; Beth Ann who brought lunch, stays with me to ask the doctors questions I am supposed to be asking but can't and then ordered a car service to pick up Kim in New Jersey (as we cannot allow anyone to drive now) to come to our family meeting tomorrow at the hospital. She told me to STOP asking her why she is doing these things for me—she keeps murmuring to no one in particular that this is all a privilege for her—really?

I am grateful to Robin, who had meetings all day and said she would be here after work but then when I said I needed her, she said the heck with the meetings and just came to my side; for my son and daughter who are doing what they can to support me while seeking support for themselves; for Joyce and Libbie and all of my neighbors who go in and out of my house like it belongs to them: for Joyce for agreeing to bring my ninety-one-year-old mother and Mark to the hospital tomorrow for the meeting (I would not wish that particular job on anyone, but Joyce did not flinch.); for Pastor Dan (Joyce's son-in-law) for talking Mark off yet another limb; and for Fran for cleaning my fridge because everyone keeps bringing my mother food.

For my RWJF work colleagues Pam, Colleen, Sherrie and Cathy for taking my mother out, and to Beth for the cinnamon buns. And for the Oser's home. At night, they listen, but only if I want to talk—they let me be. And finally, for a peaceful trip to the Basilica for a much needed touch base with God. No big answers, and I am really too nervous to be totally comforted, but it helped. For the palliative care team, who have been very caring, to the hospital pastor, Nancy.

Specific Prayer Requests: Strength for me and my children, and peace for my beloved. I am so scared and nervous. Strength for those in my very inner circle who are holding me up—it is tortuous on them as well. I am not sure what tomorrow will bring. I know my Robert Boy, and I know he does not want all the brutality that has come his way. I know his utmost thoughts are about me. I tell him that I will love him forever, and I will never leave him.

Reflection

My emotions were all over the place: fear, love, disbelief, gratefulness, horror, and sorrow. If there was an emotion to be had, I had it. I was already so lonely. I needed to discuss all of this with Bob, but that was not possible. I relied on our many conversations we had over the years about our eventual deaths. Neither one of us could bear the thought of being without the other. I knew his wishes—we had living wills and were preparing for my mother's death. We had our cemetery plots all arranged. Having the privilege of living with two veterans—my mother, a former Air Force nurse, and Bob, an infantry sergeant in Vietnam, we had an automatic in at the local veteran's cemetery. All of us. We would be together. Bob arranged everything, as he always did. He even brought my mother and me to the cemetery twice so we could be comfortable with the arrangements. My mother said she wanted to be under a tree, but that we could not guarantee. Bob and I did not care where we were, as long as we would be together.

Even though I dealt with death as a nurse and lost a father and a brother, nothing compared with the pain of losing Bob. He was me, and I was him—kindred spirits. Yes, of course, we were both very independent and had our own careers and our own interests, but after thirty-seven years, we were one. The ripping apart of the deeply woven interconnected vines was more than I could bear.

***

ENTRY   10/5/2016 at 6:51 a.m.

"LOST MY BEST FRIEND"

I lost my best friend last night and the world lost one of the most giving souls in the history of forever. So many people have been praying, and you deserve to know what your prayers have answered.

Yesterday, which was a year in length, Kim, Mark, Matt, Karen, Kristen, and my mother, Jackie, came to the hospital to hear and process the best advice that the palliative care team had. Beth Ann and my favorite ICU nurse, Kathy, were also there to help with questions. Actually, knowing Bob with my inner soul, I was the one who questioned the doctors about all they were continuing to do and why—I stopped counting the machines and tubes and bags that were hanging around my husband....was it ten, thirty, fifty, one-hundred? They became part of the background.

Bob told me many times that he did not want to be hooked up to machines. He would have never approved. Bob (Or was it God?) startled me awake from sleep the other night to demand that all the banging, poking, alarms, tests, and x-rays (the constant alarms that drove me insane) be stopped. In my dream, Bob kept yelling twenty times one sentence—I DON'T WANT THIS, I DON'T WANT THIS, I DON'T WANT THIS and the voice got louder until I awoke. *Although I would give anything to have my best friend sitting next to me in any kind of condition at all, I had to stop this—not for me, my children, nor the hundreds he serves—but for Bob, the ultimate giver of all times. He doesn't want help ever, and he did not want this kind of brutal life where all he would have to look forward to every day was a swarm of help.*

My pain is deeply profound, but Bob is at peace. I usually got my own way with him—those who knew us understood how spoiled I was to have a husband who gave constant unconditional love and supported me every second of my life and career. Yes, I gave in to him—no marriage can survive without giving—but everyone knew it was unbalanced...the kind of unbalanced that allowed me to be who I was. Spoiled indeed. But last night, Bob got his way, and I did not.

Although I could write a book about these ten days, there were blessings involved. Yesterday when I arrived to see him, he was awake and alert after being unresponsive. He understood everything I said to him and most importantly asked of him. I got many kisses. He smiled at me and his children, and he was able to kiss me many times (Kim said she got the most, but I know I did.); he heard Matt tell him that all my bills would get paid and that I would be okay; that Matt would always help me. At first, I questioned my decision and thought that we could handle caring for Bob in any condition. I was worried that my children would think that as long as Dad could blink and kiss, why would we let him go—but it was God's and Bob's way of miraculously giving me his last gift...

always thinking of me. He lived for easing my pain and troubles constantly and always with humor—our survival technique. He came back for just a while to let me know that it was all okay and that he would love me forever. He said he understood what was happening. He smiled at me and let me know it was okay. Kim said he was never really human to begin with—only angels give as much as he does, and he came back as an angel to give us all this gift.

I was relieved that Kathy was on duty that day. I don't think I could have gone through this with any other nurse. She cared like no other. She asked me if I was ready, and I said I was. She gave my husband some medicine to relax him more and more, and in the afternoon she began to dial down the breathing machine. She helped me move Bob's 6'4" 230 pound body to the side so that I could lay next to him. She brought her iPad to his ear and asked what kind of music he liked.

His vital signs remained strong throughout the afternoon. His heart remained vibrant. Kathy dialed down the machine again and noted that she was very surprised at how strong Bob's heart was in the midst of so much medication and decreased oxygen. I reminded her to look at the pictures again to see how strong he was when he arrived at the hospital. He had just finished another thirty miles of bike riding when he fell—of course he had a strong heart.

I called for Pastor Nancy to bring words of comfort to Bob and me. She, too, had a knack for compassion and the right things to say. A stranger showed up to let me know that Pastor Nancy was at a retreat on campus and could not come, but she was there in her absence. I sent the stranger away and told her I was sure she was nice, but she was not Nancy—I only wanted Nancy. Could I make just one demand in my time at this hospital? Beth Ann saw how agitated I was becoming and in her role as my "pushy friend" as she liked to call herself, she went right to the top and demanded that Nancy show up. Beth Ann was nice—she is always nice, but she knew this last request was critical to my well-being. Nancy soon stood at my side, concern in her voice, and love in her heart. She took me in her arms and prayed. We all prayed—Kristen, Karen and me holding Bob as tightly as we could, and then they left the room. I wanted it that way.

Kathy's shift was ending, and I was petrified to be left without her. She knew this. Another dial down. More medication. His heart kept beating, each one a reminder of Bob's love for me. Sixty times a minute, sixty times I love you. Kathy reached over to Bob and told him it was okay to go — I had given him permission. His heart still kept beating.

Kathy came to me at 7:20 p.m., her coat on, her purse slung over her shoulder. In ten minutes, she would be gone, and Bob would still be here. I told her it would be hard without her. She asked if I wanted her to stay, and I hugged her, crying into her shoulder, and nodded. She threw her coat and purse to the side and took her position next to Bob and his machines. She dialed it way down, warning me that it would be hard for him to get oxygen in. Yet, he hung on. This time we both told him it was okay. I kept telling him I loved him. Finally, Kathy said the only way to let him go was to completely shut the machine off, and through tears, I gently nodded. One last breath—completely dependent on the machine—and for the first time in thirty-seven years, I was alone. Kristen and Karen walked me to my home away from home. They were there, but the loneliness shook me to my core. I walked into the Osers' home and informed them it was all over. How does one actually say what just happened? There are so many words I don't like—passing, death, widow. So, I simply whispered, "It's over."

Blessings for Today: Always my inner circle support team. I could not have survived without Kristen, Karen, and my children. I don't know where Beth Ann came from, but she anticipated my every need as her "greatest honor and privilege"— aside from giving me Bob back, she gave me anything else I wanted and needed. She brought food, linen table clothes and napkins, real silverware, pictures and flowers, and made me sit and eat. She brought Nancy to me. For Joyce for navigating Philly traffic to get my mother to me and for her constant support and prayers. For Robin, who is on her way now to bring me home (my husband's home) and will support me walking in the front door for the first time in ten days. That will be a crushing moment, and, I know, a process.

For my nurse Kathy, who cared for Bob and me so much and helped me to make very painful decisions yesterday. She told me yesterday with tears in her eyes that she needed to work on her own marriage and that our story had inspired her. I wish for everyone to have a nurse like her.

Finally, for all who have been praying, I read your words and prayers of comfort constantly, and they have sustained me. Bob would hate my writing this— but it is my job to let everyone know that an angel has been in our midst.

Specific Prayer Requests: No one can bring my Robert Boy back to me, so we will skip over that one. My prayer is that everyone take some kind of lesson from this— whether it be about caring or giving back, being there for your family, or looking for the best in people and situations. Okay, well, I still need your prayers— remember me, the spoiled one. I need help in transitioning. I don't know how to do life without Bob. I have no idea—none! And actually, I don't know all that I need help with—I think God might know, but I don't know it all yet. I have never faced a journey like this before. (I know others have.) Pray for my children and that we continue to make good and honorable decisions. I told Bob that I would be with him soon— but not too soon—as I have a lot of work left to do. He has honored my work, and for him and for the people I serve, I will continue. I am blessed to be part of the Robert Wood Johnson Foundation and Red Cross families—two organizations that will allow me to find meaning and purpose in my life.

Reflection

I was shocked to see Bob in the alert state that I found him that morning, and I questioned our plans to let Bob go….to turn off life support. I thought Kim and Mark would fight me if they saw their Dad alert. I had to prepare them. Nurse Kathy said it was called a death rally and was not uncommon. It was an uncommon gift to me—a miracle arranged between Bob and God. It was just like him to always make sure the kids and I were okay, first and foremost. At the end I did not know what I did not know. I was numb, fatigued, in shock, oblivious, lost, and alone. For the first time in my adult life, I could not discuss with my best friend what had just happened and what I needed to do. I no longer had a best friend—here one minute and gone the next. How on earth did that happen? I was absolutely incredulous.

***

ENTRY   10/6/2016 at 6:12 a.m.

"ARRANGEMENTS AND HARD TO READ STUFF"

It was most hard for me to come into my neighborhood. I knew it would be, and I cried, but Joyce and Chris were here, who had just finished cleaning my house (and Rita helped earlier), so I had people with me—and, of course, Karen and Kristen, my mother, and then soon, Kim, Matt, Mark and my grandchildren. Pastor Dan came and asked about Bob, as they had never met, and then asked about arrangements. It was all so confusing—I did not understand all of the decisions that needed to be made.

For ten days, I was in a protected cocoon—just me and Bob, really, and all the machines, bags, tubes and such, yes, but you know what I mean—it was just me and my man. It was all very simple as I look back. No one really bothered me about things—until the end—so it was routine. I woke up every morning and went to Bob—it was just that simple.

Now I am home, and people are asking me things that I don't want to answer. Bob and I already had plans for this weekend—why are you asking me to change my plans? I like and even love all of you, but we already had plans, and they did not include you! Asking about eating, what to eat, when to eat, services, visitations, bills, should I use the red or blue magic marker for my pumpkin Nana?, hotels, airplanes, airports. Did you not know that you were not all in the plans? I am happy to see all of you, but you say more are coming and they need to know which airport, which hotels, when this and when that.

Ask Bob, will you? We always made our weekend plans together. Bob and I made these decisions together—you say you want to know what Bob wants. Well then, ask him, will you? He is upstairs watching television. It must be a good show he is watching because no one can drag him away from it to help make these decisions about what he wants. This is all supposed to be about what you want, Robert, so why are you not helping me with these decisions? It must be a science fiction show—I can never get you away from the television when you are watching science fiction…all those monsters saying weird things. I never understood it.

Bob told me to always wake him up when I could not sleep, no matter what. He said that he always kept a clear conscience and never lived with any regrets, which is why he always slept so well. It was always okay for me to wake him to help me process something, but he is not helping me now, and all these people keep asking me questions. Bob said that I could always wake him up, but he is frustrating me now—he is not waking up. Can't he just answer just some questions, and then I will let him return to his science fiction show?

My two-and-a-half-year-old granddaughter Abby told me yesterday that she was sad that Bob was not here for her. I said Pops is always here, just in heaven at the moment. And when I put her to bed last night, she said she only wanted to pray for Pops, but first had a question for me. She wanted to know why Pops was in heaven and not with me, and I told her that just like she and I were best friends and loved spending time together, that's how Pops now felt. He had a new best friend named God, and they wanted to spend a lot of time together just like us and that made Pops very happy—so we should be happy for him. We said our prayer, and she fell asleep next to me. At 3:00 a.m. I woke up spontaneously like I always do and then Abby did as well, even though she never does. She has never woken in the middle of the night. But Pops woke her up so I would not be alone for a few minutes. I worried about what she might tell me, but it was only to say she was hungry. This is how I knew it was Pops—he was ALWAYS hungry.

And now I will start a new day and have no choice but to go on. I have a lot of people counting on me. When you see me—if you could spend just one second telling me how Bob made you laugh, how he helped you, what lesson he taught you—I think that would be good. I know you want to say you are sorry, and I accept that—no one is sorrier than me. Bob loved humor. Tell me how he made you laugh, and perhaps I will do the same.

Blessings for Today: Any quiet moment like now that I can reflect on who Bob was; my neighbors who do everything for me (And yes, this is NEW JERSEY!); my family surrounding me; and others coming to my side and to the funeral, although none of this was in my weekend plans. My Abby, who looked up at me while she was on the potty and said, "You know, Nana, I sure love you."

Specific Prayer Requests: I cannot say that Bob will get his way on this funeral thing—he hated any kind of recognition or attention. He had integrity and compassion and just lived by those values and more. He never wanted recognition for those things, and he thought everyone should live by those things and not need recognition. So my prayer is for guidance to recognize him in a way that would be most meaningful to him. When he sees that his services might bring ME peace (always thinking of me first), then I think he would make this one allowance.

Reflection

I grieved that Bob was not here for me and Abby. I could not understand what happened, yet I was forced to try to make sense of it for Abby. I loved her so very much, as did her Pops. They lived for one another, especially after Bob became her babysitter. All I could do was give Abby rote answers—maybe to convince her, but mostly to try to convince myself.

This was the beginning of some kind of psychological shift in my brain. I guess it was a protective mechanism. I was convinced that Bob was still with me. It was unfathomable that he was not with me. He said he would always be with me, and I believed he was, but I was not sure where. My mind made up all kinds of places where he might be, and it was strangely satisfying to know that he was out someplace or simply upstairs. I talked to Bob as if he were there. If someone asked me what happened to Bob, I could explain what happened to him and say that he was gone. But my mind would never really allow me to believe that for a very long time.

***

ENTRY   10/7/2016 at 6:58 a.m.

"THE ART OF RE-ADJUSTING HEARTS"

I searched for my heart this morning as I woke up (I am sleeping, but only due to drugs.) and realized it was not where it was supposed to be. It did not take me long to find it, however, as it was in my throat. Go down I tell you—go down where you belong so I can think of the blessings. I need to focus on the blessings…somehow when my heart travels to my throat it's not as easy because all you can focus on is breathing and surviving, and moving your heart back to where it belongs. It's the grief, you know. I miss Bob terribly today. My little Abby is sleeping, and when she awakens, she will help my heart go back to where it belongs for the day, so I will wait for that.

I asked Abby last night who she wanted to pray for and she said that she only wanted to pray for Pops. When I asked her what she wanted to say she said, "Well, I know God is with Pops and is watching over me, but I think they are also making sure I eat my broccoli." Pops loved many other things much more than broccoli (believe me!), and it did not sound like what he would do, but Abby knows that people who love her want her to eat healthy. She knows the difference, and well, however you want to interpret it, it was touching and funny nevertheless. She helped readjust my heart back to my chest where it belongs. She's my little heart re-adjuster.

I heard yesterday that there was a bad hurricane, and that Red Cross volunteers are needed desperately to serve—Bob and I both get these alerts into our emails. I also heard this from my best childhood friend, Lori. She cannot come to Bob's services as she is in the thrust of it now in north Florida. I am thinking of many others who will not be able to come to Bob's services because of their need to flee and serve. I wanted to see them and tell them how much they meant to Bob, and also to feel comforted by Red Cross volunteers, but many will be absent. Bob's got the big picture going on, however. He would want—and truthfully I do too—every last person to be doing their job to flee and serve. People are suffering today because of this storm, and there will be more suffering ahead. I am selfish—I want Bob here with me, and I want those he knows and loves to be at the services for me. But he knows there is suffering, so that will be his priority in the next days and weeks to come. He will spend his energies helping people somehow suffer less—my pathological giver. Do you hear me, everyone in the path of this horrible hurricane? Bob will be helping you!

Blessings for Today: Gail McGovern, the president of the Red Cross, called me two days ago. She is what some would call a big, important person, and she is indeed a VERY BIG IMPORTANT PERSON, but she is also a friend to Bob and me. We have loved and respected her from the beginning. She has had to make difficult decisions over the last several years about transforming the Red Cross and even letting people go, but Bob and I have always called ourselves "Gail McGovern loyalists." Bob even stopped listening to NPR a few years back when they said nasty things about the Red Cross. She is a role model to me. I admire her business skills, her compassion for humanity, and her ability to always let others know how much she cares—the perfect combination for her role in life. She said she wanted to do anything she could for me and Bob at this time, and she created a National Red Cross Award in Bob's name, a decision that was so unexpected that it blew me out of the water. Like Abby, Gail is a heart re-adjuster.

Each year, the Red Cross will name one person for excellence for disaster service. Even though Bob does not need or want recognition, I can tell you that he has been moved by this one. We have both been so moved by this gesture.

The funds from this award will come from people who donate to the Red Cross in Bob's memory, and I just learned that my other very important family, the Robert Wood Johnson Foundation (RWJF), will match five times what everyone else at RWJF will give. RWJF—and my family members there—heart re-adjusters!

Specific Prayer Requests: This one comes from Bob and me—that those in the path of this terrible hurricane stay safe and well and that those serving have the wisdom and strength to work tirelessly. I can only imagine that the next recipient of the Bob Hassmiller Award for Excellence in Disaster Service will be among you. It will be a hard decision to name just one, as thousands leave their own families to serve others—that's just what Red Crossers do. God bless those who are serving today, and those who will serve in the months and years to come—they readjust hearts forever.

Reflection

The notion of paying it forward was being actualized to me nearly every day in all kinds of ways. I felt such enormous pain, but such enormous pride in the way my husband lived his life, and the privilege I had to be his wife. Two very strong emotions co-existed side by side—no wonder I was weak and exhausted.

I was also caught up with the fact that people's lives around me went on, and I was incredulous that they could go on, in spite of such a loss. Was this transference—the notion of transferring your own feelings to others? My mind continued to play cruel psychological games on me. I could hardly stand on my own, but when I did, I found myself simply walking in circles.

***

ENTRY   10/8/2016 at 6:30 a.m.

"CIRCLES"

I will have a visitation service today for you, dear Bob, and a memorial service for you tomorrow. Okay, you know that is a lie. I cannot lie to you. I have never lied to you. You would not want this. But we want to honor and remember you. There are so many people who want to honor and remember you. But I know you don't want this. You never needed to be honored. Be there for us, however. Even though this would make you cringe, still please be there for me. Come with God, your new best friend, as I now tell Abby. God has always been part of your life, but I know this has brought you closer.

Abby understands best friends are there for you forever. She says Tessie is there for her always, so she misses you but accepts that you are with your new best friend because she knows that best friends are always there for you. You always told me that I was your best friend, and best friends are always there for each other. One of the last texts that we exchanged two Saturday nights ago, the night before the accident, was: Me: "Good Night My Forever Lifetime Partner" and You: "BFF." What happened, best friend? You left me. Why?

There will be people there tonight and tomorrow who are not part of my inner circle. I am a fairly private person. You would not think so reading this blog, but I am. I don't accept friends on Facebook (FB). Why does everyone need to know what I am doing all the time? You liked telling people, and you always told them about me, your grandkids and the Red Cross. I always yelled at you for putting so many pictures of me on FB…do people really care? But you said you were proud of me and wanted people to know, and same with the grandkids. But family was my business, and only open to a tiny number of inner circle people.

We have secrets—issues—doesn't everyone? I liked only having a small inner circle know about any of this. I did not mind going out on occasion to be with those who are one circle out from the inner circle, but that was about it. Circles 1 and 2—that's all I ever really needed, but you and I were mostly just Circle 1 people. And mostly we just liked being with each other…Circle 0.

So why I am I allowing us to venture beyond Circles 0, 1 and 2? To honor you? To help me? I am not sure. They say it will help me—all of us—all the circles with grieving and remembering, and then we can move on. Really? Move on? Is that what this is about…moving on? I don't feel much like moving on! It will be easier for Circles 2–5 to move on, but I will tell you it will be pretty darn difficult for Circles 0 and 1. What will I say to all those Circles today and tomorrow?

I am nervous…more nervous than I have ever been. I spoke two years ago to thousands at Carnegie Hall. You were there in the audience, remember? I was not nervous…I was excited as I always am to share my RWJF and Red Cross messages with small and large crowds alike because I believe so much in what I am doing and the messages I am conveying. I am confident. Today I am nervous and unconfident, and I am not sure what the message is. I am always sure of the messages I want to convey, but today I have no script—no one wrote any script for me. I am winging it with Circles I did not ask to be with. Can you and God help me today? I think if the two of you are there—my Circle 0 friend with your new BFF— that would help us all.

Blessings for Today: My daughter Kim, who in Bob's eyes never did one thing wrong. Honestly, we have discussed this, my Circle 0 friend and I…he is firm on this! I saw a few minor things here and there…tiny really…Bob saw nothing except a perfect being. Bob and Kim were their own Circle 0. And for the last few days it has been on Kim's shoulder to put together all these remembrances, with Mark's help, of her Circle 0 Daddy. She is so overburdened, losing hair, breast-feeding and soothing her crying four month old baby, but she told me last night it has helped her to put all this together…like me writing to you has helped. You will see pictures, hear scripture, sing songs, feel inspired, laugh and cry and know more about my Circle 0 friend than ever before. I really do thank you for coming and being with us in spirit and helping all of us honor my Circle 0 friend. I say that I don't want you there, but now that I am writing this…it is beginning to sound okay. I am still petrified to see you.

This journey has been about going beyond the Circles you are comfortable with, I suppose. I have allowed people into Circles 1 and 2 to help me, and these people say they feel privileged to help me. You are teaching me and my Circle 0 friend some strong lessons about being there and sharing and paying it forward. And now today, more Circles. Just be patient with me.

Specific Prayer Requests: That my Circle 0 friend and his new BFF are there with us all. That is most important. That others, no matter how many Circles we are talking about now, are inspired by your life and your new BFF. So, I will stop here now at 7 a.m. as I hear my Abby calling out to me to start a new day…she and her Circle 0 BFF, Tessie.

Reflection

It remains bizarre to me that as private as I am about my family I could write this blog. It was a combination of trying to make sense of all of this and honoring Bob. I have this enormous fear that everyone will just move on and forget about him. Not the Circle 1 folks, of course, but others, yes. I want the world to know what an extraordinary soul inhabited this earth for a time and the difference Bob made to those who knew him.

***

ENTRY   10/9/2016 at 7:42 a.m.

"COGNITIVE DISSONANCE...OR WHAT TO BELIEVE AND NOT BELIEVE"

I made it through one required event...the so-called visitation. So many people—good to see them, but perhaps, I would have "enjoyed" seeing them at another time, thank you very much. Bob, of course, would say all he wanted was his family sitting around remembering the good times. He would not want such a fuss, but I will say to him that these were all people who cared greatly, both family and friends (Circles 1–5), and took the time and the love to come. So, let's just put that one aside, Bob. On this one, we compromised. That's what you do in marriage and in all great relationships...you compromise. There were people sitting around talking about you, and that's not my fault that so many people cared about you. I could not control the numbers—that's your fault. You cannot peg this one on me.

I did not know what I was going to wear before Bob's service. With five minutes before it was time to leave, I saw red pants in my closet and then a white blouse, and then a navy blazer. I was married on the 4th of July, both of us wearing red, white and blue and it was always our most special day. Bob would have liked that I was dressed like a flag...he was really big on flags. He always said he lost his independence on Independence Day...and we both laughed and knew that was the truth!

My daughter and son put together an outstanding slide show and the songs, scripture and support were all over the top. I was so proud of everyone who shared their own special stories about Bob, especially my children, Mark and Kim. It was beautiful and I was grateful and was so inspired and uplifted, but I cannot stop thinking about how out of order this all was.

I go in and out; I don't know what to believe and not believe. That's cognitive dissonance, right? I don't use that phrase a lot, as I was never entirely clear on its meaning or when to use it. I think it's about conflict, about what to believe and not believe and how some things seem, even though they are really not that way. I don't know, but whatever it is, I seem to have it.

What to believe? That all will be okay (Yes and no…mostly no, at the moment); that I will move on (right now, that would be in the no category); that you hear Bob (tell me please what he is saying; I need to know); that you will be there for me (yes and no); that humor will get me through (yes and no); that Bob will be here for me (in what way do you mean?). Do you know that my washer machine stopped working yesterday, that I got a hospital bill that sent me to my knees, that the garbage had to go out or was it recycling day? Not sure I got it right. That Abby is asking why the doctors and nurses could not fix Pops; that I don't know how to work the thermostat to make people comfortable in my home; that I don't know where the tree clippers are to cut the branch that is about to fall; that Abby wanted to watch Minnie Mouse and I could not get the remote to work. What buttons do I press? You knew the buttons, I did not; that I get lost driving. The list goes on endlessly—just how will he be here for me…you tell me!); that having faith will save the day (I am holding onto this one…Mary texted me yesterday that, "the Lord is near to the brokenhearted and saves those who are crushed in spirit: Psalm 34–18…this seems like something I can believe).

Here is what I do believe: that for whatever reason God brought you into my life, and you made it a better life—actually a great life. Yes, we had challenges, but we always faced them with humor and faith. But what I saw and heard yesterday is that you did this for many. Someone told me that you were not really human, that you fixed all holes, sometimes holes she did not even know she had. Yes, that would be true. You are the best hole fixer I ever met. Reminds me of my song to you:

> The Spy Who Loved Me…the words that say,
> *Nobody does it better; makes me feel sad for the rest*
> *Nobody does it half as good as you*

Baby, you're the best
Nobody does it quite the way you do
Why did you have to be so good?

And therein lies cognitive dissonance again. WHY DID YOU HAVE TO BE SO GOOD? If you weren't, then it would not hurt so badly. It feels good, but it feels bad. I know I had it good…the spoiled one…and that's why it hurts so much. Is that what cognitive dissonance means? I'm still not sure.

Reflection

I wondered if it was worth all the pain to have loved in this way—to have been married to someone so wonderful. I hurt so badly and saw no end in sight and swore I would never put myself in a position to feel this much pain ever again. I realized that many people have lost loved ones. I wondered about their pain. I wondered how people bore this. I thought about the Holocaust and war and how people lost loved ones for no good reason. For the first time in my life, I thought about the fact that we are here and then we are gone. For what? What was the purpose of all of this coming and going?

***

Blessings for Today: Matt, who cannot always be here with me in person, but is definitely in the category of major league hole-fixer. He tells me that we will work through all of this with me…that he will handle things for me. He picked me off the floor when I showed him the medical bills. He says all the right things, and I believe him…no cognitive dissonance here. I believe in my soul that Matt's words to Bob in the last hours about taking care of this family is what gave Bob permission to go. Also, blessings for Mark, who is doing all he can at the moment for me and our family when he feels so despondent himself. He has a tremendous heart. For Chris/Jeff; Libbie/Paul; and Gary for opening their homes to allow out-of-towners to stay in my neighborhood. For the Polson and Lich families and Karen and Ray who came so far and others who came near and far to stand in the rain and only had a brief chance to tell me what Bob meant to you. It was important for you to tell me, and it was so important for me to hear. It helped Mark and Kim tremendously.

Specific Prayer Requests: That everyone be lifted up in the spirit of Bob's memorial service today and be blessed for having known this wonderful man—this hole fixer—the one who was too good to me. That I will somehow be able to pay all of this forward. Your love and words and support mean everything.

Reflection

The memorial service took place that afternoon. What I wanted to do was scream at everyone in attendance about the unfairness of it all—that my husband was ripped from me when we had so much to live for, and that I had no idea how I would ever go on. And that no one could ever begin to understand how desperate and alone I felt. I loved the slideshow that my children put together of Bob, and for a few brief moments, I felt a touch of happiness and pride that I had known such an extraordinary man. An out of body experience. I was particularly grateful for the words of Nurse Abby, who was the first to see and speak with Bob when he arrived at the trauma center. It was she who gave me the words, through email, to recite at Bob's memorial service when I would have otherwise been dumbfounded to find anything close to how I felt.

I thought about how many people were in the church and how I loved so many of them. But truth be told, it would have been so much better to have had such a wonderful gathering of friends and family for a much happier occasion.

***

ENTRY   10/10/2016 at 3:00 p.m.

"OUT OF ORDER"

I wanted to get this message out earlier, but my Abby woke early and in a startled voice. "Nana Nana, I have to make some phone calls." She has a little red toy calculator which never really worked…she really cannot use it as a calculator anyways, so to her this was always her cell phone. I handed it to her. When I asked who she had to call, she said that there were people falling off bicycles all over the place and she had to find out why. We called Frankie (made up name) and she asked him what made him fall off his bike. Frankie said that he went over a bump and lost his balance. And then she handed the "phone" to me and told me to tell Frankie that she loved her Nana. We then called Mary, who fell off her bike and was with Pops in Heaven. She told me that she is not getting very good answers from all the people she is calling…and then she called Tessie, who was also in a recent bike accident. Tessie told her that she was feeling so much better because Abby loved her so much and that seemed to do the trick. And later as she journaled (she scribbles incoherently in a Red Cross notebook), she told me today's story was about how her Nana and Pops always take such good of her. The End. So, that and Chuck E. Cheese is what occupied my morning.

I took it as a sign that Bob was speaking through Abby. I desperately wanted to remain connected to my husband in any way, shape or form. So, I chose to believe he was speaking to me in this way. Whether real or a protective mechanism, it didn't really matter.

I know now that these events were also desperate pleas by Abby to stay connected to Bob as well, and of course, to try to make sense of all of this. I wanted to believe, as Abby indicated, that love would make it all better. I thought it would eventually help. But at the time, nothing was making anything better. I just wanted Bob back. I lied to Abby, however, and told her that Pops was happy being with God. At least it helped me to practice those lines. Perhaps one day I would believe it.

I am a big planner—my days, months, years, vacations, family gatherings, all my presentations, meetings…everything! Yes, I know that sometimes things do not go as planned…I miss planes, the video I wanted to show for a presentation doesn't work. Hey, I am flexible enough to understand all of this and go with the flow and always stay calm. Important people that I want at meetings don't show up, but Bob leaving me was really out of order, more out of order than I know usually how to deal with. Way out of line, do you hear me? This was really brought home to me when I called the funeral home where I had made arrangements last year for my nearly ninety-one-year-old mother. The funeral director had to ask again… "What did you say? This is not about your mother? But you made plans with me based on your mother, and now you are telling me this is about your husband? Did I hear this right?" Yes, you did. This was out of order, I said—really out of order.

It was all planned, the way Bob and I talked frequently. We just did not know who would go first: Jake, our twelve-and-a-half-year-old dog, my mother's sidekick, or my mother. Bob and I talked about what might work best for the two of them, always making sure both were well cared for and making arrangements for both. We worried constantly about them. And Bob, who was seven-and-a-half years older than me, planned for how we would live out our years. He would go first when he was in his nineties and then I would follow several years later. We planned for that, emotionally and financially. We had all our trips planned out. Really?! It all sounds incredulous as I write this—as if I really had any control. SO OUT OF ORDER!

My husband retired so he could help be my mother's caretaker. All so out of order. I know friends who have lost children, spouses and the like…so I am not the only one to get this lopsided deal. I realize that and grieve for everyone who gets lopsided deals. I think of the kids at Sandy Hook, and the Holocaust victims…anything to give me some semblance of reason (reason?) for this crooked, out of order tale. I know I am not the only one…but God, did you realize all the effort I put into this planning? I am a really good planner—one of the best.

So maybe it's more about this: I really have no other thing to hold onto, so this is a reminder that life and death are out of our control…and even as I write this—I hate it—but have to accept it.

Reflection

My mother realized the cruelty that Bob was taken before her, and she felt guilty. She said that she would have rather died. Even Mark has said that God took the wrong person—that he should have gone instead. I lived through days of wishing I could just be with Bob, the way we had planned. I told my hairdresser, Issa, who was a good listener, these things. He finally told me that I was talented and that God had many ways that he wanted to use my talents. He said he could not quite say how it would all turn out, but that I would find ways to make sense of this, package it, and deliver it back to the world. I held onto this.

***

Blessings for Today: My little Abby and her fortitude to keep sending me messages as she tries to process this. I love her in infinite ways that I cannot explain. All who helped with the memorial service. And the ladies in my neighborhood who decorated the club house for me and made sure the family had a private dinner afterwards…thanks to Joyce, Colleen, Fran and Rita. The blessings that came from seeing so many at the visitation and memorial service for Bob…all so out of order…but all so loving and so grateful for all your presence and support.

Specific Prayer Requests: That I can find care for my mother. I am desperate to do so. I do want to eventually return to my job, but I cannot without care for my mother. That I can take all of this an hour and day at time…planning as I might…but having more understanding about who is in control. It does not appear to be me. Matthew 6:25–27 tells us, "Therefore I tell you, do not worry about your life, what you will eat or drink; or about your body, what you will wear. Is not life more than food, and the body more than clothes? Look at the birds of the air; they do not sow or reap or store away in barns, and yet your heavenly Father feeds them. Are you not much more valuable than they? Can any one of you by worrying add a single hour to your life?"

Reflection

I was drained and weak, yet trying to hold it together. I was gratified to talk about Bob in such a public way. Something he would never have wanted, but to make me happy, he stood for it. It helped Mark and Kim to work on such an extraordinary video of their Dad. Bob would have liked that they worked on something together, like that.

***

ENTRY   10/11/2016 at 9:41 a.m.

"GIFTS AND THE POWER OF ONE NURSE"

Although this has been the single greatest tragedy of my personal life, there are gifts. Some stare you in the face and you can't miss them. They walk in your front door with food or just start cleaning your house, or they make you sit down so they can rub your back, or they say I will be right there to be with you and then they actually show up (Second shift: my beloved Jane Polson here now from

Nebraska to relieve shift one, my beloved Kristen and Karen from Ohio)…clear gifts. Cannot miss these. And some are more subtle…like the red, white, and blue outfit that Bob picked out for me to wear at his funeral service.

And how Bob rallied before leaving us with smiles and kisses and understanding and acknowledging what was happening, and his peace. And how we got to say good bye…well this was not so subtle. It scared me, until someone had to say, accept this gift—this is his gift to you; many people don't get to say goodbye. And Matt, who told Bob he would be there for me and as the man of integrity and love that he is. He is here, the financial genius and Mr. Fixit. And then there was Nurse Abby.

Nurse Abby reached out to me after Bob was airlifted to the hospital in Philadelphia. I saw an email (subject line: With Love) in my inbox for a while, but I did not recognize the name, certainly did not connect it to her, so I let it go. A few days before his memorial service, however, I decided to look at this email as it came in a second time…"with love." She said that in all her years of nursing she had never before reached out to a family…she worried about her being "unprofessional" and worried about administrative consequences…but Abby felt compelled to write to me.

I read, at Bob's memorial service, the entire two emails she sent instead of using my own words. She spoke for me. So, even though Abby said she did not know why she felt compelled to reach out to me, I knew it was another gift from Bob and his new best friend God. Three Muskateers. Abby is an earthly angel and a nurse, and I will never forget her. I will never ever forget her skills as a nurse and how she packaged that with kindness and compassion.

Here are a few short excerpts of what Nurse Abby sent to me:

"My heart continued to ache in the coming days as I pondered over how tragic it is that a person can be healthy and enjoying life one minute and then suffer a life-changing, devastating injury the next. Despite years of health care experience, this set of circumstances weighed heavily on me. Perhaps it is because Bob reminded me so much of my own bike-riding sixty-eight-year-old father, or perhaps it is because when I looked into Bob's eyes to explain what I needed to do, I felt a soul-piercing sensation that Bob was a wonderful man.

Whenever I am preparing to assist someone into a state of sleep, I tell them to "think happy thoughts, let your dreams be good ones while you sleep," as they drift into unconsciousness in what I hope is a more peaceful and relaxed mindset...I am sure as I gave Bob these instructions and he closed his eyes, he was envisioning you. As a follow-up to what I said previously regarding someone being so lucky to have a person like Bob by their side, I'd like to add that I am so thankful a person like Bob was blessed (rewarded!) to have someone who cared for him so deeply and made him so happy. Love stories like yours don't happen too often. As an oncology nurse early in my career, I had first row seats to life's final moments more often than I ever wanted. As much as I needed to be there for family members during these tough moments, it was heartbreaking—especially as people conveyed their regrets to me. I get the sense that neither Bob nor you live a life of regrets and this brings joy to my heart and some semblance of sense back to the universe. I know right now you wish nothing more than Bob's presence, but I hope eventually this will provide you comfort too. Thank you for being Bob's advocate and best friend until the end."

And after she found this blog, she wrote, "Now, after learning more about Bob—his life's work, his personality, his example as a husband/father/grandfather, I know my instinct was spot on. My brief but powerful encounter with Bob had an enormous impact. Know that Bob's life had an immense impact, even on those he met only briefly, and the ripple effect has only just begun.

Blessings for Today: Nurse Abby and the lessons this has for nurses and all health professionals...that their clinical skills mean everything in the world to us... Don't ever stop honing your clinical skills, but your compassion is life changing.

Specific Prayer Requests: Pray for those who are lost and suffering... You or those you know...or those you don't know...and for life-changing compassion.

Reflection

Few things have struck me as so profound as this one nurse. You may have to be a nurse to truly understand the full meaning. Sure, you can relate to and love her compassion. However, the way that she felt absolutely compelled to reach out to me and to tell me intimate things about my husband was not of this world. It is not something nurses normally do. Care for people in real time, sure, but not to reach out in this way afterwards. I truly believe with all of my heart that Bob was speaking through Abby. It is just too out of the ordinary for one nurse to feel so compelled.

She later told me that she felt an enormous spiritual and psychological pull to reach out to me and tell me specific things. She couldn't explain it fully, but just that the pull would not ease up until she found me and spoke to me. Bob, I will never forget the power of Nurse Abby reaching out to me, and it sustains me still.

***

ENTRY   10/12/2016 at 8:46 a.m.

"SESAME STREET: THE LETTER FOR TODAY IS D"

So, this is what I would say to all of you at the moment—unsubscribe to my posts if and when this gets to be too much for you. I probably would at this time. You have your lives to live. Although I lived at the corner of "happy and healthy," we still had our challenges. I liked to keep things simple. If I ever watched television—and it was very little—it always revolved around one version or another of the Home and Garden Channel. Very simple…a couple had a housing challenge, they said what they wanted, and the stars of Home and Garden simply made it happen. Very tidy and happy and satisfying.

My favorites are Chip and Joanna because they remind me of Bob and me. Not that we had their skills—clearly not—it was more their personalities. Joanna says what she wants in the house, and Chip said, "I trust you…that sounds great." But more than that, Chip is corny and a jokester like Bob, and Joanna always rolls her eyes. I was famous for my eye rolls. What I would not give for a little corny now, so that I could roll my eyes. People laughed at us all the time—Bob's corniness and my eye rolls. Sometimes I would pop Bob on the shoulder just like Joanna does to Chip. I watched five minutes here and there of Fixer Upper with Chip and Joanna just to be reminded of what the corniness and eye rolls felt like.

So, here is where I should give you the big warning: "Be advised that the following message contains graphic language that might be offensive and disturbing to the reader." Here is where you should go no further if you want to go on with your happy productive day (which you should!). I wish happiness and joy for everyone. We need more in the world, so go on.

For me, this is Sesame Street—a world that is not real to me—with fictional characters who have costumes on…and they are happy. I keep thinking of words that start with the letter D. Today's letter, boys and girls is the letter D: Deceased, Dark, Divided, Drugs, Despondent, Disgusting, Dependent, Desperate, Down, Disintegrated, before my very eyes. Here one moment and gone the next. Did Cookie Monster eat him? I am not sure why this happened, but Kathy, who lost her husband in 9/11, said it is a fruitless question and one that we will only be able to answer when we are gone ourselves.

Disturbed, Disenchanted—more D words. Kim, who is struggling mightily, said that I should always try to end on the positive. She likes the word Delicious. Daddy Boy, as she refers to him, was simply delicious in every way possible. Happy and delicious—you wanted to just eat him up.

I thought how the letter of the day used to be H: Happy, Healthy, Home, Helping, Homogenous, Holidays, and Heart. Bob had the biggest heart of all. Too much of a heart. When I asked him where he wanted to live throughout our lives and when we retired, he always gave the same answer: he said his home and heart was with me.

One early post-Thanksgiving Black Friday morning, we were waiting in line at Best Buy. It was freezing and dark, and he said it was stupid to wait in line for an hour in the cold and dark just for a half-price television. I caught him. I said, "Ah ha, you always said as long as we were together that nothing else mattered." But he said I took that out of context— it did not mean waiting in line in the dark and cold for a half-price television. So, we left and simply walked into Walmart and bought the same television for almost the same price. Compromise.

Blessings for Today: Hearing back from Nurse Abby about how overwhelmed and honored she was that she was the focus of my blog yesterday. She told me that she recently had to fill out a survey for her work on nurse burn out, and the last two questions asked her to provide answers to the following: "In the past month, what work-related event has caused you the most sadness?" and "In the past month, what work-related event has caused you the most happiness?" Here is her response: "The answers, 'Bob's death' and 'Reaching out to Sue' were obvious replies for me. And so I wrote them, clicked send, and spent the next hour or so reflecting on things before I drifted off to sleep. I thought about how meaningful it has been to connect with you. I had no idea you were a nurse when I first came looking for Bob's family in the ICU that day. It would be an honor to be able to connect with anyone during such a sensitive time, but the fact that you are a nurse and are woven from the same fabric, makes this all the more special to me." She also said she will be here for me…and said she means it! And I know she does.

Specific Prayer Requests: I don't know. You read my blog. I think some of you know better than me what is needed. I am depressed, and that starts with D.

Reflection

I was consumed with dread and found it hard to speak to people in ways that wouldn't scare them off. Very few people truly understand the loss of a beloved spouse. So I took to this blog to fill blank spaces with the depths of my soul. The world, I supposed, was going on, but I only felt grief and could speak of grief— nothing else. For those who didn't want to hear it, we would part ways.

***

ENTRY   10/13/2016 at 8:13 a.m.

"TOO MANY DOORS"

I don't like malls. I never have, and I never will. There are far too many doors to go in and out of, and too much stimulation and too many choices. I never understood why people need so many choices in life. Bob and I mainly went to Eddie Bauer and Columbia. We biked, hiked, walked, swam, explored and just hung out. Those two stores had all we needed and more, to do exactly what we

wanted to do. Many times, like now, we just kept the same clothes on for a few days at a time. Who cared? We had better things to think about than clothes. Yes,

I had to buy work clothes, so I shopped twice a year at Chicos and Talbots. That was it. We kept it simple.

We spent a lot of time last winter at the Freehold Mall, but that was when we had Abby and outdoors was not an option. The Freehold Mall has a carousel, a kids train, and an ASPCA animal adoption center, where we pet the animals and rejoiced when one was adopted. That's it—there were no stores. We wandered, sang, and enjoyed being together. Bob pushed my mother in her wheelchair, and I pushed Abby in her stroller. We were a happy team, and we knew the routine: the train first, then the animals, then the carousel, followed by pizza and "brownie milk." We loved our winter routine. Once, we went into the dollar store for a BIG lollipop, but that was it. Don't tell Kim.

I have far too many doors to go into now, most of which I did not and still do not want to go through: "Trauma Bays;" ICU rooms of any kind (I was never an ICU kind of nurse, so I have always tried to stay away from those kinds of places); funeral homes; and the cemetery gates tomorrow. I am scared to go back to work and enter through those doors, as well as the doors of Newark airport and the train station—all doors that I must go through to "move on". I have made it through some of these doors already and am still standing. With help, I will get through the other doors, but there are other less tangible doors that are even scarier.

The less tangible doors are those called shame (I can never live up to the kind of man Bob was, and I did take you for granted at times—you spoiled me terribly); guilt (I should have told you not to bike ride on that day...that we had the trip of our lifetime that we were about to embark on within days and it would not be fun if you got a broken arm or twisted your ankle...so be careful...I thought that but never said anything...Would you have listened and stayed off the bike?); I'm not good enough (what have I ever done to deserve all the love I am being given?); fear (of the unknown and facing life without you); anger (that I had to spend the last two days working on caregiver plans for my mother and you were not here to help me).

I have more decisions to make...why are you not here to help me? I don't want to spend my time doing this but must; loneliness; the revolving doors of despair and disbelief (I know, the D words again...I got ever so gently zinged by friends yesterday who offered many other D words that I might focus on like Dedicated, Devoted, Divine, Durable and Dependable. I had to laugh at Kim Harper's D word of the day…Donation…I really appreciated the offers of so many other D words! They all made me smile…all so much better than my own D words).

There are other doors, however, that feel a bit better—actually a whole lot better, but are still a bit scary…There are doors called love; faith; support; friendship. Love is still a scary door for me as it is mixed in with the door of underserving; double doors if you will…you know the kind; one swings in and the other swings out…what did I ever do to deserve your love and support? It blows me away every day. I know Bob was great and wonderful, so I am trying very hard to accept all your help and love on behalf of him. As you know it would make him cringe—he was always first in line to help, and maybe he still is. Yes, actually, as I write that I believe that he is first in line to STILL provide me with love and support, he and his new BFF (the door of faith)…just a few (hundred) people behind him to lend a hand and prayers and beautiful words. I think it would be okay with him for others to help me (Circles 1–5)…as long as they were not trying to help him. I think he would like this and be so grateful to all of you for helping the love of his life.

It is hard for me to humbly accept your love and help and thank you is never enough. It has humbled me to my knees. I have one friend who texts me IMMEDIATELY after I send out my blog every day, and she tells me what she thinks; I have two friends who email me late at night…or late for me…9:00 p.m.…to make sure they know I am okay…and they always have sage advice and loving words…they understand this walk, so I trust them and email them back. Others text me sporadically, but faithfully…just a few words or a few lines. Others say their words are far too personal for open view of all who go to this website, so they email me privately with beautiful words that help. Some call—you are brave to call—you actually have to hear my depressing voice. Not fun. You all tell me things that you have been more inspired to do, as a result of this "situation" and some tell me you are using this in your classrooms to teach compassion.

Blessings for the Day: I really don't like a lot of doors, but some are good doors, and you have forced me to see beyond simply the door of Sue and her Circle 0 love, Bob. I loved that door the most. I would give up all your doors for just having that one door back, but I am grateful for your help in getting me through the hard ones—almost all of them. You have become my doormen, letting people into my building who are trustworthy and faithful. And to Frank, who will fix my two broken toilets—the doors to bathrooms are really, really important too!

Specific prayer for the day: For my children and Abby, who continues to ask everyone she meets why people fall off their bikes and get hurt and have to live someplace else. She wants to know where people sleep when they are no longer with us and if they get to watch their favorite television shows. Matthew 7:7–8 promises, "Ask and it will be given to you; seek and you will find; knock and the door will be opened to you. For everyone who asks receives; the one who seeks finds; and to the one who knocks, the door will be opened."

Reflection

My emotions were all-consuming. Fear, dread, anger, grief—so much grief. And continued disbelief that all of this really happened in the first place. But I was also bombarded by love, kindness, and compassion. They fought each other daily for my attention, and it was draining. I lost weight and the muscle tone I had developed from doing all the activities that Bob and I loved to do…bike, hike, swim, and dance. I could barely walk, and when I did, it was usually only in circles.

***

ENTRY   10/14/2016 at 3:31 p.m.

"AND THE AD SAYS: HEALING NEEDED. INQUIRE WITHIN"

Most days I know where to begin with my message for the day, but today I struggle. Today is the day that we took Bob to the Veterans Cemetery.

I have always been so proud of my husband and his military service in Vietnam. He was shot twice and received a Purple Heart. He never swayed from loving his country. He never went on and on about why he had to go and the stupidity of it all. He was never bitter or said that he hated his country or the government. Yes, he was scared, but he went, proud to serve his country. We have never lived in a house without a flag flying 24/7. He frequently visited the Vietnam Memorial in Washington, D.C., to pay tribute and remember his entire platoon, almost all of which died. His patriotism fit in with our decision to get married on July 4th, and it is why I wear a ring with diamonds, sapphires and rubies.

The service today was to be extremely meaningful. It was for family only with full military honors. A flag in his honor from our President. The service would be short; fifteen to twenty minutes; as the waiting list for the chapel and getting in is so long. I could not say I was looking forward to it, but I wanted this for Bob, and obviously, he thought it would be a good idea at the time we signed up.

Instead of a calm morning, emotions were raw, sharp and with little sleep. Grieving was at its height, setting an unexpected bad stage for the final good bye. A screaming match between my children ensued, and I was shattered and heartbroken. Easy to expect these kinds of things at these times, but as I tried to mediate I was shaking and heartbroken. I understand everyone's emotions and everyone's "side" so well at these times. There was no side for me to take except for Bob's, and we were both heartbroken. He cried with me. I do not want to go into any more details, but we were a family broken and crying instead of at peace with this final good-bye. I know what you are all thinking now—these people really need HELP! Stop writing these blogs and go out and get some real help! And yes, we are moving towards that, but just have not gotten there yet.

I rode in the car with my close family friend Jane, who knew she was signing up for combat duty when she offered to come. But I don't think she knew fully: this is the land of the traumatized and the severely wounded, and she would be serving right at the front lines. We rode silently for the forty-five minutes to the cemetery. As we approached the chapel, Jane simply said, "just let this be between you and Bob and God…block out the rest." I followed her instruction and felt all the better for it.

Pastor Dan conveyed some scriptures, and then I took over, knowing that our twenty-minute shot at this military chapel was slipping fast. I said to my small family that I wanted us to do what we do every Thanksgiving and Christmas, and that is to go around the room and say what we most appreciate about each other. I offered to start. I said that my husband's sense of humor could get me through anything in life. And indeed it could and did. I said that Mark had a sensitive, brave heart and was trying so hard to help in ways that he could…I love his heart and how he takes care of his Grandma; that I love Grandma's sense of adventure; that Jane has been with me through thick and thin and never asks why, but just asks when; that Matt loves my daughter with all his heart and takes care of everything— his wife, his kids, and now helping me; and that my daughter is my heart—she has my heart, always has and always will—and she knows it. Everyone chimed in and said with kindness and contrition how much we all meant to each other…each one getting a special recognition from the others. Bob would like most that we did this. That we did a family hug and then cried together. Pastor Dan (knowing of the morning screaming matches) said when this happened, it was divinely inspired and perfect. Thanks to Jane for moving me to this plateau in the first place. Of all the ceremonies of this entire week, Bob would have liked those twenty minutes the most.

I did this for you, my dear Robert Boy, so that you could have some faith that we would somehow be okay…that we would make it—not easily and not without hurt and anger and crying and shouting—but somehow, we will make it, dear one…my best friend. Do you hear me? Did you see the hug afterwards? We hate that you left us. We are really more than angry, but I don't want this to be in vain for you. We always said that we must leave this world a better place, you and I, and I am trying so hard for you, but I need your help….you and your new BFF.

Blessings for Today: That your life was NOT taken on the battlefields of Vietnam—that I eventually met you and that we had thirty-seven years together. And that I think we will all try very hard to make you proud. We will slip mightily at times—like today—but we will keep trying. You are my hero, and I just want you to know that I will give it my all and that together as a family perhaps we can all help each other.

Specific Prayer Requests: For all those serving in dangerous posts in our military services. I am proud of you for serving your country. You are in good company with my husband and many other brave men and women. Pray for Mark and Kim and for those of you who know very specifically about them and their needs…you will know how to individualize your prayers. And for those of you who have been hounding me about self-care, I hear you! I will get there. I do have my little Abby for starters, and when she sings to me I hear Bob singing with her. Their favorite is: Twinkle Twinkle Little Star. Keep singing, Abby, keep singing.

Reflection

I resented that I needed to play the mediator in my family. It was a role that Bob and I swapped on and off, depending on who was most up for it on a particular day, but on that day, I had to step in. That was the beginning of the realization of how every single role that Bob and I shared were now being squarely dumped onto my lap. Not only the tasks of daily life, including fixing things, paying bills, maintaining automobiles; but the emotional and psycho-social roles as well. The one role that went by the wayside was the humorist. Bob had a way of keeping things light, with humor, and I had no skill or desire to use humor. A huge and devastating void.

***

ENTRY   10/17/2016 at 7:48 a.m.

"HOPE AND JUSTICE...AND THE CURSE OF 3:00 A.M."

Bob had a saying that he repeated every day of his life. When someone asked him how he was doing, he always complimented the person who asked. If I asked, he responded, "If I were any better, I would be married to Sue Hassmiller...Hey, wait a minute, I AM married to Sue Hassmiller, so that must mean I am great." He said the same to friends and coworkers: "If I were any better, Abby and Jeff, I'd get to work with you every day...Hey, wait a minute, I DO work with you every day, so I must be great." Or, "If I were any better, I would get to help people at the Red Cross... Hey, wait a minute, I DO get to help people at the Red Cross, so I must be great." If Abby asked, he said: "If I were any better Abby, then I would be your Pops...Hey, wait a minute, I am your Pops, so I must be the happiest Pops in all the land, and you are my fairy princess." The ultimate optimist.

Sometimes I would ask him when we were handling hard times (at least in my book) how he could keep telling people he was great when that was not really the case. He'd first look at me incredulously and then say, "Are you kidding me? Do you know how much harder other people have it?! We are not going through half as much as other people." Well, Robert Boy, I cannot get above this one...I need your help on this one. I know I have blessings, but I cannot fill in that sentence like you always could, and you faced some difficult circumstances in your life, worse than many. A very young marriage that did not last, getting shot in Vietnam, a mother who drank too much, losing a father too young to a medical error and more.

When people ask me how I am, I say a variety of things, but never that I am great. You would not expect that of me, would you? I imagine that if the tables were turned, you might say, "If I were any better, then I would have had the greatest fortune for any one man to have in a lifetime to have been with the love of my life for thirty-seven years…Hey, wait, I was with the love of my life for thirty-seven years, so I must be great." Would you really be able to say that and mean it? I've heard you say that mantra of yours in very dire circumstances, but could you really say that now?

I am getting by every day, mostly because there are tasks to do and people to visit with—very kind and wonderful people, including my children and grand-children, but then the door of the bedroom closes, and I am alone. Medication helps, but it seems to only last until 3a.m., the bewitching hour. Flashbacks of what could have happened differently; that magic clock to turn back the time (still have not found it); the brutality of the procedures you endured for ten days (I relive each procedure); the accident itself and how I imagine it; what people said to me and what I knew you were thinking as you lay there only able to look at me. I remember every minute of being with you in the hospital and how I could not fix things for you. I could only whisper many things in your ear that will stay between the two of us. My insides and body shake. I have flashbacks throughout the day when people are chatting about something or another, and I go in and out listening to them and envisioning you. But mostly, my body shakes at 3:00 a.m. to think of all of this. I pray—I always pray—I try to relax and meditate as Dawn taught me. Eventually, the medication kicks in, and I can sleep again. I don't know if I believe that saying that "it is better to have loved and lost than never to have loved at all." Too much pain for now.

A colleague of mine, Laure, sent me an email the other day and said she was up at 3:00 a.m., googling even more about Bob (really, Laure…3:00 a.m.?) She sent me a link of an interview that he did about being the CEO of a small national association for ten years. You can read it if you want, but to me the most telling question from the interviewer is the following: "What would you say is the most important responsibility for an association leader today?

Bob: "Easy. It's the CEO's job to accept blame and give away credit [chuck-ling]. It's only a problem when you get it reversed."[2]

Blessings for Today: I attended Lifetree Christian Church yesterday, the same church that held Bob's memorial service. I did not announce that I was coming, but did ask Joyce, (Pastor Dan is her son-in-law) what time the service was in case I showed up. And dress was important. I do not like to dress up. She said, "The pastor wears jeans." I thought it all sounded promising, especially the jeans part, so I informed my daughter and family that we should go. From the moment I walked in, it was meant to be. A neighbor, Nancy Costa, was the prayer leader that day, and said she had prepared for a long time, but since the events of last week she had some other things to say. Her tribute to Bob in a church filled with strangers who never knew him was such a gift. Thank you, Nancy. She used the scripture that we found in Bob's Bible, all marked up about what God expected of him. Micah 6: 6–8 reads:

> "With what shall I come before the Lord
> and bow down before the exalted God?
> Shall I come before him with burnt offerings,
> with calves a year old?
> Will the Lord be pleased with thousands of rams,
> with ten thousand rivers of olive oil?
> Shall I offer my firstborn for my transgression,
> the fruit of my body for the sin of my soul?
> He has shown you, O mortal, what is good.
> And what does the Lord require of you?
> To act justly and to love mercy
> and to walk humbly with your God."

And then Pastor Dan's message was on justice and revenge—something I could really relate to. Pastor Dan even used a quote from Bob's all-time favorite movie, *The Princess Bride* ("You killed my father. Prepare to die!"). How did he know that Kim and Bob watched The Princess Bride repeatedly? That we walked Kim down the aisle to this movie's theme song? Did you know this, or did Bob tell you to slip that one in to get our attention? And he too, cited Bob in his message—the man he never knew, but came to know through us these past few weeks—a man, who he learned, always tried to act justly, love mercy and walk humbly. He also quoted Micah 6:6–8. He sent Bob's credo to the congregation, and I knew I was where I was supposed to be for that moment. Pastor Dan said to everyone (but I felt he was speaking to me…and perhaps he was) that in the end justice will prevail. He did not say I could have it now, but it will come, so I will hold onto that.

I cannot end without thanking my dear and blessed friend Janie, who leaves to return to Nebraska today. She helped me with really, really hard stuff—sorting through the mounds of paper, looking for deeds, titles, leases, and more. *She made important* "to do" lists for me of tasks that Bob used to take care of and was patient when I became distracted and could not follow the list exactly, and she took my mother to McDonalds every morning for her English muffin and coffee. You will be missed.

Specific Prayer Requests: That I can remain open to finding blessings in all of this pain and somehow help others through similar pain. For Kim and Mark—for Kim who says she needs help, and Mark, who is not quite sure that he really needs any help at all. That we can all understand and know the scripture that Bob gave us to hold onto: Micah 6: 6–8.

Reflection

Attending the church service was my first foray into the world as everyone else knew it. Until that time, I stayed in my cocoon with only family and close friends, who might remotely understand my loss. They did not get scared away with all of the grief pouring out of me. Walking into a group of strangers was scary, yet I did it. Getting out in a semi-sheltered environment, albeit with strangers, was the right thing to do. I was trying to follow my boss, Risa's advice of listening to my heart and following its guidance.

***

ENTRY   10/18/2016 at 7:14 a.m.

"TO TELL THE TRUTH"

There was a popular television show that ran from 1956 to 1968 called "To Tell the Truth." It may be too early for many of you to remember, but I remember it well. The show featured a panel of four celebrities whose goal was to correctly identify a described contestant who has an unusual occupation or has undergone an unusual experience. This "central character" is accompanied by two impostors who pretend to be the central character; together, the three people are said to belong to a "team of challengers." The celebrity panelists question the three contestants; the impostors are allowed to lie, but the central character is sworn "to tell the truth." After questioning, the panel attempts to identify which of the three challengers is telling the truth. In essence, this panel gets to decide who they think the real person is…the special person…the one worthy of being put on the panel in the first place.

Of course this reminds me of Bob…how among a very large lineup of imposters, he was not lifted up as the special one—the one who got to stay—the one who was identified as telling the truth about who he really was…what he stood for…the person who won the game. I was in the audience…I was cheering for you to win the game, my Robert Boy. I cheated as they told the audience members not to yell out the truth or give answers away, but I was yelling it out anyways (rules are for others). We all were yelling and praying that the panel would be able to determine the real person from all the imposters. So many other imposters! (I know I am not supposed to judge other people's lives, but this is my blog and I can do and say whatever I want!) Yes, I am making judgment. I am, I am!

The imposters on Bob's show were liars and cheaters. They stole, they murdered, they hurt people, they were mean people who used guns to kill, they bullied, they used people to further their own gains, and they have no conscience about any of it. But somehow they lied, and the panel believed them—they got to stay. Why did they not believe Bob? He was the real hero. I called Bob the real hero of our family. He directly helped people every day. Maybe it was because Bob was too humble, and he did not speak up loudly enough and was not convincing enough to the panel. How could they not believe him over so many cruel and unjust and horrible people? Did the panel not know that this man stood for truth, justice, humility and helped everyone on this earth to a fault?

It should have been so clear to the panelists, but they got it all wrong. Did the panelists know how much more good he had to do, and that he promised his family he would always be there for them? Now his grandkids will not know him. He lived by God's word—why did the panel not know this? What was in the panelists' heads, who chose imposters over this man, Bob Hassmiller? Maybe this is a lesson in…actually, I don't know what the lesson is. I keep looking for lessons, and all I see are people, who are good and help mankind, die, and there are horrible people who get to live—the imposters. If anyone has an answer, please let me know: Why do the imposters stay, and Bob had to go?

Blessings for Today: My third shift, Lori, is here today. My childhood friend from Florida arrived at midnight. She left her job and home, like all my other shift workers, to be with me. Two years ago, we celebrated fifty years of friendship and met up in New York City. We told three girls in their 20s in our hotel elevator that we were celebrating fifty years of friendship. I could tell they thought we must be very old, but they congratulated us anyways. I am hoping the third shift will be easier, but I cannot guarantee Lori…grief changes from hour to hour. You have all earned a piece of Bob's Purple Heart. I found it the other day—there was just one Purple Heart, but you have all done combat duty to have a piece of it. Maybe Lori can help me understand why imposters get to stay, and truth seekers have to leave.

Specific Prayer Requests: That I can figure out how to help myself and somehow find my will again. I currently have no will. I promised Bob that I would not give up, however…that I would keep doing what I love to do with my job, family and volunteer work. I am a person of my word…always dependable, and promises are very important to me. This is what I promised Bob, the truth seeker and non-imposter. It is hard for me to keep my promise when I am struggling to understand why others have not kept their promise to me, but I will try somehow. There are a lot of truth seekers who are helping me.

Reflection

The stages of grief are not always straightforward. I find myself going in and out of them at someone else's will. Certainly not my own. Disbelief, and thus conjuring up stories and notions in my own mind about where Bob is (at work, helping with a disaster, upstairs reading) and then anger and physical pain when somehow I am jolted back to reality. It all takes so much energy. Just to get up in the morning takes energy. I am weak in mind and body and look to others to make decisions for me. Even the simplest of decisions take energy from a source that is depleted.

***

ENTRY   10/19/2016 at 7:22 a.m.

"LETTER FROM YOUR DEAD HUSBAND"
(IF YOU READ NO OTHER BLOG POST, READ THIS ONE)

I have so many thoughts and demons floating around in my head…voices that I don't want to hear like a bad and cheap amusement park where the rides are going around and around and upside down and backwards and jerking you around, and people are screaming to go on this ride or that ride, or to play this game or that game. It's easy to win it all. Really? You are an imposter for saying that—go away. It is all too noisy, and the ride operators really do not care if you are safe or not. It's just a job; they don't care. The roar of the rides, the smells of all things bad that we should not eat, like fried Oreos. Someone is sitting in a mansion someplace right now because of the very crazy idea of fried Oreos making a bundle of money because everyone is eating them.

And all I want to hear are two voices: Bob's and God's. But the noise is deafening. So much great advice is coming my way, and I don't want it to stop—it is my connection to many of you, so hear me and don't stop…but I long most for the mantra of, "Be still and know that I am God"…I have repeated that from the beginning. It is the only scripture I can remember and repeat with my depleted brain, to be honest. Be still and know that I am God. I am not good at being still and now am really lousy at it. All this pushing and shoving and noise. But I hold onto that scripture anyways.

One way I can hear Bob's voice is from a letter he left me called a "Letter From Your Dead Husband." He has left me an updated version of this letter every year for the last ten years or so. It started when we were hiking in Arizona and he decided to tell me all about the financials and what I should know. Really? He wanted to ruin the hike by discussing things I didn't care about. Couldn't we just enjoy the walk, nature and each other? Bob insisted, and I gave in, but to be honest it went in one ear and out the other. I cared about a lot of stuff, but numbers and investments and deeds and bills and everything that is supposed to be really, really important I did not care about. Besides, it spoke of being gone and separated from Bob, and that was not going to happen, right? Why have this conversation if Bob was going to keep his promise and never leave me and always take care of me? I trusted him on this one. We had plans, really great and wonderful plans…So couldn't we just hike, please?

Bob knew that he had to take a different approach with me, so every year he wrote me a letter called "Letter from Your Dead Husband." This was the only way he could safely and lovingly let me know every single detail of every single thing I would ever need to know financially and much more. At some point, Deborah, a financial consultant with her own local TV show, featured Bob and me. She found the advice novel and useful to her TV audience, so we agreed to be interviewed on air. Bob explained why he did this, and I politely said how I thought this was probably the ultimate gesture of love and care—to ensure that your loved one does not have the burden of financial worries and where papers and passcodes are. I think maybe she read about how he did this every year in an article he wrote for Motley Fool.[3]

Bob felt so strongly about this that he shouted from the rooftops for all who would listen to please do this for your loved ones. It will matter, he said. He knew this deeply as his own parents left absolutely nothing—no words, no wills, and no instructions. Bob vowed never to do that to me, nor should anyone do that to someone they love.

I got out the letter this morning. I certainly did not understand all the many pages of numbers in between, but my extraordinary son-in-law did. He took the letter, and like a perfect recipe for Mom's Apple Pie, it was all there. No guess work. Matt has helped me to gain a financial footing, but he could never have done as well as he has without the detailed instructions from Bob.

The parts that I paid attention to were the first and last paragraphs:

"Dearest Sue: I want you to know that I've enjoyed every minute that I've been able to think about our future together as I've done this financial planning. But, if you're opening this letter, something has happened. This makes this planning all the more important, and please know that I have done all in my power to care for you and your future."

And then it ends with, "I want you to find someone else who will make you happy. Having said that, I suggest you establish a pre-nuptial agreement to protect you. I always want to ensure you are protected. I hope you know how often I've reviewed these numbers to ensure that you and I spend as good a time in the future as we've done to date. I TRULY LOVE YOU and want you ALWAYS to be happy. Now put this away and hopefully you won't need this for another forty years."

Blessings for Today: I hate this part of my blog, but it might be the most important. I feel my biggest blessing has been ripped from me, so why this self-enforced paragraph about blessings? What happened to the forty additional years you promised me, Robert Boy? I would rather wallow at the moment, thank you very much. But my message to you is to please, everyone, take care of your blessings. Of course, it is so hard to go on—Bob wants me to find another who can make me happy. Are you kidding me? I know he meant well, though. But to know that I have this letter with detailed instructions, and Matt to decipher, eases part of the pain. I cannot imagine anyone who could have loved me more in every possible way. "It is better to have loved and lost than never to have loved at all." I still don't know about this one, but I see a glimpse of it in this letter.

Specific Prayer Requests: Follow Bob's advice. [The link to the video is in the endnotes.[4]]If you are the financial person in the family, write a letter now to your loved ones. I make it through hour by hour only…and for those of you who have been hounding me from the beginning to see a grief counselor, I have an appointment today at 4:00. I will tell the counselor about this letter and much more. And pray always for my children, Mark and Kim, and my son-in-law Matt, who like Bob, truly and deeply understands the significance of this "Letter from Your Dead Husband."

Reflection

This letter and its instructions have guided me to this day. It meant that in the deepest wallows of grief, I did not have to think about what the passcodes were and where important papers were stored and whether the bills would get paid on time, not to mention what the bills were in the first place. Bob's letter was the ultimate act of love. I have counseled many to follow suit.

***

ENTRY   10/21/2016 at 8:09 a.m.

"KEEPING BOB ALIVE AND THE ADVENTURES OF 'POP'SICLE"

I find myself desperate to keep Bob's spirit alive. This is not a judgment, rather a fact of life, and one that I understand very well: People have moved on. They have their lives. The "events" are over, and, well, as I said…everyone must move on. I would not want it any other way. I would not want the world wallowing around with me. NO! Of course not! But for me, life stands still. I don't want to have conversations about the upcoming Presidential election, (Okay, bad example…Who in their right mind does?), Halloween, which television show to watch, what brand toilets to buy (I had to do this the other day and it drained me for the entire day), or ANYTHING. I do have these conversations in order to respond to all the wonderful people in my life who came to my rescue and who are still there for me: "Yes, the weather is warm," "Yes, the trees look simply lovely this time of year," "OH, wonderful, your grandchild got into Princeton, so wonderful." And it's not that I am beyond being polite or acknowledging everyone; it's just not where my mind is. It is not what I care about right now. You understand, right?

Someone told me today that I have made progress…I suppose that means I have gone from being immobile and thinking of only Bob, to now being more mobile and thinking of only Bob. It's all relative. I agree progress has been made, but I still cannot converse for too long about the mundane when there are bigger and more relevant questions and issues for me, including how to get care for my mother.

So, that's where Popsicle comes in. I have been spending a lot of time with my little angel, Abby. She asks me to pray for Pops and has many questions about where he is sleeping, if he has water to drink, and if he is able to watch his favorite television shows.

Abby has an array of stuffed animals, and Tessie, with her distinct personality, is her favorite: "Tessie does not feel like cleaning up the toys;" "Tessie loves you so much;" "Tessie is not tired yet;" "Tessie hates carrots. She thinks that's what bunnies should eat, not us;" and "Tessie fell off her bike and has many bumps and bruises, and I don't know what to do." And out of my mouth the other night came the introduction into our nighttime story time of a beautiful new animal...a cat named "Pop"sicle. Tessie needed another best friend other than Abby, I said. Of course, Abby called Bob "Pops"...so I thought a cat named Popsicle could help me keep Bob's spirit alive.

As I described to Abby, Popsicle is the most beautiful cat that ever lived on this earth. He has beautiful gray hair and startling green eyes and purrs over every-thing...such a happy kitty...and most important, he loves Abby and Tessie the most. And silly Popsicle, he has this crazy habit of climbing trees...and when Abby said she did not think that cats could climb trees, I told her they absolutely can. And in the adventures of Popsicle and Tessie, that crazy little cat is forever climbing the highest tree he can find because he gets so much pleasure out of being up high and feeling like he can fly and looking over everyone, especially Abby and Tessie to always make sure they are okay.

I brought Abby to my computer, so we could order a real stuffed cat with beautiful green eyes that you never wanted to stop hugging. Abby chose one that to her seemed most like Popsicle and huggable beyond belief. Abby was thrilled when Popsicle arrived. To all of our delight, Tessie and Popsicle became fast friends. They dance together and hug all the time...and they LOVE to hear stories about themselves and how they each helped each other and Abby to stay safe from spiders and hawks and rats, or whoever or whatever happens to be the villain in the story for the night. It's always the same theme. Abby is happy walk-ing along with Tessie and Popsicle; she comes across danger; that crazy Popsicle goes and climbs the tree to get a better perspective on what's going on below; and together Tessie and Popsicle keep Abby safe and protected. Abby gets it, I think, that Popsicle is about her Pops, just as she sensed that Santa Claus was really her Pops last year. She loves the adventures, and I love this very small way of keeping

Bob's spirit alive. The adventures of Popsicle will go on. It makes us both happy. Just look at the picture I am sending along of Abby holding her Pops last night…I mean Popsicle!

Blessing for the Day: That I had a beautiful and PUUURfect Popsicle of my own for thirty-seven years, and that between Abby and me, we will find a way to keep his lessons alive: to protect those you care for, even if you have to get out your claws sometimes; to hug and dance with your best friend often; and to climb as many trees as you can to see the bigger picture in life and know what is really important. I am also so blessed that there is a National Red Cross award named after Bob…that blessing still blows me away, and the number of people who have donated to that cause.

Specific Prayer for the Day: That Bob's spirit and the lessons he taught us will come to life in as many people and ways as possible. That my faith will be lifted up to understand and take comfort in what I had and what I do have now and the promises of the future. That I can, in all of the business of life and the new chores I must now take on—and all that I am unsure of—somehow find ways to take care of myself and stop feeling so overwhelmed with this new life. And for my children—always for my children.

The desperation to keep Bob's spirit alive is all-consuming at times. I lie in bed and remember every crack and crevice of his body; jokes that he told; advice that he gave; warmth that he conveyed, praise that he showered on me. I hang onto all of it. Keeping him alive for me, but also for others, especially Abby.

***

ENTRY   10/22/2016 at 8:13 p.m.

"DISTRACTIONS, THE QUEEN OF KATWE, AND RESETTING THE PIECES"

I cannot figure out if I like or dislike distractions. Obviously, distractions give temporary relief from dwelling on very difficult circumstances. However, there is guilt that goes along with being distracted as well. I feel that, and certainly all the books on grief that people give me tell me the same—survivor's guilt, it is called. It's true. I am not supposed to take pleasure, or at least I feel that for the moment.

There are certainly enough chores and tasks related to this circumstance. (I don't like using certain words, so I tend to use incident or circumstance.) I became extremely frustrated two weeks ago that one organization was not returning my calls, and when I felt it was imperative that they did so, I used the word "KILLED," but I did that to make them stand up and take notice. I had to, and it worked…so that one time, it was okay to say it. But, I will say it again if I need to!

So, back to the distractions and chores. There are old chores (I went grocery shopping at Trader Joe's for the first time in a month with help from Lori) and the new ones (endless paperwork about notifying organizations about who in our marriage is still here and who had an incident). All distractions and all take me away on endless journeys to meet the "to-do" list for the day, and all ugly reminders (at least for the moment) that this life marches on. I don't like marching on without Bob. He and I were inseparable (except when I traveled for work), and we did every single thing together. He was the only regularly attending guy in my Fit and Firm and Water Aerobics classes. Yes, he ADORED Lisa, our fitness instructor (everyone knew that…and she adored him, too), but he also did not want to pass up five minutes without me. I realized that after living in New Jersey for nearly twenty years that I had never been to Mercer County Park without him. I walked there the other day by myself…BIG MISTAKE! Next time I definitely have to bring another walker along with me.

Today, Lori decided that I needed the distraction of a movie. I didn't really go to movies, and Bob always refused, as he said they would come to television eventually, so we really did not go. However, today it served as the distraction of the day. We researched last night which movie might serve as the best distraction. We crossed out anything with violence and beautiful love stories, so Queen of Katwe it was. It is a true story about a young girl, Phiona, growing up in the slums of Katwe, Uganda, who learns how to play chess as a distraction from her own "dire circumstances." She becomes excellent at the game, but not without struggles, and victories and championships along the way. It fit the bill and was actually a great movie that I would highly recommend. Of course, when you are struggling with difficult "circumstances," you tend to look for signs that God or Bob is speaking to you. So, it served that purpose as well.

When Phiona had struggles with a particular chess tournament and wanted to give up, her coach simply reminded her that she needed to reset the pieces in her mind, but keep playing the game. Don't give up. His words were meant for me, right? I will never have the same pieces as I have had for the majority of my life—pieces that I was so used to playing with, touching, manipulating, moving around, cheering on, crying with, loving with. I will never have those same pieces again, so I am to reset the pieces, but not give up the game. I get it.

Unlike Phiona in a ninety-minute movie, it will take me far longer. The pieces are all over the place and out of order, and I feel like I don't belong in this story. Funny, as Phiona's coach also said to her that "sometimes the place you are used to is not the place where you belong." I will have to give that one some thought as well. I do know, however, that Bob would NEVER want me to give up the game. He always said, "Hassmiller's don't give up." So, there you have it: I have been spoken to.

Just as Phiona reset the pieces in her mind, I am being forced to as well, and I will. I am not a ninety-minute miracle movie though, so I will need to be patient with myself (not easy), and others will have to be patient with me, too.

Blessings for Today: All of my full-time chief operating officers who have come to my rescue; some who have come to live with me for a while (Kristen, Karen, Janie, Lori, and Kim, of course) and those who reside outside of my household who are just as powerful at nourishing my spirit. There are a few who even try to get me to chuckle by sending funny pictures and some jokes. There is nothing to do except pay it all forward.

Specific Prayer Requests: Patience with myself. I hate this story. Help with resetting the pieces that I never wanted to reset in the first place. I had no need at all to reset. Strength to keep moving forward, even when I have to take four steps backwards and use the "K" word with people who are not listening to me.

Reflection

Resetting one's life after thirty-seven years seems near impossible, yet out of necessity, the resetting has already begun. Against my will. I want everything to remain the same, yet everything is different. From the emptiness in the house to the taking on of new chores, to the relationships I will no longer have, to the trauma I am enduring. The reset button is constantly being pushed. I would love to be able to push the reset button and get life back the way it was, but that is impossible.

***

ENTRY   10/25/2016 at 7:59 a.m.

"UNRULY CLASSROOMS"

I cannot say that I have been a stranger to grief…it has touched me in my decades of life, including the loss of my brother and father. Bob also came from some extremely challenging circumstances…we have both had events in our lives that would have thrown some people under the bus for a lifetime, including some very difficult child rearing events. I keep that in mind when I have met people, even now, and they are incapacitated with an event or at least dwell on it to the point that it becomes a life focus and an excuse for much. It makes me pause to think that I have made it through that particular "thing." Clearly, I am judging here. And of course, now, I see, who am I to judge? I cannot judge and we cannot judge another's grief. BIG LESSON HERE! But I do have to say when you have been through circumstances and are able to come out the other side, you are more able to be helpful to others. Bob and I made a pact that we would get through everything no matter what it took—and quite simply, that's the way it was—and it helped us to help each other…and others.

Humor helped a lot, as well as perspective, prayer, and confiding in people who we thought might understand. I heard in church on Sunday that the happiest people pay when nothing is owed. Bob lived that fully. That was always his attitude; that no matter what, his job was to help others—there were always people who were worse off.

But for now, I have taken many steps backwards. Rather I have fallen into a hole. Taking steps backwards is much too mild a way to describe my profound grief. I frankly don't know what to think at the moment, however. That's what profound grief is— a swirling and swishing of emotions like an unruly classroom…the worst kind of unruly classroom with kids talking over one another at all times and yelling out things that are disruptive and deceitful. Like a few of my teacher friends who have told me that all the bad kids were put in their classroom. That's how I feel: someone has put all the bad ones in my class this year. Some are louder and more unruly than others, and it's taking a toll.

Take those rascals "pain" and "shock," for instance. Boy oh boy, when they buddy up with "tears," it really takes quite a bit of energy to put them in their place. "Disbelief" is ever present and circles the classroom every so often smirking and claiming that none of this is really true and that you can wish it all away. I actually like "disbelief" and frequently call him to the front of the class to recite his poems and show the beautiful pictures he has drawn, and they are comforting. This really did not happen. I like the little guy, but he is getting smaller and weaker and being pushed around a lot by little miss "anger" and that really manipulative "bargainer"…together they are BIG TROUBLE, especially when it comes to debate time…they scream at each other and to God (How dare they?) and it scares the other kids a lot. It is so scary that I threaten to send them to the principal's office but they just laugh at me and throw things at me and say, "We dare you. You cannot get rid of us that easily," and I can see that they are right. "Self-doubt" sits at my side and just cries to see how these kids are being so disruptive.

"Humor," normally someone I like a lot, all of a sudden has been drawn into the clique of "guilt." "Self-doubt" reminds me that there is no place for "humor" at this time and pushes her aside, and "guilt" agrees fully. No laughing allowed— you must spend more time with "pity". "Pity" is feeling left out.

But I don't like "pity" (never have!), yet "guilt" and "self-doubt" say "pity" is not so bad if you just give her a chance. "Pity" is very easy to get along with, they reason. You don't have to fight with her like the others—just give in to her, and she will be your life-long companion. But I want her to go away. I will flunk her if I have to. She never tries or turns in her homework, anyways.

Why can't "courage" take a little more initiative here? Good thing "love" is in my classroom this year and "care." To be honest when they walk in the room, the other troublemakers cower a bit. Oh, the others are strong—don't get me wrong—but "love and care"…they have what us teachers call "great potential." They are trying the hardest, so I make special places in the class for them. I give them special assignments, and they shine. You are not supposed to have favorites, but they are at the top of my troublemaking heap. I want to bring in some special tutors for them so that they can reach their full potential.

I want to see more of "courage" and "strength" and "fortitude," but they are in another class at the moment. Why can't we share students so I can see more of them? I hear they are running for class officers this year, and they run as a pack. They have a tough competition with "guilt," "self-doubt," "fear," and "anger" running against them. But I will vote for the CSF team…that's what they call themselves…CSF. "Love" and "care" are serving as the campaign managers I understand—they are in the same corner. I hear "confidence" is supplying the capital. Good for "confidence"…he must have had a good teacher last year to be so active in this campaign and to put his life on the line this way against "anger" and "guilt" and "self-doubt." "Revenge" is supplying the capital for these opponents, and I know there is plenty in her storehouse to keep that campaign going for quite some time, but I have heard that "love" and "care" have been storing up for many years.

Finally, "Faith" is so calming. Amidst all the troublemakers that talk over each other every hour of every day and at 3:00 a.m., I can always depend on "faith" for the long haul. I wish she could be in my classroom next year. Maybe I will ask to teach the class above me next year so that she can stay by my side more often.

Blessings for Today: I found a wonderful grief support group yesterday with seven people who understand this notion of unruly classrooms very well. They are good teachers, have lived with and are living with spousal losses and all those nasty students. Here, I thought I had them all in my classroom, and low and behold, they have them as well! These people are all in front of me, however, so have teaching experience that is helpful and have a few more of the good students. For the first time since this horrible event, they made me smile and not feel guilty for doing so. Sounds small to you perhaps, but that was an insurmountable task. And Robert Boy, I just want to go on record to say how terribly I miss you. You were and still are my favorite student, and I don't care who says I play favorites.

Specific Prayer Requests: Patience with insurmountable paperwork and applications and well, the very unruly classroom that I am navigating at this moment. And selling cars. I feel like I am in such unchartered waters and need support, with nasty students yelling many things at me. Pray for the good students to succeed. They will in the end—it will just take time, tutoring, and little Miss "Faith," right?

Reflection

The voices and emotions that I hear and feel are traumatizing and exhausting. Naming them helps to keep track. And being able to identify the good emotions and to call upon them is also very helpful. It is a fight and struggle and continues to weaken me physically and emotionally. Physical activity, even simply walking or lifting things, (activities that I would not have given a second thought to) are all difficult.

**

ENTRY   10/27/2016 at 10:04 p.m.

"DIPPING A TOE IN THE WATER OF REAL LIFE"

Nine years ago, Bob and I sold our first Princeton Junction home and right after the closing, he brought me to Taco Bell for some news. "Good news or bad news?" I asked. He said he thought good news, but I would have to determine for myself. He was as nervous as I had ever seen him. Was he going to ask me to marry him again? I thought that I would say yes, but this time I would put a few more conditions on the deal. I knew more now, so why not bargain for a bit more out of a nervous, begging man asking me to marry him again? However, right then and there, over two soft tacos, he said that he had given away a good portion of the proceeds of our house to the Red Cross. WHAT?! More money to the Red Cross—didn't we already give enough? He said it's all done, and he could not undo it, so he hoped I was okay with his decision. WHAT?! I loved the Red Cross too, but couldn't we space this out a bit?

He said this time it was different—that he was so proud of all the work I was doing on behalf of nursing at the Robert Wood Johnson Foundation and the Red Cross. That he wanted to combine my loves into an annual award program that allowed Red Cross chapters to compete for who had done the best job with integrating nursing into their work that year by implementing programs that could be sustained and replicated. He said that he needed a way to honor me and this work. Okay, Robert Boy, so just tell me you are proud…Did you have to give away all our money too? Couldn't you just give me one of those nice, schmaltzy cards of yours and tell me that you're proud of me? I would believe you—really, I would! But then I asked the only reasonable thing I could think of at the time and that was if there was going to be money left over for vacations. I did not want to give up my vacations with Bob…so if that was the case, then he could forget it, Buster. But, when he said yes, I decided to settle into what he had done, although I found the whole thing rather embarrassing…the name part, that is. I liked that we would be helping the Red Cross and nursing. In the end, I thought that if famous movie stars or sports figures, who did far less important work than nurses, could have names all over their foundations, then perhaps it was okay in our case.

Every year, we traveled to the American Red Cross awards ceremony, where we got to announce the winner of the competition and hand over a check and an award. And indeed, I am very proud of what the chapters and their nurses have done. This year, on October 26, the Bob Hassmiller Excellence in Disaster Services Award would be announced after the Susan Hassmiller Award for Nursing Excellence. I was looking for one small excuse to dip my foot back into the world. Being with my Red Cross family would be a first step to try out my weak sea legs. I checked with close Circle 1 people to ask if I should go, and all gave their blessing as long as I would be accompanied by another Circle 1 companion. And as soon as I asked Carol Chang and she said the honor was all hers, I decided to accept the invitation to attend but declined a speaking role.

So, there it was—on the one month anniversary of this terrible accident, I sat in the safety and surroundings of my Red Cross family, crying as Gail McGovern announced the Bob Hassmiller Excellence in Disaster Services Award. Her speech was followed by a short video of a day in the life of a Red Cross Disaster Action Team member, who are the real HEROES of the Red Cross. They are the ones who help every day and the ones who give out those Red Cross blankets that you all see on television footage of disasters…the same blanket that I kept on Bob while he fought for his life.

And now that blanket covers me, and I am reminded every night that I was married to a real hero for nearly thirty-seven years, and that he would want me to remember the good. It is so hard and painful now, but I remembered the good at the ceremony. I will, my best friend, I will.

Blessings for Today: The awesomeness of the award in your name. I know you hate the idea, but it is for the real workers of the Red Cross. Let's keep our minds and hearts on the bigger picture here and know that this will recognize great service. For Gail McGovern, awesome leader of the American Red Cross. For Carol Chang, who spent an exhausting sixteen hours with me and made me smile more than once.

Specific Prayer Requests: On the plus side, pray for so many talented and committed Red Cross staff and volunteers who do so much good every day. On the minus side, I don't know how to stop from feeling so overwhelmed and exhausted. The unruly classroom keeps rearing its ugly head.

Reflection

It was so hard to step out, but once done, it felt like an overwhelming accomplishment. I know Bob wanted me to be there. Funny as it might sound, I felt Bob was still grappling with the acceptance of an award named after him. The tables were turned. Now he knew how I felt when he arranged for the Susan Hassmiller Award for Red Cross Nursing. In fact, just as Gail McGovern was announcing the Bob Hassmiller award my phone rang a number of times. It was my mother, yes, but somehow I felt Bob was behind these calls, trying to distract me from the whole Bob Hassmiller Award idea. I told Carol, and we smiled knowingly.

***

ENTRY   10/30/2016 at 6:50 a.m.

"CONVERTIBLES, BEACH BOYS, AND NO REGRETS"

The absolute known in our family was that Bob did not need or want anything materially. Birthdays? Christmas? Anniversaries? Please nothing. He would agree to a celebration and a cake if we shared a meal and talked about what we appreciated about one another, but he never wanted presents. I snuck him into stores a few times a year under the false pretense that I was looking for something for me, and then I dragged him over to the men's shirt department. He told me he had more shirts than he could ever wear, and besides, he was retired. He'd say he didn't want it, and he walked away and meant it. Sometimes I yelled at him, and sometimes I just threw it into the basket and bought it anyways. Sometimes he wore it, and sometimes he didn't.

But then, all of a sudden, a big birthday was upon him, and he became obsessed with having a convertible…an old style Mercedes convertible—a classic he would say, one that he could fit his tall frame into. This from a man who only got rid of cars when they were barely able to move…200,000 miles…no problem…she still had legs, he would say. Also, he reasoned that all those shirts and pants and shoes over the years that he never bought could all be rolled into the price tag of one car. And he threw in the fact that he never once spent a nickel on a barber. Since I had met him, I had cut his hair. Ridiculous, I cried! No one needs a convertible. Besides, I reasoned, you could get sun cancer from all that exposure. No argument worked. All he did was ask me to approve a price range that he could work in. I didn't want to give him a price range because I didn't want a convertible….did he not hear me? Back and forth from March through May. He kept looking, and then one day he said he found it—the perfect car for him.

I was still against it, but a friend of ours pulled me aside one day and told me that a few of her good friends just lost their husbands and that if this was truly something that Bob had always wanted, I should reconsider. It was about fun, but it was also about having no regrets. Somehow that made sense to me, so I relented on the grounds that he deserved to have fun…if this was how he chose to define fun…and boy, did he ever.

For a few short months, after he bought it, he was a kid again. His license plate said: "NVR2Old," and he set out to prove this point! He wore his "Abby's Grandpa" hat backwards, and then his hat that said "Abby and Johnny's Pops" after John Robert was born. He immediately bought the Beach Boys Greatest Hits. He pulled in one day, music blaring and announced that he finally understood why the youngsters play their music so loud. He sang every song at the top of his lungs: "Fun, fun, fun 'til her daddy takes the T-Bird Away;" "Round, round, get around, I get around;" and "Good, good, good, good vibrations."

The ultimate for him was when his best girl would go for a ride with him. Having given in, I decided to completely take the plunge and sing along with him, only balking when he drove it faster than I felt comfortable with. I told him I finally understood this. It was fun! In fact, it was a blast!

"Do you love me, do you surfer girl? Surfer girl, my little surfer girl."

"I do I do love you…your little surfer girl loves you.

"I may not always love you; But long as there are stars above you; You never need to doubt it; I'll make you so sure about it; God only knows what I'd be without you; If you should ever leave me; Though life would still go on believe me; The world could show nothing to me; So what good would living do me?; God only knows what I'd be without you."

So yesterday, I sold the car. I had to—it was Bob's car and no one else's. Always remember that your little surfer girl loves you and she is so happy that you had your car for four months, and you were a kid again, and you sang at the top of your lungs.

Blessings for Today: Our living will had a section that asked how you wanted to be remembered and Bob wrote this: "He acted on his beliefs. He always supported others; he loved and he laughed a lot; he absolutely loved and adored his wife and family; he regretted little and was thankful for a lot." Bob lived his life with love, compassion, humbly before God and the world, and with no regrets.

Specific Prayer Requests: Another person who lost her husband told me last night that it gets worse before it gets better. My heart sank even lower, if that is possible. Grief is the price of love, and the more you love, the more you grieve. I am not certain how this can hurt anymore…how much more pain is possible, but I am sure glad I gave into that convertible. So, my prayer is that I can somehow remember the joy amidst the grief and sorrow. Matthew 5:4 says, "Blessed are those who mourn, for they will be comforted."

Reflection

There were a number of things that drew me to Bob. He always had an inner confidence, was never hesitant to keep to his integrity, and lived without regrets. We were different in a lot of ways (sometimes annoyingly and even angrily so), but these basic values were the glue. I read recently that communication as the entire key to a good marriage is overrated; what really maintains the staying power is basic mutual respect. I think that really affirmed what I felt. We always had to work at communicating, visiting counselors a few times during our time together, but we never lost our respect for one another.

***

ENTRY   11/1/2016 at 8:24 a.m.

"WHAT'S IN YOUR BUBBLE?"

About a year ago or so, Kim, the eternally optimistic extrovert, announced that she was tired of smiling at people and saying good morning and not getting a response. How could people NOT respond, she wondered? She was giving it her all, as she always does—her best smile and her very best good morning. I detected a teachable moment.

First, I said, you have to make sure people hear you (I am hard-of-hearing, so I am always sensitive to people speaking audibly). You need to realize, too, that to some people it may not be a good morning. Maybe something is going on in their lives, and they just cannot smile today. I showed Kim an effective four-minute You Tube video produced by the Cleveland Clinic[5] that showed patients and hospital staff walking around the hospital for different reasons. As music played in the background, their "thought bubbles" appeared on screen. Their thoughts ranged from, "I am so excited about being a new father" to "my nineteen year-old-son is on life support" to "my tumor is malignant" to "my tumor is benign."

We rarely really know what is in a person's heart and mind at any given moment. A year ago, this was a teachable moment…an academic exercise to let an optimistic extrovert know that not everyone can smile at any given moment even if approached by the most beautiful smile imaginable. They just can't, and we have to accept that and perhaps, if we feel called, we can say a little prayer for them and whatever is in their bubble.

I remember the video now and think a thousand times over how sensitive we need to be to each other's bubbles. I now pass people on the street (in the rare times I venture out), and they smile and say, "How ya doin?"…and they have no idea what is in my bubble. Even people who are familiar with my circumstances do not and cannot fully know what is in my bubble. It is far too complicated. I don't want to burden people with what's in my bubble. But I am not just concerned with my own bubble. Now, I understand more deeply than before the bubbles that others are carrying around with them, and eventually, I want to be really there and present for others and what might be in their bubbles. I hope people with bubbles of fear or anxiety or anything else troubling can reach out and get help. I have reached out in the last few days to ask a few others, mostly people who have lost their spouses, to tell me what is in their bubbles and to tell me their stories.

We have the choice to touch upon others thoughts and hearts, but like me in the past, would not always take the time. It takes time and care to want to understand another's bubble. Some people are better at this than others. There are people who I have come across in my circumstances who could win bronze, silver and gold medals for deciphering bubbles.

Blessings for Today: That there are people in this world who are Olympic champions in bubble deciphering. So many of you have touched my life this past month. They will help teach and bring the rest of us along (including me!). They not only decipher bubbles, but translate back what they think those bubbles are saying and are encouraging and lift up hearts and spirits.

Specific Prayer Requests: Pastor Dan said that the happiest people know they are not okay today, but they know that they eventually will be. I am holding onto this one. I think we all should. Also, prayers for my mother, who will be ninety-one this Sunday. She knows (her own bubble) and has said that things are "out of order"…that she should have gone before Bob, and I am angry because Bob went first and because I feel this way. However, it is her birthday, and we will celebrate a life well lived. It will be hard to celebrate, but Abby loves cakes, balloons, and presents, so she will help. Psalm 90:12 says, "…teach us to number our days, that we may gain a heart of wisdom."

Reflection

Even though I was trained and educated as a nurse and was taught about compassion and empathy, there is nothing like this lesson to teach me that there are a lot of people carrying around a lot of painful bubbles. I used to wonder how someone could be in so much pain and inner turmoil that they would want to take his or her own life. I understand pain and turmoil now. Kim now has an inkling of why some people simply cannot breeze back with a smile and a good morning.

***

ENTRY   11/4/2016 at 9:57 p.m.

"WHY?"

I know I am reverting back to previous questions, but today is the one month anniversary of Bob's departure to Heaven, and I need and deserve to keep asking "why." Why did this happen? What is the reason? I want answers, and all I get is nonsense. I came across my husband's latest multi-page results from a physical exam he had; he was in perfect shape, other than the high cholesterol and pudge around his belly. But hey, this is America. All labs, EKG, vital signs were like a twenty-year-old. I line that up with the death certificate, and nothing adds up for me. Two incongruent pieces of paper. They don't belong together, so why?

I carry on in minimal ways at the moment and am tortured by this play I am cast in, with its conflicting themes and people I don't want to associate with—funeral directors, mental health professionals, financial advisors, grief support groups, attorneys, and government agency workers who don't answer their phones. I feel like a struggling actor in a play that I have been badly miscast for, but I was forced to sign the contract and must carry out my responsibilities in a role for which I have no passion. I demand overtime pay!

I ask why to people all the time. I asked my hairdresser Issa after getting angry with him. He knew what happened to my husband, yet he greeted me with, "How's it going today, good?" I have known him long enough that I could yell at him for that kind of greeting. But in actuality, he had an answer to the why question that was not all that bad, although I will have to take more time to think about it and let it sink in.

He said that I may not know the reasons now as to why everything happened the way that it did, but that if I keep myself open and listening that the reasons will evolve. He talked particularly about Bob not wanting to live as a quadriplegic and what that would have meant for me to care for Bob and my mother. Issa said that I have more to do on earth and that I am not to squander my gifts. I countered that my best friend and number one fan was gone, and I questioned how to even go on, and he responded that Bob's support is not gone. I just have to be open to hearing him in another way and listening to others in different ways.

When I drove home, the bumper sticker on the car in front of me said, "Your purpose in life is to determine your gifts; your mission in life is to share your gifts with others." When you are in this state of mind, you look for any and all signs that help you maintain any modicum of equilibrium. Again, I know academically, in between bouts of crying and feeling sad and bewildered, that Bob would be really upset with me if I did not continue to figure out my gifts and share them. Easier said than done for the moment, but I see it.

And speaking of signs, Abby always comforts me. She, too, reminded me today that Bob is still with us. She talked about Pops all day today, as there were many reasons to do so. I told her about the white ribbons that were tied around the neighborhood trees in honor of Pops and that every time she saw a ribbon it meant that people in that house cared for and were praying for us. She liked that notion quite a bit. She helped me visit some of the trees to make sure the ribbons were nice and secure. She told me she misses Pops a lot, and I said we all do so very much, and then she said that she wishes she could be in Heaven with Pops. I told her that now is her time to be with me, but in a long, long time from now I believed that we would all be together again in Heaven. And then the clincher: When I told her tonight that I loved her more than anyone in the whole wide world…she, like Issa, reminded me that Bob is NOT absent, but is still with us. She said, "But Nana, you said that you loved Pops more than anyone in the whole wide world." And I said, you are right Abby…Pops is with us and I do love him more than anyone in the whole wide world."

Blessings for Today: That I am getting help and that I am open to help. That I have the opportunity to express myself through these blogs and when I miss a day or so there are people who check in to make sure I am okay because they have not heard from me. That some who have read my blog know that I am angry at my mother (or God or both) that she is here and Bob is not, but it is her birthday on Sunday, and people are making efforts to congratulate her for a life well lived.

And thanks to Robin and Ralph for spending nearly two-and-a-half hours with me at my attorney's office, taking notes and asking questions about a way forward, including a new will. For Marilyn for spending the day with me on Wednesday; for Wendy for coming to talk to me and Mark; for Nancy for encouraging me every single day; for Lisa's private "fit and firm" training session that wound up being a much needed sob session for both of us in addition to exercise; for Susan's visit; for Lori's daily check-ins; for Tom for providing advice on tires; and for all in the neighborhood who are still feeding me. I am thankful for the gifts of so many. 1 Peter 4:10 says, "Each of you should use whatever gift you have received to serve others, as faithful stewards of God's grace in its various forms."

Specific Prayer Requests: I am a very reluctant, forlorn, and sour actor. Ask that God continue to show me any source of light that I might hang onto, and that I do find blessings along the way.

Reflection

It strikes me that some people do everything in their power to cut themselves off from pain. They don't talk about it, they throw themselves into work, they smile, and they laugh. Others drink and self-mutilate, and incur abuse on others. Everyone is so different in how they handle grief. But in the end, purposely shutting out the pain, laughing or drinking it off won't work. We are human beings— not robots. Suffocating grief will only cause it to rear its ugly head in other ways, in other times. I am trying my best to remain open to the pain, feeling every prong it cuts me with. I do not hold back tears, sorrow, or anger. I don't stop asking why. I don't get any answers, but I will not stop. And in all of this openness, I also do not stop love, nor compassion, nor the help that others want to give. I see that is a gift to them, a gift that someday I will reciprocate. I vow to pay this forward.

***

ENTRY   11/7/2016 at 6:53 a.m.

"GRIEVING IN AMERICA"

I have many books from many of you on the subject of grief and healing. They sit on an end table in my sunroom, stacked neatly in a pile with their titles facing my view, so as not to forget the life I am now living. They are *Grieving with Hope, A Gift of Hope: How We Survive Our Tragedies, Healing After Loss,* and several more.

I started reading one (*On Grief and Grieving*) because I recognized the author, Dr. Elisabeth Kubler-Ross, an expert on death and dying. She is gone now herself, but experts turn to her and her description of the five stages of grieving: denial, anger, bargaining, depression, and acceptance. The key is that you can go in any order and revisit categories as often as needed. I resonated completely with her discussion about the changing face of the grief process in this country and what I call "Hey Folks, this is America, so let's go ahead and get this thing over with." Kubler-Ross called us the "death denying and grief dismissing society of America."[6]

I know we are a death denying society. I am part of this health care system, and I live in America, so I know how it goes: let's save everyone or almost everyone. After all, remember that I initiated the discussion about palliative care with Bob's health care team. A friend called this the "teaching hospital syndrome": the tools and machines are all available and ready for use, and there are students to teach, so let's keep going no matter the cost to the patient, literally and figuratively. Our whole society feeds into this notion, patients and family members alike—not just the doctors. If I could have had Bob back in any way, shape or form, I wanted that. I desperately wanted that. I thought there was hope, and there was in the beginning, but it was not working out that way in the long run.

And now that Bob has been gone for one month, the pressure is there to move on. This is the "grief dismissing" part of what Kubler-Ross talks about in our society. So who is providing pressure? Well, no one in particular, but the nuances and the comments and actions are there. This is America, and these are our values—to move on, to pull yourself up by your bootstraps. Don't worry, your heart will catch up. You have tasks to complete, new roles to understand, new jobs to figure out. Come on Sue: it's been a month now. Surely this has been enough time to understand how toilets, finances, car tires, tree fertilizers, contracts, social security, Medicaid and Medicare, long-term care (for mother), selling cars, tax code 32-1a (What was that number again, and why are you telling me this? Will the number really matter to me?), insurance, driving to new places, wills, probates, and more.

Doesn't all this new information and independence empower you, someone asked. Bob would not want it any other way. He would be so proud of you. Really? Is that a fact? Do you know this to be a fact? We liked our cozy little understandings, and the roles we each had…the respect for what we were each good at and the safe boundaries that these roles created in a quietly harmonious and compatible love arrangement. Is a month enough time to undo all of this? Is an eternity enough time to undo all of this?

I wonder how long I will feel so pained and traumatized and am torn between sitting motionless and (as they say) letting the waves of grief just wash over me and jumping back into the real world—my Type A personality rearing its ugly head. I already see that as time goes along that it will be or should be a very delicate balance between the two, with each taking its turn, and now grief is the dominant twin. This is not me. I have goals. I love to accomplish. I love to take on more than I can handle. I thrive on challenges. I rarely get stuck. I like moving on, so grief having its way with me is an unnatural and ugly force throwing me against a solid brick wall with no give and pushing and ripping me against my will, with my inner soul slogging about.

No one told me about this in nursing school. I learned about Kubler-Ross and her stages of grief, but no one told me how the words in her books play out in real life. No simulation labs in those days to role play these kinds of scenarios. Is this being taught today? Who would want to role play this one anyways? Simulations have a beginning, a crisis in the middle, and then an end. How would this simulation end? Nursing and medical school would not be long enough to incorporate the end point for this one. There is no end—only a transformation. Kubler-Ross says that, "In grief, just like in death, there is a transformation for the living. If you do not take the time to grieve, you cannot find a future in which loss is remembered and honored without pain."[6]

Blessings for Today: I have a lot of people supporting me—my army, as someone said today. People who share their love and words of care on a daily basis and provide me with feedback on how they think I am doing. When you don't exactly know how you are doing, it is good to have an inner circle (and an outer circle 1–5) of people telling you and giving honest feedback....including books to read.

Specific Prayer Requests: Forgiveness for judging so many who have gone before me when I did not know their exact situation and thought it was time for them to move on with their grief. I will be back to work soon enough, and I continue to make plans to dip my toes into a couple of safe places at the right times—some of which are coming up soon. Patience with myself and others.

Reflection

I remember a few people early on saying to me, "What's the rush?" in regards to everything I thought I needed to do. Consumed by the everyday tasks (mine and Bob's), I thought I would sink from the pressure. The pressure was enormous (at least it was for me). I found that addressing my broken heart, my children's grief, and all the tasks of daily living overwhelming. Did I do this to myself or did others do this to me? Mostly I did it to myself. The call of life as I once knew it, beckoned me, but I could not return that call. I did not know how I would navigate a new life. I learned the only way to do it is to just let it come. Do some tasks when you can and let the grief flow when it might. Grief has its own mind and timetable.

***

ENTRY   11/8/2016 at 5:51 p.m.

"BIRTHDAY WISHES"

Sunday was my mother's birthday and it would normally have been an occasion for high celebration. Actually, thanks to many neighbors and friends, and my mother's little group of long-time friends, it was. It absolutely was—for my mother—and that was what counted. She had two parties: one with her small family and another with her friends (thanks to our neighbor Judy's help!) Both joyous occasions. Joyce announced my mother's birthday in church, and everyone gave her a rousing burst of applause. Nancy gave her a wrist corsage. Mark came to church and surprised us all. Tears of happiness that our small little family was there all together and for a few moments we were there with one purpose—to make my mother feel like it was her special day. Abby and I made her a rainbow cake, where the frosting ended up mostly on the cake, but with an abundance on Abby's face and in her stomach. The candles were lit and wishes were thrown to the wind. It was not my turn to make a wish, but I wished anyways. I don't turn down a moment in the day to wish.

That night, I found a handwritten note from my mother on the kitchen counter as my "gift in return." My mother stated...put it right out there...that she was so very sorry that we were celebrating her birthday and that she was still here and Bob was not. And that she feels the enormous hole as well, but it is just too painful for her to bring it up, as she sees how pained I am. She did not want me to think that because she never brings it up that she does not feel his loss on my behalf. I took that note and could not disagree, but realized through a friend's clarification that I do not wish my mother to NOT be here—no I don't! It was just the order of things that I take issue with. The hole is here, and it is real, but the hole would be ever the larger if she were not here. In the time she has left, she will continue to teach me lessons about life—if not outright, then through her actions.

My mother loved all the attention today and gave back to her visitors what the visitors could not get from me—joy, laughter, and a positive attitude to celebrate the day. For a few hours people came to this house and heard laughter and singing. It made me happy to see her have her day, albeit bittersweet.

Blessings for Today: That friends and family stepped in to be my surrogates for laughter, joy, and celebration and for well wishes to a woman who deserved to have every bit of this attention. With more cakes, cookies, and pies to start our own bakery shop, the sugar keeps flowing. A good thing, as my mother subsists on sugar and carbs. Is this the secret to a long life?

Specific Prayer Requests: That this notion of things being out of order was and is completely out of my hands. There is so much about all of this that I don't understand…all painfully out of my control. I don't like it one bit, but Happy Birthday, Mother. There is more for you to teach me. Isaiah 55:8–9 teaches, ""For my thoughts are not your thoughts, neither are your ways my ways," declares the Lord. "As the heavens are higher than the earth, so are my ways higher than your ways and my thoughts than your thoughts."

Reflection

Each one of us has been known to say glibly on occasion, "Of course we don't have control." God is in charge, or there are powers beyond our control, or fate will do what it will do. But until an event like this happens, with all the energy put into staying healthy and safe, it just never hits home right in the center of your heart and brain. The anger that a loved one is ripped from us is inconsumable. How could this be? How can things get so out of order? How can there be still births? How can a child drown? How can a twenty-year-old die in a car accident? How can a gunman take so many lives? All unanswerable pains, with the hope that one day more answers will come.

***

ENTRY   11/11/2016 at 8:14 p.m.

"A VETERANS DAY HERO FOR ALL TIMES"

Today is Veterans Day and another day to remember Bob, his character, and his service in Vietnam. Perhaps Bob's good friend, Rob Stephenson from Australia, said it best when he said the book he is reading, called *The Road to Character* by New York Times Columnist David Brooks, reminded him so much of Bob. And as I read the quotes that Rob offered of what a person of high character and moral integrity might look like, I do believe he got it spot on. As you read the descriptive quotes from the book, I hope that there is much to reflect on for all of us about who we are, who we associate with, who our leaders are, and what we teach our children and grandchildren.

"Occasionally, even today, you come across certain people who seem to possess an impressive inner cohesion. They are not leading fragmented, scattershot lives. They have achieved inner integration. They are calm, settled and rooted. They are not blown off course by storms. They don't crumble in adversity. Their minds are consistent and their hearts are dependable. Their virtues are not the blooming virtues you see in smart college students; they are the ripening virtues you see in people who have lived a little and have learned from joy and pain. Sometimes you don't even notice these people, because while they seem kind and cheerful, they are also reserved. They possess the self-effacing virtues of people who are inclined to be useful but don't need to prove anything to the world: humility, restraint, reticence, temperance, respect, and soft self-discipline.

"They radiate a sort of moral joy. They answer softly when challenged harshly. They are silent when unfairly abused. They are dignified when others try to humiliate them, restrained when others try to provoke them. But they get things done. They perform acts of sacrificial service with the same modest everyday spirit they would display if they were just getting the groceries. They are not thinking about what impressive work they are doing. They are not thinking about themselves at all. They just seem delighted by the flawed people around them. They just recognize what needs doing and they do it.

"They make you feel funnier and smarter when you speak with them. They move through different social classes not even aware, it seems, that they are doing so. After you've known them for a while it occurs to you that you've never heard them boast, you've never seen them self-righteous or doggedly certain. They aren't dropping little hints of their own distinctiveness and accomplishments.

"They have not led lives of conflict-free tranquility, but have struggled toward maturity. They have gone some way toward solving life's essential problem, which is, as Aleksandr Solzhenitsyn put it, 'the line separating good and evil passes not through states, nor between classes, not between political parties either—but right through every human heart.'"[7]

Blessing for the Day: That for nearly thirty-seven years I was married to a hero and a man who possessed the highest character and moral integrity (sometimes annoyingly so) of anyone I ever met. Happy Veteran's Day, my dear soul. And for all the men and women of our armed services who work every day to protect our country.

We brought Abby to the Veterans Day ceremony today at the cemetery where Bob is, and where my mother and I will someday be buried. I talked to her about what a hero is, what it means to REALLY help people, and what a man of character is like. She had a Pops who fit the bill, and she has a Daddy to fit that bill.

Specific Prayer Requests: That we all understand what a real person of character looks, smells, and acts like and reflect on those characteristics for ourselves (me included…certainly); and that we teach our children and grandchildren everyday about how great this country is and about the men and women who keep it that way. I pray that Bob and his legacy will continue to inspire me with the characteristics he would have wanted to pass on to his grandchildren.

Reflection

Bob was never the best looking person or fanciest dresser I dated, nor the one with the most money or prospects for money. Thank goodness I had enough wits about me when I met him to know that he was very different in other more important ways. He exuded an internal confidence that made me want to stand straighter. He saw humor in things that made me want to laugh out loud. He had such a dependable heart that I could never bear to turn mine on him, and his humility in the service he provided was and will be a continuing inspiration. A hero is someone who decides either swiftly, or with more thought if time is allowed, to step forward in a conscious manner to save a life or carry out a service benefiting another or society, without regard for payment, either monetary or emotional, in return. Bob was, and will remain, my hero.

***

ENTRY   11/12/2016 at 10:10 p.m.

"NURSE HEAL THYSELF"

Most people who know me know that I run at quite a steep speed doing what I can to plow full steam ahead through life in the name of making this world a better place. I have been a nurse for several decades, and now direct a national Campaign on how the health system might take better advantage of the skills and expertise of nurses in order to provide the best possible care for people in this country. The idea of making things better for others appeals to me greatly. I think many of us have this goal, right? At least those people do who affiliate themselves with the same kinds of organizations I affiliate with and certainly many who live in my neighborhood. I have also gotten the sense this past year that there too are a lot of angry people who may not feel this way. I understand the reality that life does not treat people equally. There are a lot of people angry and hurting and without means. But there are also a lot of people angry and hurting with a lot of means. That all does not escape me. But for me, this internal need to serve others as best I can cannot die. I won't let it. After all, it is what drew Bob and me together in the first place. My counselors and Circle 1 folks are now telling me this need to care for others first, instead of self, is hurting me.

Some people are really good at taking care of themselves and thus set boundaries, which has always thrown me a bit. What do you mean you cannot meet with me after 5:00 p.m.? What do you mean you cannot have that report ready by 3:00 tomorrow? Why are you not returning my emails within an hour of my sending a request to you? What? You are skipping that conference meeting to get a massage? How can anyone possibly stop in the middle of the day to take a nap—a waste I tell you! Yoga? Isn't that where you just stand there and then lay there and hum and do nothing? What's the accomplishment there? There are people to help; people to get back to; goals to meet.

I have to determine what makes sense for me now and at a time when the roles and responsibilities in my life have just increased tenfold, or is it a hundred fold? No one took any tasks or responsibilities away for me so that I may simply be this new transformed person who takes more time to relax and reflect. Does anyone see the contradiction here? Now, at this time, when my Robert Boy is not here and all the roles he carried out for me still need to be taken care of. There are so many of tasks of daily living that I now have to contend with (such as waiting for three hours at Walmart this morning to get new tires on my car). So, you tell me how I am supposed to slow down and love myself when I have tires to replace, appliances to fix, finances to tend to, grocery shopping, cooking, long-term care arrangements for mother, endless paperwork, accounts to change over, and the list goes on and on and on. No more job sharing. Delegate, some say. Okay, so who wants to wait three hours in Walmart to get tires replaced for me? Raise your hand now.

I see firsthand how some people have handled the stress of a lost spouse—they retire! They retire to complete tasks, to grieve, and to take time for self-care. Two people told me they went back to work within two weeks and then crashed and quit. Actually, I have heard this a lot. But I have no intention of retiring. I don't just have a job—I am passionate about my work to improve health through nursing, so retirement is not in my current plan.

So, okay—the balance—where is the balance with all these new responsibilities? Breathe. Take some deep breaths. I am into that now as I have temporarily given up on all Bob and I did to stay fit. I will not return to biking, our love and passion, and I cannot return to exercise or dance classes without him. I walk and breathe. That's enough for now, right? Walking and breathing.

I did four things today to commit to helping myself...at least for today. I walked with another widow to hear her story and for her to hear mine. I went to a church that had a convenient 5:00 p.m. service on a Saturday night and met a woman who sat next to me and introduced herself warmly. And when she asked me what brought me to her church, I told her. She claimed me as hers on this special evening, stating that I was meant to sit next to her, as she told me her personal and very assuring beliefs about my situation and shared with me a bit of her life. Then I found a meditation app that basically led me through thirty minutes of somewhat the same message.

Finally, I just returned from getting a massage from a woman who greeted me with, "Tell me what is going on in your life right now so I know how best to help you." "You really want to know?" I asked. She said, "Of course," and meant it. I don't think I ever had a massage therapist ask me that. So, I told her as well, the fourth time I told my story to a stranger today. If I thought it would have helped me get my tires on more quickly this morning I would have also told the Walmart mechanic. This woman not only gave me a massage, but spoke to me in the beginning and then at the end. Again, the message was repeated about being open to Bob being with me, and that he is okay. She affirmed that I was not yet okay, but told me I would be….that little by little I would be, but I have to take care of myself and be open to the positivity that comes my way. And when she spoke to me, I was certain that I saw Bob standing next to her, telling her exactly what to say.

Blessings for Today: I keep going back to what Issa, my hairdresser, told me about there not being a good reason at all as to what happened now, but later answers would come. I do hold onto this. Meeting and being open to people who want to speak to me in realistic and uplifting ways does help, especially people who possess great faith.

Specific Prayer Requests: It's Abby's birthday today, and she was so happy, which made Kim happy, but oh, so sad. The first of our many special days and holidays to get through without our rock and anchor…the essence of love and positivity…that's my Robert Boy. The season is upon us, and Pops will not be here for us. We all need prayers for courage and persistence in this journey and ways to care for ourselves to help with healing. Psalm 147:3 promises us, "He heals the brokenhearted and binds up their wounds" while Jeremiah 29:11 tells us, "For I know the plans that I have for you,' declares the Lord, 'plans to prosper you and not to harm you, plans to give you hope and a future."

Reflection

I have never been a good listener of my own needs. I get caught up with the business of life, accomplishing tasks, and doing for others. It was the ultimate contradiction that at a time when I had more on my shoulders than I ever imagined, I also needed to take stock, to breathe, reflect, and to take care of my body and heart. I realized that with my children and my mother, I was the last egg in the basket, and my grandchildren needed me. If I didn't take care of myself, then no one else would. Breathe—one, two, three, four.

***

ENTRY   11/15/2016 at 8:37 p.m.

"SPRINTS AND MARATHONS"

I took a huge step yesterday and traveled to a meeting in Miami. It was a sprint—it took power, energy, and strength to get over the finish line, but I made it. One would not think it was a huge step from someone who frequently travels for work, but it was monumental on every physical, psychological and spiritual level possible. Not to mention the fact that Kim reminds me that I am now her only living parent, and well, she wants me to be careful. I know, Kim…I want you to be careful too. So few eggs in our precious basket now.

I would just as soon curl up and forget the rest of the world most of the time, but I do have a goal of easing back into work. So, with the help of my dear friend Jean, who escorted me the entire way and then protected me throughout, we attended the meeting. The meeting was a nursing meeting and it was the last time these nurses were to meet. So, no big speeches, just words of recognition to a group of people I felt compelled to recognize and encourage to keep up their great work.

When I sat down after my few remarks to an audience of well-known colleagues and reflected on the meeting, I thought there were accomplishments here, thanks to the initial powerful sprints everyone made, but the ultimate success (more better educated nurses in our country) has to do with the long-term endurance of the marathon; that's where the real sustainability will come. Both sprints and marathons are important in life.

Although I appreciate and plan for the long term, I am a natural sprinter. One of the best. That's what has had me so dumbstruck about this grieving process. There is no way that I can sprint my way out. I would love to, but they keep adding more weights around my ankles, and they make me drink stuff that makes me nauseous and saps my energy. I tell them that my gift is sprinting. Why are they not paying attention to what I do best? But they look at me, shake their head, and simply say, this is a marathon. You are in this for the long haul.

Grief counselors and those who have lost spouses tell me that the grief process takes years to overcome, and you are still never the same. I know some people want me back now, exactly the way they know me, but it ain't gonna happen. Every single cell in my body is affected, and every single cell must strive to recover. I do feel at times that I will never recover, but I will need to learn how to sustain the distance for the long haul. I read that the length and depth of grieving has a lot to do with a number of different factors—the length of marriage, age, sudden loss versus illness, quality of the relationship, children, and relationship dependency.

They say that the more the couple was dependent on each other, the more intense the grief. Yes, I admit it, and you should know, that I am not that big independent person you thought I was. I was truly dependent on Bob for—do I dare say— almost everything. Whenever I asked him to do something, or I was lost, or needed something, Bob loved it. He would dance and sing, "She needs me. Like the flowers need the rain, you know she needs me; she needs me, she needs me." That big grin on his face. And he was dependent on me as well. Now, I am reading that this is a crime…this dependency thing. That is what has brought me so far down into the grieving debit column.

Blessings for Today: People who are ahead of me and who can guide me with the grieving process. Those grieving with a positive outlook remember what was best about their relationship and the blessings that they had, including the dependencies. They say, "That's what I loved most of him…that he really needed me and that's what made our relationship so special." I am not in that place yet. I still think all of this as very unfair. I resent that I have to be sitting writing this instead of on my bike, or swimming, or hiking someplace special with my Robert Boy, or simply sitting on his lap with his long arms around me.

But I do learn from and am blessed by the role models who show me. And sprints do matter. There is a time and a place for sprints. Miami was a sprint... getting over one finish line at a time and then resting from exhaustion.

Specific Prayer Requests: The endurance and patience that comes from training for marathons and the power and strength that comes from sprinting. Both are important in life. I just need more encouragement for the endurance of the marathon. Hebrews 12:1 says, "Therefore, since we are surrounded by such a great cloud of witnesses, let us throw off everything that hinders and the sin that so easily entangles. And let us run with perseverance the race marked out for us."

Reflection

Settling into the journey is no picnic. And that's just what it is...a journey. An eventual acceptance and settling in for the long haul. The road is very, very bumpy with constant reminders of what you no longer have, but with persistence and support the minutes turn into hours, the hours turn into days and the days turn into months. You have to brace a lot in the beginning for the triggers and the constant waves of grief, but you embrace the people who are there for you and who have gone before you and will show you the way if you let them. You embrace that you are even getting through in the first place, and you embrace the things that are still present in your life that are good and sustaining. Take a moment to recall what they are. It helps.

***

ENTRY   11/19/2016 at 8:12 a.m.

"LIVING WITH PARADOX"

Last August, I went with my mother to her longtime heart doctor armed with a letter. In the letter, that I reviewed and approved, my mother asked her doctor to turn off her pacemaker and internal defibrillator. It was a

good and well thought out letter really. Nothing morbid or depressing about it. All just matter of fact. She talked about her love of life and that she had a great life indeed, but that she was ready to go, and she wanted to go on her own terms. She had observed her mother and brother suffer immensely, and she did not want that. She felt both were brutal and unnecessary endings.

Her doctor's reaction to her request, however, was one of horror and disbelief. He made the statement, "I will be no part of turning off anyone's pacemaker, and indeed, if I did, they would put me in jail. You would not want me to go to jail, would you?" So, case closed. There it was—a decision my mother wanted, yet one the doctors considered a "silly notion" that he never wanted to discuss again. "Your edema looks better this month. Please come again next month. Next patient please…"

Fast forward to yesterday when we spent the entire day interviewing my mother for one particular long-term care community program that held promise. All asking my mother questions unique to their specialty, but all asking the same last question: "What is your goal for care?" My mother always responded, "I simply want to go on my own terms. I want my pacemaker turned off. I want a peaceful ending. I have lived a long and wonderful life, and I do not want to suffer anymore." My mother is not bitter. She simply knows what she wants and is honest enough to say so. The social worker and nurse practitioner picked up on my mother's desire to end her life peacefully and asked if she felt she needed counseling. Sure…why not? "But what I really want," my mother claimed, "is to move to one of the few states like California or Oregon that respect the wishes of a human being who knows what she wants. But sure, I'll talk to a counselor."

My own mind runs in parallel, but jumbled, tracks…tracks would be much too organized a way to describe this paradox. One, the need to make sense of Bob's life taken when he was still healthy and wanted to stay. AND THEN the need to make sense of a weakened, yet very fulfilled person who has seen immense suffering (as both a nurse and observer of family deaths) and simply wants the power to claim her own time in her own way. I want so desperately to work through my own emotions and bring some semblance of normalcy back to my life—the "new normal" they call it—but this process of helping my mother die, while having just tried to help my husband live is so confusing and stymieing to me and is actually very much hindering my movement forward. I think— I know—I could handle each situation individually, but to process both simultaneously is defeating much of the time.

It reminds me of being in college and wanting desperately to graduate, but they keep telling you that your credits are insufficient— you have to take more classes, and by the way, the classes that you want to take ("Great memories of Bob Hassmiller 101" or "Wellness for Your Inner Soul") are filled up, so you have to take classes that you have absolutely no interest in ("Advanced graduate level long-term care in the United States" with endless lab classes).

They say you are strong, so you can handle the advanced classes that others of your capabilities could never handle, and you wonder who these people are who are making these decisions about classes you must take and are able to handle. How dare you tell me what you think my capacities are? You look for mentors to help guide you, but the mentors are limited. They have handled one or the other side of this paradox, but not both at the same time. As you sit through these classes that you are barely passing, you keep getting notices in the mail that your credits are still insufficient—you will certainly never graduate on time, and you won't get the job that you want. You will have to study harder, pay more attention, and do extra homework. What's wrong with you? Why can't you focus?

Blessings for Today: Kim saw one bright and shining star last night and said that star was her Daddy and that he was indeed here. The way that Abby sings "Twinkle, Twinkle Little Star," which her Pops used to sing to her—the only song in his child song repertoire for which he knew the words and could teach it to her, so that is "their song" and the star belonged to all of us last night as a reminder—a small dip into my class of "Great Memories of Bob Hassmiller 101". I am longing to take many advanced classes with that title. I had one such seminar on an early morning walk when I noticed the super moon to my left and the sun rising to my right. A little grey unknown kitty with white socks (Pops was never without his white socks) appeared and walked with me for a short while, rubbing against my legs in a loving and knowing way. Why, hello there, Pops"icle." Does Abby know you're here?

Specific Prayer Requests: I know this is a situation where many would tell me to turn this whole thing over to God or a higher power. But my faith has been shaken badly. Help with the many hard decisions I have to make. For Kim and Mark, who grieve differently. Proverbs 3:5–6 says, "Trust in the Lord with all your heart and lean not on your own understanding; in all your ways submit to him, and he will make your paths straight." Psalm 55:22 asks us, "Cast your cares on the Lord and he will sustain you; he will never let the righteous be shaken.

Reflection

I am struck with the continued psychological battles I tried to understand: a mother who wanted to die but somehow could not in the timeframe she had in mind, and a husband who loved life and me and never wanted to leave—never! It was paradoxical and unfair and speaks again of the utter lack of control we have.

And I am struck by how comforting that strange cat was coming in and out of my legs on the beach so soon after the tragedy. My husband had gray hair, green eyes and could often be found in his white Red Cross t-shirt and socks. I was—and still am—convinced that was Bob. Maybe really Bob or symbolic Bob, but Bob nevertheless. I look for signs. Many in my position do. Signs that remind us that we are not forgotten here on earth. Signs of love and comfort. With the full moon to my right and the sun rising to my left, I was reminded that somehow the world goes on, and for a time I was loved deeply and profoundly. The cat told me so.

***

ENTRY   11/22/2016 at 8:00 p.m.

"PETER PAN AND THE LAND OF MAKE BELIEVE"

Sunday afternoons I spend with Kim, Matt and the grandkids. This past Sunday the weather was gray and blustery, so for the heck of it I got out a "Disney Monopoly" game. I do things differently when Abby is around—I keep up a positive front so my three-year-old continues to believe that Nana's house is a place where you can be happy. This is important to me.

Abby asked Matt, "What is this game about?" Her Daddy and I explained that it was a game about pretending: that you have real money, that you can buy things with fake money, and that you can charge people rent for fake property that you bought with fake money. Abby gets what it means to "make believe" and she got the fact that none of it was real, but all she really ended up caring about was that she learned how to roll the dice and count the dots and move the make believe characters around the make believe property.

I was immediately drawn to select Peter Pan as my token, as he best personified my mood these days. Lady and the Tramp, Sleeping Beauty, and Dumbo just did not cut it. Once I had Peter in my hand, I began to remember the story line. You never grow up, life goes on forever in Never Never Land, and nothing is impossible—you just have to dream it, and it will come true. Throw a little pixie dust my way, will ya?! I sure could use some.

That's how I lived my life—dream it, plan for it, do it, give back, and it will all be okay. Like magic, everything will turn out. I think most of us feel that everything will be okay…one foot in front of the other, right? We must believe we will be okay and that everything will turn out well, or else we would not function very well. It did not escape my notice as a nurse that people did die, but that was for other people. Other people lost the loves of their lives—not me. We all know or can at least say there are no guarantees; that life is short; that we have to make the most of every moment; "I suppose it's like the ticking crocodile, isn't it? Time is chasing after all of us.".… All the clichés that we should believe, but don't until it happens. So hard. Please, I say, please pass the pixie dust!

Tiger Lily says, "she did not believe he could have really gone, because for her, to leave the person you loved was impossible." Right, Tiger Lily, I'm with you… it's impossible. So what happened? And more here from Peter Pan to Tiger Lily or is it from Sue to Bob:

"I knew I'd miss you. But the surprising thing is, you never leave me. I never forget a thing. Every kind of love, it seems, is the only one. It doesn't happen twice. And I never expected that you could have a broken heart and love with it too, so much that it doesn't seem broken at all. I know young people look at me and think my youth seems so far away, but it's all around me, and you're all around me. Tiger Lily, do you think magic exists if it can be explained? I can explain why I loved you; I can explain the theory of evolution that tells me why mermaids live in Neverland and nowhere else. But it still feels like magic.

"I like to think that one day after I die, at least one small particle of me— of all the particles that will spread everywhere—will float all the way to Neverland, and be part of a flower or something like that, like that poet said, the one that your Tik Tok loved. I like to think that nothing's final, and that everyone gets to be together even when it looks like they don't, that it all works out even when all the evidence seems to say something else, that you and I are always young in the woods, and that I'll see you sometime again, even if it's not with any kind of eyes I know of or understand. I wouldn't be surprised if that is the way things go after all—that all things end happy. Even for you and Tik Tok and for you and me."[8]

Blessings for Today: Sometimes I just don't know what to grab at for blessings. Sometimes I just want to dream and just make it all come back again. Wendy says, "You know that place between sleep and awake, the place where you can still remember dreaming? That's where I'll always love you, Peter Pan." So, that's where I will always love you, Bob Hassmiller. That's where I'll be waiting.

Specific Prayer Requests: "Never say goodbye because goodbye means going away and going away means forgetting."[8] (Peter Pan) John 14: 2–3 says, "In my Father's house there are many dwelling places. If it were not so, would I have told you that I go to prepare a place for you? And if I go and prepare a place for you, I will come again and will take you to myself, so that where I am, there you may be also."

Reflection

I never thought of Peter Pan as a spiritual story. It was about make believe and never growing up, boys getting into trouble, and a little fairy spreading pixie dust. The lines in Peter Pan came to life for me, however, as I found it far less about make believe and more about relationships, love, and how love stays connected for real—no make believe there. I have felt the seeming impossibility of having a broken heart and conveying love. And, I so desperately never want to forget. I continually celebrate when I am able to visit Bob in that place between sleep and awake. I so treasure when I can remember. And, I hold onto the fact that I will be with Bob again—that it simply cannot all be so final. Is that make believe, is that Pixie dust, or a dream? I choose to believe that somehow, someway, I will be connected once again to Bob. I choose this as my reality…as my faith.

***

ENTRY   11/23/2016 at 8:42 p.m.

"STEPPIN' OUT FOR THE NEXT GENERATION"

When the accident happened, I canceled my entire work life, and even now most of it is still canceled. My world used to be big and bold and included the nation and the world. Now it has shrunk drastically: it is only about me, Bob and those closest around me. But, I found myself with an appointment that I somehow did not cancel and was unsure of why.

It was not a presentation I would have even normally accepted, as the commitment was to "only" one school, Villanova. I was scheduled to speak to up to 400 nursing students and faculty about the role of nursing in enabling people to live healthier lives and to experience greater well-being. The event was in the same city where Bob spent the last days of his life, and I was not anxious to return there....in fact petrified. I accepted the engagement initially because I have some "RWJF Future of Nursing Scholars" (outstanding students who complete their doctoral degree in nursing in three years with RWJF support) at Villanova, and I wanted to be there for them. But with ten days before the presentation, how could I cancel? I worked to concoct a solution as my heart raced anxiously at the prospect of actually moving forward with this. Bottom line was that I had to remain authentic to myself and my circumstances—I could not give my standard presentation.

So, to remain authentic I decided to invite my good friend and hospital angel Beth Ann to present for me while I gave "some kind of intro" to the nursing students. To me, the ability to go forward with this commitment was all about the students and the message I wanted to give to them as future nurses. So, with the concurrence of Beth Ann and the dean at Villanova, this arrangement was secured.

On Monday night, I walked into a packed auditorium, sat in the easy chair next to Beth Ann on stage and proceeded to tell the hundreds of nursing students and faculty that although I was honored to be there, I would not be presenting the intended lecture. Instead, I wanted to share with them a story about what happened to Bob, my husband and best friend. I said that there were three very special nurses who stood out among all nurses in regard to their care and compassion, and that I wanted to describe them and the effect they had on our lives.

I told them about Nurse Abby, and I read both her emails that she sent me after his accident. I said how I would never forget her touch, care, and the concern in her eyes.

Next I shared the story of how Beth Ann, an experienced nurse administrator, never left my side for the ten days I stayed at her hospital. Her gifts of compassion, touch and rugged proactive advocacy, and ability to make people jump through hoops for me will never be forgotten. The story she published in *Health Affairs* of how she almost lost her husband and what she had to do throughout her ordeal gave me insight on how she used her experience to "pay it forward" with me.

And then I described Kathy, the nurse that helped me throughout Bob's last day and night. How she cared for me with words and hugs when machines had to be turned off and medication increased…and how she would not go home when her shift ended, knowing that Bob and I still needed her. She stayed with Bob and me to the end. To the very end.

I told the nursing students that I am known for encouraging students to continue on with their education, to use their critical thinking skills, to understand the research process, and make sure they aspire to be leaders on boards and more. However, I said that the most important ingredients to me and Bob were care and compassion, and if you don't have that, then there is no nurse. I told them that as they ventured out into the world of nursing and they became frustrated or overwrought with paper and computer work that they were to remember why they chose this profession and what their care, concern, touch and hugs mean to patients and families. Don't forget to touch. Don't forget to hug. Beth Ann told me later that you could hear a pin drop, and not one person had their smart phones out—these days a compliment, right?

My plan was to exit stage right as soon as the presentation was over, but students came up and wanted to share their thoughts and their hugs with me. The last nursing student in line thanked me for having the courage to come to Philadelphia. She squeezed me hard and then asked what she and her classmates could do to repay me for coming, and again, I said that I wanted everyone in the room to hear my voice in their ears and minds for years to come about what it means to be a real nurse and to make a difference in the lives of patients and families in the same way these nurses did for Bob and me.

Blessings for Today: The opportunity and gift to speak to future and graduate level nurses about how the gift of giving is the most meaningful piece of being a nurse. And how one of the students found my professional Facebook page and followed up with a lengthy note about what my words meant to her. Bob's life mattered to me more than anything in the world, and if I can convey how nurses have the honor and privilege of respecting and honoring each and every life they come into contact with, then this will not be in vain. I must make Bob's life matter.

Specific Prayer Requests: Tomorrow is Thanksgiving. I am angry and overwhelmed, but am also thankful for a lot. It is very hard to be without the person who made every Thanksgiving special and came up with the idea of making sure we went around the table to each say what we appreciated about every single person there. My family will gather separately the hour before the others arrive to continue this tradition.

Reflection

The gnawing feeling in me of not letting this horrible tragedy happen in vain is what I hold onto. To honor Bob's life is to find ways to bring lessons—including love and compassion—to others. I know he would say, "Now, that's the Susie I know!" To pay it forward. I remember my hair dresser Issa's advice that I should not be preoccupied with why all of this happened but should instead look for opportunities to share lessons and pay it forward. He assured me when I doubted everything that I would find my way and find these opportunities, and he was right.

***

ENTRY   11/27/2016 at 6:58 a.m.

"ATTITUDE OF GRATITUDE"

What Would Pooh Say? Never in my wildest dreams did I ever imagine spending the holidays of 2016 without my Robert Boy. I hate this more than I have ever hated anything. Many times I still think he is simply upstairs reading or away on a disaster call. Although I am fully cognizant of what happened, it doesn't stop me from thinking or hoping he will walk in the front door. And I know what he will be wearing, including his hat. That's just the way this goes. Of course, I have awakened to the fact that almost all of us grieve at one time or another, but it doesn't make it easier.

"If you live to be one-hundred, I want to live to one-hundred minus one day, so I never have to live without you" (Winnie the Pooh)

"It's snowing still," said Eeyore gloomily.

"So it is."

"And freezing."

"Is it?"

"Yes," said Eeyore. "However," he said, brightening up a little, "we haven't had an earthquake lately."[9]

So, now against my own will, I must adjust. I don't feel like adjusting, but there is no choice. I can adjust with great bitterness, which quite frankly feels the much better choice at the moment—or I can choose to remember the good and some of the blessings along the way and somehow turn this into a way to help others (or help myself). Yes, myself first.

Mind you, for me this is a forced choice at the moment. Like, do you want to eat your peas or go to your room or stand in the corner? I don't want any of those choices. Or a multiple choice question that omits the choices of "not sure," "depends on the context," "I don't feel like it at this time." Can't I just choose "none of the above"? But NO, this is a forced choice question, and you must answer, they say. I can delay my answer, though, right? I don't have to take the test just yet. I still have time to think about this. I am choosing "I don't feel like it at this time." They will give me a pass for now. After all, I still have enormous feelings to sort through, minute by minute…hour by hour…but they are asking that I think about this for the future. Try it out they say—see how it feels to notice something positive. You don't have to fully commit at the moment…just try.

"I knew when I met you an adventure was going to happen, " said Winnie the Pooh.

So here are my attempts, and this part is not really hard at all. It starts with those who came to my rescue. I could not have survived without all of the first responders. The ones who triaged care and responded with actions immediately and without question, and with great love and hugs. And now the sustainers.

Piglet sidled up to Winnie the Pooh from behind and whispered, "Pooh…"

"Yes, Piglet, what is it?"

"Nothing," said Piglet, taking Pooh's paw. "I just wanted to be sure of you."

Life goes on as it should, and still people throw me life preservers each day. And sometimes it's not what you think, or who you think will come to your rescue and help you the most. People surprise you. The blessing for me is that there are a special few who are still hanging in there with me almost on a daily basis. Others less frequently, but always with words, books, songs, and care and deeds that matter enormously. I am grateful.

Piglet: "How do you spell love?"

Pooh: "You don't spell it, you feel it."

So a new journey begins—a journey I did not choose. I have begun walking—sometimes going forward, sometimes going backwards, and most times just walking in circles, just being and praying and taking it in and trying to make sense of it.

"Don't underestimate the value of doing nothing, of just going along, listening to all the things you can't hear, and not bothering, " said Winnie the Pooh.

Blessings for Today: I cannot think of a day in my life when I have been more grateful for those of you who have stood by me and my family and are still standing with us, long after the required amount of standing.

"Piglet noticed that even though he had a very small heart, it could hold a rather large amount of gratitude, " said Winnie the Pooh.

Specific Prayer Requests: I know this journey is long and torturous. I also know that there are things that I can learn along the way and later use to help others. Pay it forward. It is easy to stay bitter. After all, I feel bitter and wronged and that my family has been wronged. But someday, I want to have an attitude that is centered around gratitude and faith. I am not there yet, but prayers that I will get there.

"Sometimes, if you stand on the bottom rail of a bridge and lean over to watch the river slipping slowly away beneath you, you will suddenly know everything there is to be known, " said Winnie the Pooh.

"If ever there is tomorrow when we're not together…there is something you must always remember. You are braver than you believe, stronger than you seem, and smarter than you think. But the most important thing is, even if we're apart…I'll always be with you, " said Winnie the Pooh.

Reflection

I took much comfort in the words passed between Pooh and his friends. The author of Winnie the Pooh truly conveyed the truisms of love, loss and life. I hold onto words that bring some meaning to a morass that I don't understand.

I search for meaning constantly and go back and forth between so many emotions. I hold onto words and love that people send. Their intent is always important. Some people stay away, as it is too much of a reminder of their own mortality, and they don't know what to say, but just saying you don't know what to say is perfectly okay. The words and the intent behind the words are what matter. And as Pooh aptly pointed out, sometimes you cannot spell love, but you can sure feel it.

***

ENTRY   11/30/2016 at 7:34 p.m.

"I GOT THE MOUSE!"

Our house backs up on two sides to dense forest, and the forest has lots of critters. The peskiest are the mice. The other critters manage to stick to their own terrain, albeit they consider my backyard part of their terrain. The mice, however, seem to think it's perfectly okay to enter our home. Every year around this time. as winter approaches, a mouse or two show up. My job has always been to scream, jump on the bed, and call for my Robert Boy to remove the pest. And Bob always comes dutifully with a towel ready to throw on the mouse. I never quite understood the logic of using a towel to catch a mouse, but I think Bob always thought that would be quicker, and he wanted to put me out of my misery as quickly as possible. Stopping my screaming was definitely a motivation for him. Mind you, he has never ever caught a mouse with a towel. Step two is always to run to the store to get the yearly mouse traps, and then, yes, the job is done.

So, about two weeks ago when a mouse ran across my bedroom floor, my first inclination was to scream and jump on the bed, but then suddenly, I realized that my screams would not produce my beloved husband. So, what did I do? I ran to get a towel. Why? I am not sure. I really had no idea how to catch a mouse with a towel. Apparently, Bob did not either, but I figured that was always the first step. Then I remembered there was a leftover mousetrap from last year, so I set it (without screaming) and put peanut butter on the little mouse plate. The next morning the peanut butter was gone and so was the mouse—he had gotten away. So, I bought "guaranteed 100%" mouse traps, but they did not work either. I figured that the mouse had moved to greener pastures, since I had not seen him for a few weeks. Then lo and behold, at 4:00 a.m. on Monday, I heard a crash coming from my bathroom closet—he was back! I set the original trap out with peanut butter and hoped for the best. The next morning I awoke to a job well done—this time both the peanut butter and the mouse were no longer. And then I did the impossible—I removed both the mouse and trap from my premises.

So, why do I tell you this story? Because I believe *so far, this has been about my biggest accomplishment since the incident.* It was huge: I strategized how to catch a mouse, caught it, and disposed of it. You have to give me that. I was aglow all day from this feat. I took a picture to show no one in particular, but to remind myself that I did it!

I have been consumed with tasks of all kinds. It used to be that (to put it simply) I had one hundred jobs and could delegate fifty percent to Bob and twenty-five percent to my mother (when she was driving), and then I could give extraordinary energy and devotion to the twenty-five percent that I had left over. People thought I was Wonder Woman, but I had the best darn support system going—that was the big secret. We all knew our tasks and carried them out superbly.

And now I have everyone's job and no one to delegate. Every once in a while I have someone who will help me with something (have I mentioned Matt with the finances!), but basically, it is me, myself and I. I am overwhelmed constantly between trying to figure out how to run this house, physically, mentally and financially.

LADIES and GENTLEMAN: focus your attention on the talented magician in the center ring and watch as she tries to decipher long-term care strategies, policies, companions, Medicaid spend down, annuities, VA paperwork for Bob and mother, while talking to lawyers, accountants, appraisers, reading stories to and bathing grandchildren—all while standing on one foot and with no memory to speak of, fatigued to the bone…and catching (and disposing of) a mouse single-handedly. Applause please!

For her next trick, she will return to work, while jumping up and down, balancing plates on her head, discussing toilets with plumbers, selling cars, taking her mother to wherever her mother happens to need to go to for the day, negotiating prices and job responsibilities with elder home companions, and then listening to people tell her they are impressed with the progress she is making. You're kidding, right?

I appreciate the progress you think I am making, but I HAVE HAD IT with tasks that don't belong to me. Do you hear me? These do not belong to me. Why does everyone keep assigning me tasks that are much better suited for others? And besides, this magician has not yet figured out the disappearing act. Her husband disappeared, but she has not yet been able to make him reappear. What kind of magician am I to only be able to perform half a trick?

I asked my technically savvy neighbor last night if he could replace all the old Xfinity television equipment and wires with the new equipment that had just been delivered to my house. He offered to show me how to do it. Please, just do it yourself, I begged him. I cannot do one more task, and I don't want to learn how to wire televisions…do you hear me? Let me take you to the sewing store, and let us look at patterns and material and special sewing needles, and buttons and ruffles. Let me teach YOU how to sew. Do you want me to teach you how to sew? If not, then why do you expect me to want to know how to wire televisions? Yes, I know…kind of sexist. Hey, I can teach you how to catch a mouse—I know exactly how to do it now (and without screams).

Blessings for Today: I CAUGHT A MOUSE…and DISPOSED OF IT all by myself without screaming! I think if I can catch a mouse, then I might be able to do a few more things that I have never done before, but I refuse to learn how to wire televisions. I do have limits. Matt told me that I should put a list on the mirror of all the things I have to do and then next to it a list of things I have accomplished, so the progress will seem more real to me. It seemed like a really good idea, until it turned into yet another task, so I gave up on it.

I do have wonderful people who have helped me along the way. The day-to-day tasks will always fall on me now, but thanks to Colleen, my wonderful assistant at the Robert Wood Johnson Foundation, who has tenderly welcomed me back to work in the softest way possible. Thanks to my colleague Wendy for walking me into the building the first day so I would not have to enter alone and then checked on me three times in three hours. And to Robin for greeting me with a dozen yellow roses to warm my office. And to Rachel and Amy in Human Resources for making life easier for me in every way possible. And to my colleague Beth, who simply emailed me and said it was good to hear my voice and have me in the building after I called in to a meeting from my offices instead of garnering the courage to walk to the conference room down the hall. She emailed me: "Sue trying to muddle through is more amazing than many of us on our best days." She must have heard that I got the mouse!

Specific Prayer Requests: I need to be a tad bit kinder to myself and take things a bit easier. I have high expectations, and I'm trying to do too many things for too many people. Matthew 11:28–30 begs us, "Come to me, all you who are weary and burdened, and I will give you rest. Take my yoke upon you and learn from me, for I am gentle and humble in heart, and you will find rest for your souls. For my yoke is easy and my burden is light."

Reflection

The tasks still continue to overwhelm me, but not as much as in the beginning. Even in my extreme state of grief, I had expectations of what I needed to accomplish. I should have prioritized better. Bills need to get paid, but other things can be put on hold. When you are in grief, you already have trouble making decisions. I wish that someone who had experienced losing a loved one could have helped me prioritize. As time has passed, I see that I simply could have let some things go. That said, the mouse simply had to be caught!

***

ENTRY   12/2/2016 at 9:03 p.m.

"KISSED BY A FAIRY PRINCESS"

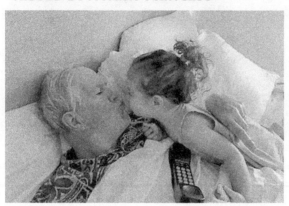

Abby spent the night with me and woke up too early. Her "Goldilocks" cot resides next to mine, the Mama Bear bed. It was just about impossible to get her to go back to sleep, but it was still dark so I tricked her into thinking that it was the middle of the night. I did break down and let her come up into my bed. So, up she climbed.

She snuggled next to me and lay her face directly in front of mine. I immediately thought this was NOT going to work, and I fretted about her intrusion into my space. But then I heard Bob's voice: Tell her she's my fairy princess. Remind her that I loved her kisses so much, and that she was and still is my fairy princess." So, I asked Abby if she remembered Pops kissing her all the time and then shaking in a subtle yet dramatic way, hands flying around just a bit, feet doing a little jig saying after each kiss, "I've been kissed by a fairy princess!" Saying this as if every kiss really mattered—and to him it really did. He savored each and every one of Abby's kisses.

When Abby told me that she remembered, I told her outright: "Abby, Pops just told me to tell you that you are his fairy princess, and he will always love you. He loved your kisses more than anything. She smiled and kissed me as if to say, "Please pass this one along to Pops."

It is my mission for Abby to remember Bob, and I know this is what Kim wants as well. Six-month-old John Robert will never know his Pops, but I keep hoping there is a chance that Abby will remember him. They were very close: Bob babysat for the kids at least once during the week, and we watched Abby on Saturdays or Sundays. We devoted all of our free time to these treasures. I feel an equal sadness between my not having my Robert Boy and the kids not having their Pops.

I am unsure how much I should say to help Abby remember her Pops. Always in a positive and uplifting way, I remind her what Pops loved about her, what we loved about Pops, and how Pops and God will always be there for her. In our prayers, we always, always ask God and Pops to watch over us and protect us. She knows, in her own way, that her new cat, Popsicle, is meant to remind her of Pops. I tell Abby that if she is ever sad or afraid that she can always call upon Pops to help her, and I believe she will. Just like I now do this, she will too.

Last night, I asked her what her wish was. 99.9999% of the time she wishes for a dog (a wish that stands unfulfilled), but she responded that she wished she could fly so she could visit Pops and God. I told her that would be a really great experience. Then she asked the dreaded question: "Nana, what do you wish for?" I told her that more than anything, I wished that I could see Pops again. She jumped in my lap and said, "Well, right now, you have Abby!"

Blessings for Today: Pops was such an enormous and positive force in all of our lives, and it is not hard to keep such a positive force alive. Many of our family and friends will gather in Milburn, New Jersey, this Sunday to walk or run the annual Run for the Red 5k to raise money for the Red Cross. Abby and I will walk together, and I will wear the Red Cross hat that Bob always wore. We will walk to honor Pops, and he will be with us.

Specific Prayer Requests: That Abby will remember her Pops and the way he loved her—that special feeling inside when someone loves you so much that nothing else matters. I desperately want my grandchildren to know what an extraordinary Pops they had, and I want them to emulate his goodness—that is not too big of a prayer request, right? That the Red Cross 5k on Sunday will surpass all financial goals to help people in need, and that all participants arrive and leave safely. "I look at you and see the rest of my life in front of my eyes." (Unknown)

Reflection

Even with the passage of time, Bob's spirit and character remain vibrant in our lives. The tears still sneak up on us. Kim cried to Abby today that she missed her Daddy. Abby ran to get four objects from her room that she instinctively knew would be meaningful to her Mom: a Raggedy Ann doll, a furry, blue stuffed bear with a funny little hat, a bear that a dear friend had made out of Bob's favorite clothing, and Popsicle. Abby said, "The Raggedy Ann doll was yours, Mom, when you were my age. You were a happy little girl then, and I want you to be happy again. The furry, blue bear was a special gift Pops gave to you when you were little, and you kept it to remember that Pops loved you. The Pops bear is made of his clothes, and we can touch it to remember what he liked to wear. And Nana gave me this cat because Popsicle is short for Pops and it would help me to remember that Pops will always be with me, so go ahead and hold him, Mom. Pops is with you right now, and he will always be with you."

***

ENTRY   12/6/2016 at 8:26 p.m.

"AUTOPILOT"

I am in an airplane traveling to Orlando, where I will go to my condo in Naples as an escape and to take care of condo business. I have mixed feelings about going to my condo as it is filled with ONLY memories of Bob and me—our place to get away. I am not sure what I will face when I get there, but I am going because I have to…for business reasons and for…well, to see if my place with the original intent of getting away from it all will still hold that special designation. I simply don't know right now.

Two years ago, I fell in love with this condo, and Bob made it happen. I am originally from Florida, and I always wanted a piece of that state to call my own. It is a highly unassuming simple condo. One would say that it is NOT updated, and I like it that way. Our real-estate agent, who Bob and I both adore, pointed out that it is not updated and in the long run not best for resale, but I was not thinking of resale. I thought of the serenity I felt when I walked in the door. I loved the comfortable furniture, seashells of all sorts, lighthouses, color, abundant windows, the great location, and the porch with non-updated patio furniture that overlooks a preserve with a pond and a fountain. It is a place that invites anyone and every-one to come on in and eat and drink wherever you like—I have no rules about where one might decide to eat. It offered a chance to take myself off of autopilot for a week here and there throughout the year.

The plane I'm traveling in right now is on autopilot. The course is pre-chartered. I am not saying the pilot's job is simple, but nevertheless, he presses some buttons and off we go. Like my life. I was completely on autopilot—my journey plugged in. I knew exactly where I was going, for how long, when I was to arrive, what it would look like, and what it would feel like—or so I thought. Autopilot. Although the journey was relatively smooth, of course, we encountered bumps.

We temporarily turned off the autopilot to get to smoother air. Some air was more turbulent. The challenges of life. Challenges that may have felt daunting at times, but back then there were two very capable co-pilots—Bob and me—working together. Check and balance. We took off, landed, climbed through the clouds, navigated through storms, and sometimes hurricanes. Together, however, we piloted a pretty strong ship. Just like this airplane I am on now, it would be unthinkable to fly a plane of this size with just a single pilot—co-pilots always work together. Sure we had passengers from time to time that we wanted to throw off, but knowing our flying skills, each mastering different sets, we knew that our plane would land safely eventually. Not so bad when you have the option of autopilot.

Now I am piloting solo without checks and balances and finely-honed skills. My aircraft, called "Life As We Now Know It" travels to unknown lands, sometimes flying in circles for days on end. I want to land but am unsure how. There is no course to plug in. There is a starting point, but no end in sight. I have experienced two new starts:

1) A false one—the day of Bob's accident.

2) The new start—the day I lost him.

The navigational computers got stuck for a long time not knowing what to do and where to go. I apparently have a real start now, but no destination and cannot use the autopilot. I have to stay acutely alert to navigate unknown skies and dart from unwanted turbulence with no discernable ground beneath me.

I am piloting people, who I treasure dearly, but they have no idea how to fly this plane either. Some are part-time passengers, but they have no more skill than me. They especially like it when I dodge a particular mountain or refuel in midair.

They send welcome messages of support from the back of the plane: "Well done, Sue, another day without navigational tools, and we are still airborne." Some have flown similar planes, and it helps to know that they have landed their planes safely again, even without an autopilot. They are my first class passengers: They have paid dearly for their seats and have earned the right to sit upfront.

They tell me that flying solo without navigational tools might land you in a very good place one day—yes, a different place but a good place with a new inner strength. (What was wrong with my old inner strength?). The trick is that every once in a while you need to look out the window at the scenery and see the sky (the big picture). If you can draw upon your inner strength, your faith, and listen to the first class passengers who were once pilots, you will survive and land. I am told I will survive—perhaps that is an end point. I am looking for an end point, and they want me to focus on the journey. One day you will land, they say, and you might even be a more compassionate person who is aware that there are many other pilots who have circled for a very long time—but who eventually landed safely.

Blessings for Today: These are my blessings: I have a support system, and I could afford to take time from work to grieve. Some people need to work to financially survive. Others are single mothers who have to go back to work and then come home and take care of their kids. I am NOT in that category. I cannot imagine a better place to work right now than where I do.

Specific Prayer Requests: I feel bitter and cheated, but I believe that over time those feelings can be tempered. I do not want to be a bitter person. I cannot live my life that way. Bob would not want that. If I must go through this, I want it to turn me into a more compassionate person—I want to be there for other people who lose loved ones suddenly. One of my biggest prayers is that when someone else is hurting that I will go to them, not turn away from them because I am afraid of my own immortality or the situation makes me uncomfortable. I want to put their feelings above my busyness and discomfort. I want to take them to lunch and truly listen to them. That is the person I aspire to be. Exodus 17:12 says, When Moses' hands grew tired, they took a stone and put it under him and he sat on it. Aaron and Hur held his hands up—one on one side, one on the other—so that his hands remained steady till sunset."

Reflection

Life is always an unknown, but especially so when you lose the love of your life. I have learned now that the smart ones still plan, but try to live life to the fullest, understanding full well that life can suddenly be altered irrevocably. Bob had a keen understanding and appreciation of the value of life. Maturity and lived experiences do that for you. But he knew that character, other centeredness, faith, and resilience were important. I, on the other hand, had to learn this and am still doing so. I have been blessed now with the opportunity to help a few others with the sudden death of their spouse, relinquishing my pilot seat. I now sit in row 1C—first class, for those of you who don't know.

***

ENTRY   12/8/2016 at 8:50 p.m.

"WALKING INTO THE CONDO"

The story actually begins two years ago when we bought our condo, and we met Claire and Jack McKinney, our warm and gracious downstairs neighbors. Bob, who played basketball in high school and part of college and never lost his love of the game, gravitated immediately to Jack after learning that he coached the Los Angeles Lakers in 1979. After coaching fourteen games, Jack sustained a head injury in a near fatal bicycle accident. Jack returned after the accident to coach the Indiana Pacers for four seasons, winning an NBA championship ring.

Bob showed proper reverence when Jack proudly held out his hand to show us his ring. Claire stepped in from time to time to jog Jack on his weak to non-existent memory and to help him follow the conversation. His ability to keep up with the conversation did not bother Bob or me, however. I understood his condition from my years as a nurse, and Bob, a naturally compassionate person, simply thought Claire and Jack were grand and this was only a minor hiccup in our quest to know each other. Jack was famous, Bob told me, and talking about basketball in whatever way Jack could was more than enough for Bob.

We spoke to Claire and Jack the few times a year that we popped into our condo, and they always welcomed us to our Florida home as if we were family. It was evident to Bob and me that they loved each other dearly. In our course of knowing them, we found out more details about Jack's bicycle accident, which was eerily similar to Bob's. An eye witness saw Jack go over the front handlebars coming down a hill; Jack never regained any memory of the incident. Although there was no eye witness to Bob's accident, we know that pretty much the same thing occurred. However, because Bob was wearing a helmet, the full force of the blow occurred to his spine instead of his head. The difference was, as Claire said last night, one great man perished from his traumatic injuries and another great man lives with them now. Claire said she considers herself the lucky one, and to watch the two of them interact, you would agree.

When I decided to visit my condo, I asked Claire to walk into the condo with me. She went beyond that simple request and told me she would have dinner for me and a bed in her condo if I did not want to stay alone in mine. She understands that she could have been walking in my shoes, and I am reminded that I could have been walking in hers. Kindred spirits brought together by similar tragedies. She relayed to me that she knew two things when she met Bob and me for the first time: That ours was a marriage of love, and that we were special because we accepted Jack just the way he was. This was important to her. Both situations remind people that life is far from perfect, and we are mortal. Both of our situations stink, but there are many in this world with really stinky situations. We are called upon to be here for others, and so, this time Claire was here for me.

When I drove up to the condo, Claire ran to the car to tell me that she needed help right away. I could see that Jack had fallen outside in front of the condo and could not get up. I ran over, and we worked together to get him standing again. I told Claire that she and Jack planned this on purpose to take my mind off of walking into my condo, and then I realized this was something that Bob would do. Yes, I decided that Bob was behind this. He does not want me to suffer, so he staged Jack's fall to distract me—and it did—it worked. It's not that walking into the condo and sitting here now is not hard—it is—but for the moment, right before I was to walk inside, it struck me that I was here for Claire, and she was here for me.

Blessings for Today: I was reminded that yesterday was Pearl Harbor Day. One can only imagine what that must have felt like for thousands of families as they heard the news and grappled for years trying to make sense of the chaos and going through "what ifs" in their heads—you always go through "what ifs." None of those families ever got to say good-bye…sudden traumatic loss. I do count that blessing…that, in the end I got to say good-bye. And, of course, the blessing of Claire being here for me, and that I could be there for her.

Specific Prayer Requests: My prayer request is for Claire and Jack as they navigate their situation. I am not even sure Claire would say it is stinky, so I won't label it as such. She loves her Jack and devotes all her time to him. I know this is a very difficult 24/7 job, however, and it takes every ounce of her stamina.

Reflection

I am certain that most people do not have a trouble-free life—although sometimes it does not seem that way. Some families have it harder than others, however. In the end, no matter the challenges, I think the ability to see some good, or some lessons and persist, can make a difference. We cannot choose all that life brings to us, but we can certainly choose how to react and deal with those challenges. Claire, you are doing an amazing job!

***

ENTRY   12/17/2016 at 10:32 a.m.

"WHEN CHRISTMAS DOES NOT FEEL LIKE A CELEBRATION"

One thing I do know is that although Christmas is a time for celebration, it is not, this year, for me. All the feelings about this holiday, including those normally accompanying the usual merriment, such as stress, anxiety, and demands have been exacerbated, along with the sadness of missing my best friend. And I think this is okay. Let's just say I don't like it, but I accept it. I have no choice.

What else might I feel at the moment? Reflective perhaps, and maybe some momentary peace sprinkled with a dash of hope. I am grappling with what else I might feel or wish to feel, but celebration does not come to mind. Not even with prompts from some that Bob would want me to be happy. I appreciate the prompts and agree that Bob would want me to be happy. But honestly, I don't think he expects that I would celebrate. I am set on this and okay with my decision not to celebrate.

I only hung a few decorations and eschewed lights and purposeful reminders—the memories will be strong and overpowering enough without all the stuff hanging around me. I am struggling with how to proceed with my new life—a life without my best friend; a life without the ready humor and strong bear hugs and soft kisses; a life without sharing stories together of past wonderful times; and a life without making plans with my best friend for the coming year. I miss those things deeply. Thus, reflection, prayer and hope will be my mode of commemorating Christmas.

So, with this decision to mark Christmas differently than others—and avoid events that would force me to keep saying, "and a Merry Christmas to you as well," I have had some trepidation about stepping into church. But, I braced myself for all of the "joy and merriment," and attended church in Florida last week. I hoped for some solace and reminders of the true meaning of Christmas. You could say I was shocked, yet pleasantly surprised and relieved—yes, RELIEVED would be a good word—that the church I regularly attend in Naples featured the following sermon by Pastor Gene: "When Christmas Does not Feel Like a Celebration." I saw the title in the bulletin and waited with great anticipation.

The associate pastor began the service with a prayer for those who would be celebrating for the first time this year without a loved one, including those who were "living without their spouse for the first time." I felt a big X on my heart and cried softly, holding Kim's hand. How did the pastor know I was wondering how I would ever get through this Christmas without my best friend? How did she know that this was just the greeting and prayer that I needed?

Pastor Gene spoke next. He said that many people suffer from depression in general, and the holiday season makes everything more acute and profound for those struggling with loss. He was particularly aware of his audience—his sheep—and their losses. It was almost as if he tallied them all up and said, "WOW—this is going to be a really tough holiday season." He even made an announcement right out of the gate that there are deeper levels of grief and depression that need the assistance of a licensed professional. He read some symptoms of grief and encouraged those who were suffering from them to seek out help. He bypassed the joy and wonderment of Christmas and acknowledged the sorrow and difficulty of celebrating Christmas. He words were honest, genuine, and authentic. I felt immediate relief that I was not alone.

Pastor Gene "somehow" knew my state of mind, and he also knew the burden and danger of social isolation and the loss of friends because they were yours and your spouse's friends. Many losses all wrapped up into one time of year. I so appreciated him calling out the fact that for many, Christmas would NOT be joyous, and that it was okay to NOT have a VERY MERRY Christmas—and that YOU MAY NOT BE OKAY NOW, BUT YOU WILL BE OKAY later. He gave me a message of hope. How did he know how to make me feel normal and not an outcast?

He continued to spread messages of hope. He knew I would not hear this in the beginning, so he saved it for last, after acknowledging my true feelings. He told us that while we would never get over our losses, we would get through this time of grief. He said that hopelessness may grip us now, but there is a bigger plan and more to this story. Our job is to be open to hearing the bigger plan—that we will be able to trust and hope again. Don't be afraid to hope, he said. I realized that hope is what keeps me going. He said that depression is the door to celebration, and God uses those who are feeling most helpless. Yes, Pastor Gene, I want to help—I don't want my circumstances to make me bitter, and I don't want this tragedy to be in vain. Good must come of this—it must! There is a bigger plan here. He said that there are things that will help—reaching out to others, volunteering, getting sunlight, praying, being around true friends who will accept your present state without trying to change it, staying healthy, and knowing that there is always hope.

Blessings for Today: I have three special Christmas decorations sitting in my foyer that were recently given to me: An evergreen center piece from Nancy; a tree ornament from Denise that I hung on the centerpiece; and an angel from Pat. A simple, yet meaningful, holiday arrangement. These gifts remind me of the season and that I am cared for and loved. I am grateful that people are still giving to the Red Cross to honor Bob's memory, and that Christmas and holiday cards have now replaced sympathy cards.

And then there is Abby. Kim explained to her a few days ago that most times a man marries a woman, but sometimes women love women and men love men, and they get married to each other. Kim told her that it didn't matter, so long as the partners involved loved and took care of each other. And then Abby said, "Well, if girls can love each other and get married, then I want to marry my Nana." And this, my friends, is the greatest blessing of all.

Specific Prayer Requests: That I will keep the big picture in mind and find some meaning in my grief. That Bob's life will not be in vain. That I will not lose the joy of the holiday season forever: Rather, I will tuck it away for now and that those who care about me most will understand and not force what cannot presently be forced. That my small family will find comfort in remembering that a great and wonderful man touched all of us for a while, and we should live being mindful of the way he lived his life with grace, humility, giving, love, and hope. Isaiah 43:2 says, "When you pass through the waters, I will be with you; And when you pass through the rivers, they will not sweep over you. When you walk through the fire, you will not be burned. The flames will not set you ablaze," and Proverbs 13:12 says, "Hope deferred makes the heart sick, but longing fulfilled is a tree of life."

Reflection

I have been consumed this year by getting through so many firsts. Bracing myself, talking and praying fervently about getting through—and then somehow making it. It helps for both me and others to acknowledge each first and what this tragedy has done to me. Acknowledgment by others is especially cleansing and freeing—it is a critical link in feeling human, connected, and knowing that we all count in the end. You are recognized as having been insulted gravely, but someone who will, in most cases, make it out to the other side. Hope helps, as well as finding ways to give back. I don't know completely why we are all here on this earth at this given time, but I do know that the more we can respectfully acknowledge each other in ways that are uniquely important to each of us is an important contribution to our existence.

***

ENTRY   12/23/2016 at 6:04 p.m.

"MOUNTAINS: CREATING, CLIMBING, CONQUERING"

So, here it is almost Christmas and the New Year, and I am trying very hard to march on for the sake of getting back to life as it now is. I am struck by what a physical toll this has been and still very much is. People tell me all the time that

I "look better." It helps to hear that. It certainly sounds better than you don't look well at all. So, yes, I think it is good to say that. I smile in pictures, but you are supposed to smile, right? It is somewhat easier to smile when your picture is being taken with your grandchild. I feel that I have always looked the same on the outside, yet the inside toll has been enormous and tells a very different story. The inside feels like one big construction site—I feel the hammers, and saws, and chisels constantly.

At first, I struggled to breathe, and it felt like I would die myself. "Broken Heart Syndrome" is real: It is an actual physiological state, where the heart muscle becomes suddenly weakened or stunned. The syndrome, which can cause death, especially in people with a pre-existing heart condition, is called stress cardiomyopathy and happens when a spouse dies shortly after the death of their beloved. I really understand this. Stress cardiomyopathy has a host of other symptoms, including an incredible sense of fatigue and doom, which is hard for someone used to having abundant energy and zest for life. It's all the chemicals and hormones that are thrown into your body to try to stabilize a constant sense of fight or flight.

The brain is the last remaining battle ground and one, I am told, that will go on for many years. For now, I experience a loss of some memory and concentration, and cannot focus as fully and articulate as clearly and with the speed I usually do. It is hard to keep up with every day "normal" conversations. I try very hard, though. It is a battle of wills: Sue wanting to get back and her physiological responses reminding her that this is far from over. Progress yes, for sure, but the toll is deep.

Dreams are another manifestation of the battle of wills and the time it takes to grieve. They underscore how the body has to deal with the processes of acceptance. I have no control over my dreams, and they speak loudly that this is far from over. I fully realize "on paper" that I no longer have my best friend in his physical form. I can even scream that Bob is gone when a frustrating situation arises or someone upsets me. I have filled out mounds of paperwork, and I know the right boxes to check (although I still cannot utter the W word out loud). But my dreams do not let me give in. In my dreams, there is no W box to check off in the marital status category. In my dreams, I am Wonder Woman—the savior—the protector. The battles are still in motion: The blood transfusions, the car that I prevent from driving into the ditch, the power in my voice as I tell the funeral director that this is not so, therefore, please take his business elsewhere, thank you very much. All last physiological and psychological attempts to fight a battle I was unsuccessful with in real life. I carry on with tasks when the sun is up and go to my battlegrounds to seek justice at night.

I am reminded of the battles it takes to form a new mountain or a new mountain range— mountains that are awe inspiring and breathtaking and filled with the beauty of nature. Mountains form in a variety of ways, but all through battles, if you will—battles of nature and geophysics. From my visits to the Hawaiian Islands, I know that the mountains that Bob and I loved to hike there originated from volcanoes. Magma keeps piling on top of itself forming hard rocks and eventually mountains. Then there are the elements—wind, snow, and ice that create the beauty that we know as rivers and valleys, hills and mountains. Thousands and millions of years is what it takes to achieve this beauty. Another kind of construction zone.

Knowing that strong and beautiful mountains are built from geophysical battles and the elements over time, it should give me perspective of what I might be able to build as a result of my own battles. I seek the strength of a mountain, but this will take time. I don't know what to do with the concept of time, however. People tell me that grief takes time, but time is so short, isn't it? I need patience with myself, the process, and others who are anxious for me to rebuild. I also know there are peaks and valleys—you go up, you plateau, you go down. I have hiked enough to know. Now I will need to understand that to get to the other side of grief, I will have to follow suit. Go up and down and all around until somehow all of me understands, accepts, and rejoices once again. And then someone might say to me: "You look good, and your insides don't seem so bad either."

Blessings for this Week: Returning to work was hard, but it gave me practice trying to focus on my passion to enable more people to have a fair and just opportunity for health and well-being. I need to take it a bit easy, as I got overwhelmed. Wonderful colleagues welcomed me back. Some not knowing what to say and saying nothing, and some stating they didn't know what to say, but in just saying that, it was the right thing. Colleen, my assistant and protector, for her organizational and spiritual gifts—both are so deeply felt and appreciated.

Specific Prayer Requests: Kim is worn to a frazzle and needs special strength. Prayers that John Robert starts sleeping through the night—this would be among the greatest gifts our family could use at this time. Grieving and constant interrupted sleep don't make for a smooth healing process. She deserves a medal, but more than that, she deserves some sleep. In the spirit of the holiday season, I ask for prayers for peace and goodwill towards all. Isaiah 54:10 says, "Though the mountains be shaken and the hills be removed, yet my unfailing love for you will not be shaken And nor my covenant of peace be removed, says the Lord who has compassion on you." Matthew 17:20 reads, "He replied, Because you have so little faith. Truly I tell you, if you have faith as small as a mustard seed, you can say to this mountain, 'Move from here to there,' and it will move. Nothing will be impossible for you." And Psalms 121:1 says, "I lift up my eyes to the mountains—where does my help come from?"

Reflection

During an integrative healing session I learned how grief affects the body, and I am still amazed by the physiological toll of grieving. I think hearing that helped. Knowing that I would wither for a time, but there were things that I needed to do to rebuild. I am grateful that my best friend, Lori, introduced me to yoga early on in my journey. I couldn't even keep up with the seventy- and eighty-year-olds at the Senior Center at that point, but it helped to have a starting point for reconstruction. Walking became my salvation and my launch pad for other ways of staying active. Just walking was all I could manage at first. I walked anxiously in circles and later chose destinations—a neighbor's house, a store, or around the block. A beginning.

***

ENTRY   12/26/2016 at 7:31 a.m.

"TICK TICK TICK"

So, Christmas is just about over—one more hour to go. I liked keeping Christmas simple this year, with some meaningful conversations. Simple gifts. Themes of memories and conversations of Christmas' past—and what would Dad be doing. He would have been sitting in the red chair smiling and thinking how great it was to be with his family. That's what he loved most—just being with those he loved. This has been a blessing in the midst of a crisis—focusing on things that matter.

We enjoyed Matt and Kim's home cooked meal and Abby and John's warm hugs and laughter We attended two Christmas Eve services…just in case one would not do the trick. I sang for the first time. Silent Night, Holy Night seemed appropriate—once at the first service and then again at another church an hour later. It felt comforting and right to sing Silent Night, Holy Night…All is Calm and All is Bright…Sleep in Heavenly Peace. Good solid uneventful times within the confines of a tragedy.

Check the box—Christmas is over! That's the goal, they all tell me—just get these holidays behind me. Let the clock tick away: Tick, tick, tick. Anything to get time behind me. Sally said, "Settle quietly until the day passes by." No fanfare—just try to settle quietly. I liked that advice.

I pretended mightily, however, that Christmas was just like any other holiday—or tried to anyways because of everyone telling me that it would be so hard. I would show everyone that I could survive Christmas without too much backtracking. I responded that all days are hard, and Christmas would be no different! I wanted to believe it; perhaps if I said it emphatically enough, it would be so.

In the end, trying to convince myself that Christmas was just another day did not work all that well. It especially did not work when I tried to wrap a few presents; it did not work as I opened cards; and it certainly did not work when we opened the few gifts that we exchanged, waiting for Bob to open his.

One friend wished me a "Merciful Christmas." I really liked that best. And then she added "Mercy Christmas" as a sign-off to her words of care to me. I resonated with a "Mercy Christmas". I never once said Merry Christmas back to anyone this year—how could I? Try me again next year.

I watched Forrest Gump tonight and felt a kindred spirit as Forrest described his Jenny at the beginning of the movie. He said, "From the time we met, we were two peas in a pod, me and Jenny…she was my special friend. She taught me how to climb, and I taught her how to dangle." And that about sums it all up for me. We taught each other so much—I will hold onto that. And then at Jenny's gravesite, Forrest tells her, "Momma said that dying is a part of life, but I sure wish it wasn't." Indeed so, I shouted back at the TV.[10]

Someone told me a few weeks ago that it was Bob's time to go, but I don't believe that. The feather in Forrest Gump flies on, showing, I suppose, that we have no control over destiny. And then, Forrest adds: "I don't know if we each have a destiny, or if we're all just floatin' around accidental-like on a breeze. But I, I think, maybe it's both." I am still trying to figure all of this out.[10]

Tick, tick, tick: twenty minutes to go, and I can check the Christmas box off. Then my clock will reset for New Year's Eve and Day. Different stop watches for different times. I pay attention. I've read that when there is a crisis or life-threatening event, time can march very slowly in order for you to take it all in—for you to pay attention. Time would not march this slowly unless I was meant to pay attention. And I am.

Blessings for Today: I liked the simplicity of this Christmas. Even Abby said her favorite gift was construction paper that she could use to make snowflakes with her new "safety scissors". Kim received an angel statue from Matt with an inscription that reads, "stars are the openings in the sky where our loved ones shine down to let us know they are happy." And Mark is now working for Lyft. My mother, who enjoys art, is on a kick painting dogs with water colors, and is happy about that. Let me know if you want your dog painted.

We celebrated Christmas as it was supposed to happen, MIND YOU, after an accident that I DID NOT think was supposed to happen. I like the fact that it was a big box to check, and it is now behind me. My biggest box to still check is July 4—my anniversary—but that clock will be set later.

Specific Prayer Requests: For all people who are grieving and very, very sad—that they have a merciful holiday season. For everyone for whom this was their first holiday box to check. Time stands still for a while so that we might pay great attention. Sometimes we just need that. To stop and pay attention. Tick…tick …tick. Joshua 10:13 says, "So the sun stood still, and the moon stopped, till the nation avenged itself on their enemies."

Reflection

I still think that it's a good thing that grieving has the distinct ability to make time stand still. It allows you to focus every cell in your body on your loved one and what happened, and—try as you may—to rebalance. It means that nothing else matters but what you are enduring, all your thoughts, emotions, and circumstances surrounding it. Everything else that is happening is a mere illusion. You wonder how people can just simply go on living. You realize that events and holidays happen, but they, and their meaning, are distractions. You count the moments—tick, tick, tick—to get the distractor out of the way so some semblance of balance might begin again. The stop watch starts anew until the next meaningful day for you and your loved ones arrives.

***

ENTRY   12/28/2016 at 11:25 a.m.

"THE MAGIC TREE...AS TOLD TO ABBY ON DECEMBER 28, 2016 AS A BEDTIME STORY."

Once upon a time there was a little girl named Abigail Grace who had a brother named John Robert. They called each other Abby and Johnny. One day, Abby woke up and wanted to walk in the forest. She had heard about a magic tree and wanted to find it. Johnny wanted to go as well, but he was small and could not walk very well. Nevertheless, they took off walking.

They entered the woods and looked around. They played with the leaves, throwing them at each other and giggling. They walked more and jumped over logs and crossed a stream. Johnny began to complain that he could not walk any farther, but Abby encouraged him on. She made up games to try to distract him. He said that his legs were not working well and that he had to stop and rest.

Abby did not want to give up, but she did not know which way to go, as they were now deep in the woods and all the trees looked alike. She was beginning to think they should turn back, but she knew that if she was ever scared, she could call upon Pops to help her. So, she called for him. All of a sudden, she felt a gentle nudge on her right shoulder—soft yes, but strong enough to guide her to the right path. So, she turned right and told Johnny they would see the Magic Tree soon. Johnny asked her what could be so special about this tree, but Abby said he would have to wait to see.

Again, she came to a fork in the path and wondered which way to go. Johnny wanted to give up. He asked Abby to carry him, but he was too heavy. Once again, she felt a soft nudge, but this time on her left shoulder. So, they turned left. She always knew she could count on Pops for anything in her life—just because she could not see him it did not mean that he was not there. He was just there in a different way now.

When they took the path to the left, they saw a faint light shining forth. As they walked, the light became brighter. Johnny asked Abby how she would know which tree was the magic tree, and Abby said it would have a star on it. So, they kept walking, and the light got a little brighter—not so bright that it was like daylight, but brighter than the other parts of the woods, for sure.

Eventually, they began to see fewer and fewer trees, and then, all of a sudden, the magic tree appeared. It was unmistakable—the tree stood alone, and a star shone right on the top. Abby and Johnny stopped in their tracks and looked up at the magic tree. Abby told Johnny that she had goose bumps, but when Johnny asked Abby what goose bumps were, she said never mind and that they should just be happy about seeing the tree. Johnny said that the tree was really neat, but he still did not know what made it so special. Abby said they had to touch the tree to find out.

They walked slowly up to the tree, paying special attention to the light shining on it. Abby touched the tree, after feeling the nudge from behind for the last time. Once she touched it, she knew exactly why it was called a magic tree. She encouraged Johnny to join her. They felt an immediate feeling of love and hope. They felt love for each other and love for all in their world. They gained a sense of hope that they would always be cared for and things would somehow always work out for them. That's what hope is, Abby told Johnny—that things will be okay even when it seems that things are not okay. Johnny understood that.

So, with more feelings of love and hope in their hearts than they had ever felt before, they returned home, happy that they had found the magic tree. And that's the end of the story.

Addendum: The day after I told Abby this story, the picture shown here, that Jean gave me, arrived in the mail. I had no idea that she was sending this to me and that this picture would turn out to be, in essence, the front cover of this story called "The Magic Tree." How much of a coincidence could this be? It is hanging in my foyer and will now be the first picture that people will see when they come in the front door.

Blessings for Today: Hope. My friend, Vickie, sent me a small dark block of wood with the word "HOPE" etched on it a few days after Jean sent me the picture of the magic tree. Vickie said it had been given to her when she needed hope, and she was passing it on to me, with the directive to send it on to someone who might need it more when I was ready. I love this idea of passing on hope. For now, I need it very, very, very much. When the time comes, I will pass it along.

Specific Prayer Requests: Hope remains a constant theme of my grief. In the beginning, I hoped Bob would make a full recovery. Then I just hoped he would live. When I lost him, I hoped that I could live through the pain, and that somehow my world would come back into sync, whatever that might mean. I also wanted Abby to know that she could always hope and would always be loved. Johnny was too young to ever understand Bob's accident, but Abby at nearly three years old would always remember.

***

ENTRY   12/31/2016 at 4:20 p.m.

"LOOKING FOR SIGNS"

I find myself looking for signs that Bob has not left me completely and forever. For those of you who know me well, you would agree that I am a driven person who sets goals and then works to achieve those goals. This journey of losing my soul mate and trying to find acceptance has caused me to stop in my tracks and question and ponder much—if not everything—in my life. All of a sudden, I feel an intense vulnerability to the forces of nature. Everything changes, including my senses—sight, smell, hearing, and touch. I see things that I have never seen before, and I see, hear, and feel things differently.

So, what do I mean by all of this? Well, there is not a person who I have talked to who has lost someone extremely close to them who doesn't wish for a sign that their loved one is not completely gone. This is the great mystery of life—and death: What happens to us? Your belief system obviously will dictate or help guide what you think and how you process death. But even atheists, it seems, still long for the connection they once had. I have not researched this, but I know my experience, and I am surrounded by others who are living this experience as well, or who are helping others to make this journey. I am trying to make sense of grief and loss and how I proceed from here.

I believe that there is something else when a person dies. I came to this conclusion when I was a young nurse helping a patient pass one evening. It was just him and me, as his family never made it for the end. I held his hand until there was no more life. Suddenly, the drapes in his hospital room began rustling back and forth. There was no wind inside his room, nor an air conditioning malfunction. I had no preconceptions or real beliefs at that time. I just accepted it for what I thought it was—the passing of his spirit or something electromagnetic that caused the drapes to rustle. I was not freaked out (well, maybe just a little), but ultimately after that time I believed "something" happens after a person is no longer of this world. I choose to believe: Let's just say I am really hoping, betting, and praying that Bob in some way, shape, or form is still with me, and there is something when we are no longer of this world. That our spirits in some way live on. I am cognizant of life after death being conveyed in the Bible over and over. Everyone says that Bob can live in my heart, but I am hoping for a bit more.

I am fortunate that I have dreamt several times about Bob. This has helped me to somehow feel connected and to make a bit more sense of my world. Most people tell me that at the very least, they want to dream about their loved one to enable some long lost or really significant piece of information to be conveyed. Consider the dream scene in Fiddler on the Roof and the significance it played in turning around some important series of events. People of all cultures and beliefs look to dreams to help them assimilate important events or to provide signs. Everyone hopes to maintain a sense of connection to a lost loved one.

I have lost other loved ones in my life—even family members—who did not have the same attachment to my soul that Bob did. …so for me at least, my desire for signs stems from my perceived closeness and significant attachment to Bob. I have also experienced other signs that have conveyed to me Bob's continuing presence in my life. I hesitate to convey those signs in writing because I do not want anyone to negate, pick apart, or invalidate the signs I have seen, smelled, heard or experienced. In general, however, I have heard that some people believe signs can be conveyed through smell, touch, movement (like I experienced when caring for my dying patient), music, coincidences, and unexplained electrical occurrences.

I also learned that children might experience these signs more often than adults because their thinking and feelings are purer and less filtered. Abby has innocently conveyed some of her experiences to her mother and me. I am also reminded of Nurse Abby, who contacted me shortly after Bob left us for good, and her unexplained need to be in touch with me to share Bob's experience in the trauma bay when he was first admitted. Her decision to reach out to me—which completely goes against any norm that nurses maintain in their jobs— was much more than a simple coincidence.

The good news for those who believe in an afterlife is that they are less likely to experience mental health issues such as anxiety, depression, and other disorders, according to studies. Makes sense to me. Believing in some kind of afterlife offers important support and can ease grief and life in general.

I am on a quest to keep Bob alive in some way, shape, or form. I have said before that I want his legacy to live on, but this goes beyond leaving a legacy. I am searching for signs that Bob still lives on in some spiritual way to decrease the trauma of "here one moment and gone the next." It's a way to make sense of death—the promise of some kind of eternal life comforts me. Others may not be comforted, saying that life after death is nonsense, downright unscientific, and may reek of hocus pocus. But this is a personal journey. And this is my journey.

Blessings for Today: I never remember dreams, so for me to remember a few dreams here and there about Bob is something I treasure. My dreams generally still revolve around how I save Bob from falling off of his bicycle. In the most recent one, he injured his arm and leg, but we were back dancing again after months of physical therapy. We always danced, and we still do. I also treasure my openness to new experiences, including the heightened sense of seeing, hearing, feeling, and touching. All with the understanding that this comes from a new sense of vulnerability and with a new understanding for others and their own personal journeys.

Specific Prayer Requests: To help those on this journey to ponder, explore, pray, and be open to signs that their loved one is near—if that brings them comfort. Isaiah 26:19 says, "Your dead will live, Lord; Their bodies will rise—Let those who dwell in the dust wake up and shout for joy—Your dew is like the dew of the morning: the earth will give birth to her dead. Ecclesiastes 12:7 tell us, " and the dust returns to the ground it came from, and the spirit returns to God who gave it," and Job 14:14 says, "If someone dies, will they live again? All the days of my hard service I will wait for my renewal to come."

Reflection

I will always look for signs, and there continue to be many. Some may be small and trivial to you, but they are meaningful to me. Others are downright spooky and unexplained. Recently, Johnny, who is two, told Kim that Pops comes to him at night sometimes and sits in his special reading chair. Kim and I accept Johnny's words as signs. And now, as I sign onto an e-travel site as Sue Hassmiller to prepare to take a trip on August 22, Bob's birthday, his name appears under the login name. As many times as I log in and out trying to bring the site wholly back to my name, his name remains under August 22. It is a sign.

***

ENTRY   1/2/2017 at 12:50 p.m.

"DENISE AND THE NEW YEAR"

To take better care of myself, I signed up for a special massage offer that included three massages at a really good price. I arrived at my appointment, walked in the front door, and proceeded to a door with the word "office" on it, thinking that was where I was supposed to check in. When I opened the door ever so slightly I heard a scream from the next room, "What are you doing going into my office?!" I responded that I was there to check in for my appointment. The voice angrily instructed me to go to the lobby and didn't I know I was supposed to go to the lobby, and why in my right mind would I ever go in a door that said "office"? Perplexed, I went to the lobby and the voice said, "If you are in the lobby, then you must take your shoes off now!" A woman introduced herself as Denise and further "greeted" me by saying that I was early and she was still on her personal time. She would be with me when my time officially started and not before. I said fine; then could I use the restroom? She told me that I could not use the rest room until right before the massage. Whew!

It was a surreal situation. I was trying to take in the encounter with Denise while processing how I felt about it at the same time and wondering if she would be giving me a massage. Yikes! I could see intense anger in her eyes as she handed me an information sheet to describe my condition and why I was visiting her place of business. Keeping to my mantra that my husband's death would not be taken in vain, I described in great detail Bob's accident and my hope for relaxation and therapy. Denise deserved nothing less.

When she returned to read the information sheet I had filled out, she was stunned. She asked me more details, and I cried as I relayed the story to her. Part of me wanted to walk out, but I did not. I actually felt intense pity for her and felt this might be a teaching moment. Although she may not have deserved it, I said a little prayer for her and her anger issues. She muttered that she should not have yelled at me, but I should have realized that her office was not to be intruded upon. Even in her apology, she could not let it go. After the massage—yes, I let her touch me—she apologized again and gave me a card for a free massage.

The point in relaying this story is perhaps four-fold.

First, it is not my place to judge. Denise might have deserved to be judged and lashed back at, but for whatever reason, I simply was more in the mood to forgive. Even if you start out strong and confident, an unexpected trauma is soul shattering, and it makes you feel very vulnerable and fragile—and you are sensitive about judgments. You care about people judging you, and you think twice before judging others.

Second, I do NOT want to be Denise. Being that bitter and angry and lashing out is unattractive. She was a good-looking young woman, but her anger and hostility made her ugly. When you are intensely angry and bitter, people tend to run the other way—just the opposite of what you might need in desperate times. We can continue to harbor intense anger and feelings that we have been treated unfairly, or we can reconcile our feelings towards a more congenial nature.

Third, try not to take things or words personally. Know that people are angry (or assign other emotions) because generally there is an underlying insecurity and/ or deep sense of sadness or feelings that they have been unjustly wronged. You will probably never have the opportunity to fix the wrongs that people believe they have, but you just might be able to let it go. Most times the anger is not about you. I try to take this advice in general, even though it is not easy, especially if the relationship is an established one.

Fourth, surround yourself with positive people, who are trustworthy, honest, kind, uplifting and encouraging. In our very short time on this earth, most of the time we can choose our friends. Being around negative, angry and deceitful people will sap you of your energy and your soul, and like a flower without water, it will be hard to bloom. Along with guidance from my Bob/God duo, I have carefully chosen these past few months the people with whom I speak, take advice, and spend time. These special people are helping me to unfold new possibilities.

Blessings for Today: Although I live with challenges, including my loss, juggling and coordinating care needs for my mother, and other difficult family issues and decisions, I have most assuredly witnessed the very best that humanity has to offer—hands down! It is helping me choose to not be bitter. Many have also reached out to me to specifically tell me how something I wrote in a blog has helped them or a friend. This means a great deal.

Specific Prayer Requests: That the love, support, and prayers heal my body and soul and create a human being who will be vigilant about paying it forward. Now that I understand the needs of people who grieve, I want to help them. I did not know before—I simply did not know. I want to ensure that Bob's wishes and example are always carried out, and that he and God look down upon me and say that they knew that I could make it. It may have taken me awhile, but they were rooting for me. Prayers for the world, as tonight I watched CNN, and while you are at it, you might as well pray for Denise. James 1:5 says, "If any of you lacks wisdom, you should ask God, who gives generously to all without finding fault, and it will be given to you." John 14:27 promises, "Peace I leave with you; my peace I give you. I do not give to you as the world gives. Do not let your hearts be troubled, and do not be afraid."

Reflection

The lesson of not judging has helped to carry me forward. A number of times people have said things that I find insensitive, but I remember that I too have probably said some insensitive things to people who are grieving. I can take stock of the insensitivity, identify why and how it made me feel;, and then, for the most part, move on. Discussing it with likeminded grievers helps to both affirm my hurt and to move on. On a few occasions, I have politely confronted people who said particularly hurtful things. For the most part, we took it as an important lesson learned followed by a hug. As for Denise, she still gives me massages—all lessons learned on that front.

***

ENTRY   1/7/2017 at 4:30 p.m.

"BIG SHOES"

Bob wore a size thirteen shoe, but that's not what I mean by big shoes. What I mean is that he left behind positive examples for all of us to ponder and perhaps follow. He was not perfect, mind you. He was the greatest procrastinator I ever met—if the absolute deadline was 2:00 p.m., he would turn in his project at 2:00 p.m. and not a minute before. People who worked with him will be nodding their heads right now. The April 15th tax deadline was a mere suggestion to him. He sought extensions regularly. I never understood it.

I always wondered why people spend so much time worrying about getting something in on time when you could do it early, get it behind you, and go on living. But what I learned about Bob was that he never worried about getting something done like I would have. He simply tucked away the deadline, and when it approached, he kicked it in. Things that had no real deadline like hanging pictures, fixing lawn furniture, or fertilizing trees would sometimes never get done, even when I gave Bob a deadline. Made me CRAZY!

Food was another issue. My Robert Boy could eat nearly an entire bag of Doritos or peanut butter combos instead of what one might consider a normal meal. Sometimes he got into a health kick and tried some kind of low-fat chip. But the idea was that it had to crunch when you ate it, but not like the way an apple crunches. Neither one of us really cooked, so our options were more limited, but I always thought eating an entire bag of anything could not be good. Many times I would ask him, "What goes through your head when you eat something that bad for you?" He always responded that he simply thought it tasted really good. No other thoughts—it just tasted good.

So, the idea here is that no one is perfect, and marriage is a series of negotiations. If you choose to get married and stay married, then you know it is hard work. What I could take away from Bob's life—and I really knew it before the accident—was that Bob did not care about the small stuff. Lots of times I wanted him to care about the small stuff, but he just didn't. He truly rose above it all and grabbed me and danced at any given moment on any street corner as if no one was watching, just to prove it. As previously stated, he survived a number of tragedies including being shot in Vietnam, a "too young" marriage that did not work out, a mother who drank too much, and a beloved father lost early from a medical error, so he had become quite adept at rising above trivial things. Within thirty seconds of my complaining to him about something or someone, he made me laugh about it and convinced me that it wasn't worth the effort. Sometimes if I thought it was REALLY WORTH THE EFFORT, I had to make him help me or deal with it.

I wish he were here to help me with my grief. He would have words of wisdom, either taken from his own life or lines from a favorite movie, such as *The Princess Bride*.

Buttercup: "You can't hurt me. Westley and I are joined by the bonds of love. And you cannot track that, not with a thousand bloodhounds, and you cannot break it, not with a thousand swords. And when I say you are a coward, it is only because you are one of the slimiest weaklings ever to walk the Earth!"[11]

He might also share scripture, but in the end, he would always find the humor in it. He always made me laugh.

When we were in the ICU, there were so many things happening quickly and decisions to be made, and all I wanted to do was to discuss the situation with him. I did not have my go-to person to discuss all the options. I did not have my humorist to make light of the situation. Somehow, he would have been philosophical and then funny, and we would say one more time that we had made it through yet one more hurdle in our marriage. Strangely, I did try to channel him—it was all I could do to help me understand what he wanted, but I acutely missed the real conversation of, "What in the heck is going on here? Let's see what our options are."

I dreamed last night that I was sitting on the bench inside my front door. I sat with my head down and my shoulders slumped, thinking that I could not possibly be in charge of such a massive undertaking. Bob and I divided our duties, but he had all the hard stuff—bills, finances, mortgages, cars, and investments, though he would say that he had all the stuff he loved. I would also say that I had all the stuff that I loved—a good negotiated arrangement of thirty-seven years. Since retirement, he took on other things, including my mother's care, baby-sitting the grandkids, grocery shopping, and the condo's rental and management. In other words, I was a kept woman. But I knew this—I really did not need to learn this lesson. Now I have jobs that I love and jobs that I hate and jobs for which I have zero capacity.

In my dream, I tried to be convincing that I could not possibly be in charge. But a male voice told me that I was in charge and capable of being in charge. I told him I wasn't, and he responded that because my name was on the list, I was in charge and capable. I could not deny that I saw my name, so I felt like this was it: I had to be in charge. I woke up feeling that since I am in charge now, I will at some point (if not now) be capable.

Blessings for Today: William Barclay—a noted author, minister, and divinity professor—said, "There are two great days in a person's life—the day we are born, and the day we discover why." I thought I had an inkling of why I might have been put on this earth. A nurse, a wife, a mother. Now, with this new found situation, I am expanding my notion of what more I might be and do. I don't think I will be able to tell you fully for a long time.

I can tell you more about why I think Bob was put on this earth. He taught me about generosity, love, humor, and giving back. Sometimes I feel he taught me more after the accident than when he was with me in person. I also hear from others how he affected their lives. People are still making decisions based on what they believe they learned from Bob.

Specific Prayer Requests: That my family and I—and others—not only come to understand why we're put on this earth, but act on it in a positive way. That I can continue to reflect and understand how I might give back, which will be a good part of the "why" of my journey. I need some humor in my life! Isaiah 14:24 says, "The Lord Almighty has sworn saying, 'Surely, as I have planned, so it will be, and as I have purposed, so it will happen." Proverbs 16:9 says, "In their hearts humans plan their course, but the Lord establishes their steps."

Reflection

The lessons—ah, all the lessons. What else can you take away from Bob's accident if not the lessons? I feel a huge hole, and to be honest, the largest void remains the lack of humor in my life. I always felt like we could get through anything with humor, and I am uncertain how to regain that. I wonder all the time, still, whether I will ever laugh the way I did. I still do not feel totally capable. I am functioning, and all the bills are getting paid, but I am still doing some jobs that I love and others that I hate. For the most part, they are all getting done—an accomplishment in and of itself. I try to rise above the small stuff like Bob did, and since I have much more to do now, I bypass some of the small stuff by necessity. I certainly believe I will make it—I have made it. I now need to make it with joy. Joy is a big goal.

***

ENTRY   1/14/2017 at 3:59 p.m.

"SPEAKING UP WHEN SPEAKING UP MATTERS"

Bob and I made the pact that if either one of us ended up in the hospital that we would be strong advocates for each other. We never talked about how

that would play out, but being a nurse, I knew more than he about what being an advocate entailed. We openly discussed and filled out paperwork regarding our wishes for end-of-life care in the context of what we thought would be my mother's more imminent passing, and we knew what we wanted. This was really important.

As time passes, I often reflect on Bob's hospital stay. I am starting to feel a call to improve the care experience for patients and their families. The ten days we spent in the ICU were very isolating. Although Kristen, Karen, and Beth Ann never left me, it was still Bob and me in our cocoon. The singular goal was survival for ten days (no matter what survival meant), and then the goal changed to a peaceful and dignified letting go (some words I just cannot say). My job—to be my Robert Boy's wife, best friend, and advocate—was focused; black and white, without a speck of gray. I told him constantly I would take care of him and never leave him, and that was a promise I would never break. We took the utmost loving care of each other for thirty-seven years, and it would not stop at the door of the ICU.

I was not a visitor, nor did I think of myself as one. I was Bob's right hand, his heart, and his voice. The clinicians knew their job well—their tasks, their signs and symptoms, their bar graphs and pie charts, their medication proto-cols, their computerized decision-making tools—but they did not know my husband. That was my job. Somehow our system and some clinicians forget to include family members when caring for their patients. Not all, but many. It is the system's fault—not theirs. Paying attention to "visitors" is not always efficient or considered necessary.

I realize that we have come a very long way in our country since I was a practicing floor nurse in how we hear the voice of the patient and family mem-bers. Other countries know how to listen to families more intently, sometimes out of necessity, as there are just not enough nurses or doctors to go around. I dis-tinctly remember when my father had open heart surgery, and visitors were only allowed in the room for ten minutes of every hour or something like that. It was hogwash then, and it is hogwash now. I traveled all the way from New Jersey to Florida to see my father. When I showed up at the ICU door, I was told to come back the next day. Really? I don't think so. I knew enough to call in the supervisor and chief nurse, but how many people would complain?

As a young nurse, I especially appreciated looking at pictures that my elderly patients shared with me. They served as a reminder of who they were and perhaps who they still wished they could be. The pictures left an impression on me. I saw the patient in a different light—a famous lawyer, teacher, grandfather, war veteran, or dancer. So, on the first day that my husband was in the ICU, I asked Kim to bring framed pictures of Bob and me, his children and grandchildren, and a few photo books of our travels. This is who my husband is: When you look at him, you should see him within the context of an extraordinary life, among people who love him dearly.

I carried my picture shrine to the next level and to the next level after that. No one could speak to me without speaking to both of us: I always held a picture of us together, smiling and revealing a privileged and happy life. If someone walked into the room to abruptly infringe a task onto a failing human body, I caught their attention and introduced us. This is who we are: Please see us and hear our voices. Know us for just a moment. This is my best friend you are sticking or suctioning or whose bar graphs you are studying. I am pleased to meet you.

The nurses took more interest in us, but they worked twelve-hour shifts, so I expected them to get to know us more as people. Kathy, the nurse who stayed with me when the time came to turn off Bob's machines, stole my heart when she told me she had looked through all of the travel pictures and was envious of such happy times. She showed me her favorite pictures and asked about them. She said that she told her husband about us, adding that she was learning to take more care in her own marriage because of her observations of Bob and me. The hospital pastor also could not ever get enough of our stories and times past.

The most striking observation to me, however, was during rounds that included white coat and stethoscope clad "intimidators." Noticing that no family members were ever present at these rounds, I simply invited myself . There they stood, outside the room of each ICU patient, viewing computers and grilling med students, talking about bodily organs and how to treat them—one organ at a time, shouting out lab values that only they understood. Individually, they were all very nice people, just like you and me. Some had kids I imagined, and others were just kids themselves. They went to church, ate meals and junk food, and drove cars. But when they stood together, shoulder to shoulder, with their white coats and strange language, they were a group of intimidators. Every morning and afternoon, I joined them. I did not have a white coat or stethoscope, but at least I knew I belonged. All family members (or at least one designee) should belong—and they should know they belong. Clinicians should personally invite family members to join in rounds, and signs should be posted telling family members that their voice matters. There should have been a crash course in "how to belong." There is such a thing as the Patient's Bill of Rights, but it is a fairly meaningless piece of paper.

I vividly remember sitting among the intimidators—as I was too weak to stand—and holding a picture of Bob. They could not possibly talk about their protocols without also looking at me and Bob. I made sure of it. I was polite and unobtrusive, but I asked questions and told them things that perhaps they should know about the man behind their charts and graphs. At the end, I initiated the discussion about palliative care, and I still wonder how long the expert care would have continued had I not spoken up.

I noticed every day that I was the only family member participating in rounds in what was a very large ICU wing. Family members cowered in the ICU waiting room, waiting for their turn to be with their loved one. Some camped out or slept in chairs or sleeping bags. The television blared in the background. Family members cried and discussed among themselves plans of action and they ate junk food to sustain themselves. I wondered if they shared their hopes and fears with any of the providers, perhaps individually with a doctor or nurse. I wondered if they wanted to be removed from the providers, who had all rights to their loved ones' bodies.

One day while I attended rounds, the physician in charge stopped his show and asked me to tell the group some things about Bob. After I described our love for each other, Bob's volunteer service, his Purple Heart, and how he lived for his grandchildren, I saw a few tears in this doctor's eyes, and then he thanked me and continued discussing Bob's care. I thanked him on the spot and afterwards. I suspect that he used me as a teaching moment to show the medical students how to connect with a patient's family member, and frankly, I was happy to be used in that way. It was a glimmer of humanity that I treasured.

Hospital Safety and Quality. As important as it is to connect with patients and their families, the bigger issue revolves around hospital errors and unintended consequences—even death. Hospitals now receive financial penalties for making medical errors, so it would make sense for hospitals to better incorporate patients and family members into the care plan. I see hospital administrators run ragged to improve their scores for a host of safety and quality measures. Hospitals spend so much money on provider training and behavioral techniques to make their providers adhere to proven protocols to improve safety and quality. While these initiatives are necessary, health systems will never ever achieve their targets unless they incorporate real ways to hear the voice of the patient and family and get them involved. Period.

Almost all health care institutions have "patient- and family-centered care" in their mission statements, and many tout their patient- and family-centered care goals. People in my industry "talk" about patient- and family-centered care all of the time. We give enormous lip service to patients and their families, but we need to do better.

Blessings for Today: I am glad that I got to be Bob's advocate and that we had discussed this kind of situation ahead of time. I am thankful that my family could help me to discuss Bob's wishes. I was blessed to have people at my side to support me in my role with the intimidators. One family member or Beth Ann took notes at each round.

Special Prayer Requests: For any provider reading this to invite family members to be that very important voice for their loved one—and to welcome family members with open arms. You are NOT the most important person in these scenarios…the patient is! Proverbs 31:8 says, "Speak up for those who cannot speak for themselves, for the rights of all who are destitute."

Reflection

Spending time in the ICU unit with Bob was the hardest thing I ever did. As a nurse, I never wanted to work in the ICU—too many procedures, emergencies, and people barking orders in life and death situations. I gravitated more towards geriatrics and public health, where I could build relationships and focus on prevention. I still cannot get over that most of the care provided came solely from computerized test results and subsequent discussion between the providers. As a nurse, I understand that this is called "precision medicine," and it saves lives.

Intellectually, I was grateful for the precise clinical care that Bob received, but I wish more providers had shown more compassion. I wanted the providers to understand who we were before the accident, and I wanted them to know our preferences and feelings. I longed to be touched, cared for, and acknowledged especially in the face of death. Clinicians need to be both proficient and compassionate. Is that too much to ask?

***

ENTRY   1/19/2017 at 9:38 a.m.

"POPS MEMORY BOOK FOR JOHN AND ABIGAIL"

Request to friends, colleagues, and family members: My birthday is coming up on January 30, and I have decided what I would like more than anything in the world—but I need your help. I want to put together a Pops Memory Book filled with stories from all of you, so that my grandchildren will know and remember their Pops. No matter who you are, and even if you did not know Bob but wish you did, please respond to this request. Please send a letter addressed to "Dear John and Abby" with one of the following:

1. Your best Bob Hassmiller story
2. What you admired most about Bob Hassmiller
3. What you would tell John and Abby about anything (life, relationships, good people).

***

ENTRY   1/23/2017 at 7:38 a.m.

"THE WIZARD OF OZ AND HIS LIMITED GIFTS"

I realized fairly early on after the accident that life would not continue as it was. I was open to this new and different possibility—we all were. My mind flashed frequently to the actor Christopher Reeves in his wheelchair describing how his life changed after his horseback riding accident. Kim believed that any part of her Daddy would be better than no part of her Daddy. Mark began to plan to be Bob's caregiver. "I can help," Mark said. "I can do this." I tried to be open and prepared as best as one could be. I thought I would get my sixty years with Bob, but just in a different way. I pictured wheelchairs, home care providers, specially equipped vans, selling the condo with stairs—everything to prepare myself for what lay ahead, but none of it was to be. What transpired was not within our realm of possibility at all. Out of my control.

So, to handle my new life, someone or something else decided for me that I was to be given this new life with new eyes and ears. The old ones would not do. Like in "The Wizard of Oz," I have been granted new body parts. Unfortunately, Oz was completely out of hearts, so I needed to keep my broken one. No amount of begging worked with the Wizard, even if I promised to kill a witch. He said there was a very long back order for new hearts, since there were too many broken hearts out there. In his time doing this Oz gig, he said he had never seen so many broken hearts, and wasn't it a pity that he could not be more helpful? He said he actually stopped giving warranties for his hearts, since they break so easily.

He told me he did not have any brains available, but the wait list was shorter. I was about to tell him to go back to Kansas where he belonged, but then he said something that made sense, so I decided to give him another chance. He said that it's sad that the people who need the brains the most don't think they need them.

The Wizard had eyes and ears available, however. I wondered why he had an ample supply, and he said it was because the directions to use eyes and ears were a bit complicated. I asked if there was a YouTube video that could help me to figure it out, but he said there is no short cut to using new eyes and ears. He would give them to me, but I had to figure out how to use them, and it would take time.

In that case, I told him that I needed a new brain. I thought that I could somehow talk him into a package deal. After all, my brain is not working very well. It forgets things all the time; it gets tired easily; and its ability to focus is hampered. He reminded me again that there were no brains, and besides, he said he knew me pretty well. He felt that with new eyes and ears I could coax my brain along. No easy fixes or shortcuts, but he had faith that I could do this. What good would just eyes and ears do? He said he had seen others do this when there were no brains available, and he felt I had enough of a brain left over to manage.

And then, you guessed it, I decided to ask for courage. I needed courage badly (not as badly as a new heart, but really, everything feels worn out and damaged).

He said he knew by the confident way that I asked for courage that I did not need any. What? Is this some kind of perverted trick? If I came to him feeble and despondent, would he give me a thimble full of courage? He told me that he only gave courage to those who really needed it, and there were people who needed it a lot more than me. He said to look around with my new eyes and to listen with my new ears to the people in our country and world to see that others needed courage more than me. A little bit of courage goes a long way these days, and I should use what I had. I was aghast at his judgment, but I realized that if I argued with him with conviction and confidence, he would never give me courage in the future. I decided to let it go.

So, I left the Wizard with a new pair of eyes and ears, half a brain, some "presumed" courage, and a very broken heart.

I am trying out my new eyes and ears. You would never be able to tell, to look at me, that my eyes and ears were any different. You think I look the same, and therefore, you presume I am the same person I used to be. You are wrong. You would probably be able to tell that I am different if you spoke to me about certain things or read my blogs.

My eyes let me take in more sunrises and sunsets, and my half brain tells me that I will view a limited number of them, so I am to make the most of my days. I see a calendar and know that my days are numbered, but don't know what that number is, so I need to use my half brain and ounce of courage to prioritize what is most important and to spend time with people I care about and who care about me.

Speaking of people, I hear when people say they love me or care for me, or that they are praying for me. I REALLY HEAR THAT and IT MEANS A LOT TO ME. I see and hear laughter, but only as an observation (like a science experiment). I can describe the laughter, but I have no feelings or inclination towards it. I am able to smile now, but not very often and only with people who I believe care about me.

I hear words that seem particularly meant for me, like verses in a song, a paragraph in a book, or some part of a sermon. I see and hear the voices and instruments of wise people—poets, philosophers, musicians, song writers, authors, and good friends. With my half brain and an ounce of courage, these words and sounds help to guide my day. With my new eyes and ears, I look for anything that might help me and avoid words that may hurt.

I hear the noise of what is going on in this country, and my half brain tells me I cannot handle so much noise right now, so I use my new ears and eyes to shut it all out—for a season. I try to hear my innermost voice and remember my dreams. I dreamt last night that I was on a plane that was flying into a massive cloud of volcano ash, and the pilot and I could not see. Is it any wonder I asked the Wizard for new eyes?

I see people who are making a difference, and I am hungry to join them. I wonder what my purpose and journey will be, and I use my new eyes and ears to listen and see signs to determine my path.

I also see things I don't want to see like bills, household and car maintenance, mice in my bathroom, and caregiving responsibilities. I cannot tune these things out or turn a blind eye. With my half brain and an ounce of courage, I will face these things. I am already doing it. I do not have a choice.

I see and hear things surrounding the brutality of the accident and the ICU that I still cannot drown out, but with pictures, cards, notes, and poetry and love from my husband in my head and heart, I can remember the beauty of my marriage. I hear and sometimes see my Robert Boy, who tells me that he does not want me to suffer and that I should never doubt that he will ever stop loving me.

Blessings for Today: That I know I am loved and cared for on this journey. That I have people who know just when to reach out to me with just the right words to say. For Toni, for bringing a special keynote presenter, Vic Strecher, a professor at the University of Michigan's School of Public Health and Director for Innovation and Social Entrepreneurship, to the conference I am attending and telling me his presentation, "A Life of Purpose" was meant just for me. Toni held my hand to lead me to the front row, so I would not miss a single word. For my best friend Lori for always believing in me and calling me every few days to listen at length and affirm what I am seeing, hearing and feeling. To know that I have to be open in order to hear and see new things.

Specific Prayer Requests: That I am not hardened by grief. It would be much easier to sit in a corner and be bitter forever. That I choose the path of openness, love, and light, and that I will reach out to others who grieve. That those who need a new brain and heart more than me are comforted. That would help all the rest of us out quite a bit!

In *The Wizard of Oz,* L. Frank Baum wrote "It was a terrible thing to undergo, but during the year I stood there, I had time to think that the greatest loss I had known was the loss of my heart." And "If we walk far enough," says Dorothy, "we shall sometime come to someplace."[12]

Reflection

I have heard of a great many stories of people who felt that they could no longer go on. The pain was just too great. I truly understand that. The pain is unbearable. However, if you believe that we are all on this earth for a purpose, then it is our responsibility to try to determine what our purpose is. We have such a short time, really. There will always be great pain and suffering, and there will always be people who need help with this treacherous journey. Who better to help than those of us who have walked the path of grief? Who better to share lessons about grief and compassion and the great attempts to walk towards light than those who have been there? My purpose is apparent.

***

ENTRY   1/30/2017 at 7:36 a.m.

"LEGACY OF LOVE, FAMILY AND FAITH"

Thank you to all of you who have sent in letters to John and Abby. I am sharing just a few of them with you:

Dear John and Abby,

My name is Cynthia, and I have had the pleasure of knowing Nana for six wonderful years and coming to know Pops through the love of your Nana. I hope that one day you will truly know and understand how much you have been blessed to have such a wonderful Nana and Pops that love you eternally – NEVER ENDING! I never had the opportunity to meet Pops in person, but I feel like I know him through all of the wonderful things that I have heard about him from people all over the WORLD. One thing for sure is that Nana and Pops love you very, very, very, very much and they will always be with you. All you have to do is close your eyes, put your hand over your heart, and whisper their names and you will feel their love for you. Because there are so many people around the WORLD that love Nana and Pops, the love for them overflows to both of you. Always remember that there are people all over the WORLD that LOVE YOU because of Nana and Pops.

With Love, Cynthia Bienemy

Dear John and Abby,

I am writing to tell you a little bit about what a terrific guy your Pops was.

Pops was my friend. He and I first met through our jobs, which were similar kinds of jobs in two different places. We were in meetings together, we led some meetings together, and we had some meals together. That was all in Virginia, near Washington, DC. Years later, my family and I moved to Minnesota, and Pops and Nana moved to New Jersey.

In 2009, the company I worked for didn't need me anymore, and I didn't have a job for about six months. I used to call Pops on his cell phone, and he would talk with me while he drove to and from Charlottesville, Virginia, from New Jersey. He helped me figure out what to do next. He really helped me a lot during those calls, and it was great to talk with him.

I got my next job with a school called Capella University, creating courses that adults could take on their computers, from anywhere in the world. One time, when I was working on a course about how people grow up, and how they figure out what to do with their lives, I thought of Pops. We decided to interview him to ask about his life—what he did, what was hard, how he got through it, and how he became the person that he was.

Pops was great. He told about some of the toughest things in his life. He told about the best things in his life. And he explained how he made it through the tough stuff, what he learned, and how he found his way to the best stuff. For several years now, several hundred people that Pops never met have taken this course and been inspired by his story. Nana has a copy of the recording.

I didn't spend that much time together with Pops, but the times we did have together were great. I miss talking with him. I'll bet there are plenty of times when you guys feel that he is still there for you.

Wishing the best for both of you, Joe Lane

Dear John and Abby,

Your Pops was a great man. You may hear people say that often, and some-times people say things just to be nice. But when they're talking about your Pops, they'll say it because it's true.

Now and all through your lives, you will find that when you're with some people you feel happy or excited or content, and when you're with other people, you may feel sad or frustrated or angry. Some people just naturally make you feel good. That's the way they are. You feel good when you're with them because you can tell that they really care about you, about what you're doing, and about how you feel.

Your Pops was just like that. When he would be around people, they felt good because they could tell that he really cared about who they were, what they thought, what they were doing, and what goals they had in life.

I met your Pops when I was working with your Nana, and even though I didn't really get to know him for a long time, he was always nice whenever we said hello. Then came a time when I was worried about applying for a new job, and he volunteered to help me. He gave me great advice, laughed with me over some of the problems, and encouraged me through the whole process.

Your Pops would make people feel good just by listening to them. He would help them to be the best person they could be, and he would be happy for them since he knew they would succeed. He also let people know that he was there to help however he could.

One of the best things you can do when you're feeling down or lonely or sad is to think about your Pops, about how he was such a great man, and that he loved you and his family, most of all.

Cynthia Vlasich

Dear John and Abby:

I am honored and so blessed to have known your Pops since he was a young man in his early 20s. He had the most wonderful smile (as if he had a special, happy secret); and always, always a sparkle in those dynamic blue eyes. Those eyes would connect and see the very best a person could ever be. He always wanted people to reach out and connect on some level. Pops told me he went sledding and was a good friend to my neighbors, the Lammlein boys, in grade school years. Their sister was (still is) my best friend. He would have been about eight or nine years old, a tall lanky boy. I'm sure we crossed paths then as well. But it wasn't until later that we truly became a sister and brother.

Pops was so very brave and fought for our country in Vietnam. He was not there long, however, as he was injured in his arm and returned to the states for rehab. He was so committed in his beliefs for freedom and equality. Pops fell madly in love with Nana some years after. He told me that he had found this amazing, special lady in Florida and was trying to make her his forever love... which he did! Your Aunt Kristen and Uncle Bob were flower girl and ring bearer. Aunt Kristen was then your age when she proudly participated in your Nana and Pop's wedding in Nebraska! Again, a most significant fact to reflect.....they were married July 4th....our most patriotic celebration! (See the theme here guys?).

Pops and Nana lived in Nebraska some time. Three significant events happened here: They found their loves ...your Mom and your Uncle Mark, and they really were involved with the Red Cross (because you see, Nana and Pops always connected and always selflessly gave). Eventually, Nana and Pops moved to Virginia. Our families shared vacations and trips—we went to Williamsburg, Six Flags, and the ocean, just to name a few. So many happy memories.

When we lost your Pops, Aunt Kristen said, "I feel I am living in two parallel universes. One being sad to leave Uncle Bob; the second universe of being surrounded by love and the best that people had to give one another." Yet I talk to your Pops, the brother I so love, and I see those thoughtful blue eyes and I still hear, "Love you, Sis!" Yes, we are all so blessed to have been touched by Pops.

So I do know this—your Pops will love you forever. When you want to talk with him, he will be with you. Often when I talk with Pops, an old hymn blasts in my ears: "All is well, with my soul." I think that is his message.

I love you all so much. Aunt KK

Dear Abby and John:

It's very hard when someone you love is no longer nearby, especially if you were very, very close to them. But I have found that if you were very, very close, they can still be nearby—but just not in the usual way.

My mom died many years ago, and I missed her terribly, and still do. But I have found over the years that she is nearby almost all of the time. I don't see her, but I feel her near me.

And she has stepped in to help me in so many ways. Once I stepped off a curb without looking and a car whizzed by right in front of me but didn't hit me. Another time, I fell off a high stool and could have badly hit my head, but I just missed the counters, which were very close together. Just this week, a truck backed out quickly from a driveway and absolutely should have hit me, but didn't.

In these kinds of times, and when especially good things happen to me, too, I just say, "Thanks, Mom" because I know she's watching out for me. So I'm not saying that I shouldn't be careful and do what I can to help myself, but it's good to have someone who cares very, very much for me to help, too. I didn't know your Pops, but I know that he is doing the same for you.

Sincerely, Joanne Disch

Dear John and Abby,

I think everyone will tell you how much joy your Pops got from helping people. The Red Cross was among his favorite organizations, he was so involved with them. In fact, not long after I met your Pops, we delivered Christmas presents, through the Red Cross, to families whose houses had been destroyed by fire. I remember him with his Santa hat; I think he may have been jollier than the real Santa himself, delivering presents, good wishes and smiles. It was such an amazing and heartwarming day; his enthusiasm and spirit were contagious. Your Pops took a genuine interest in people and was always ready to lend a hand and help out, especially to those less fortunate.

Your Pops was always so cheerful and happy. He had one of the biggest smiles I have ever seen; it almost went from ear to ear and lit up his entire face. What I remember most, though, was how much he loved his family, especially the two of you—you meant the world to him.

I spent several holidays with your Nana and Pops. On Thanksgiving, it was his tradition to lead us in Grace and then go around the table and have everyone say what they were thankful for. When it was his turn, among other things, he would always say how thankful he was for having such a wonderful and loving family and the two most amazing grandchildren in the world. He was so proud to be your Pops, and he wore his Number 1 Pops hat with so much pride. He was a kind, caring and loving human being.

Love Always, Grandma

Dear Abby and John:

Hello. I'd like to tell you a story today. Most girls and boys are lucky enough to have and know their grandparents and some of us, like me and you, are lucky enough to have super special grandparents. I met your Pops and Nana when they moved into the neighborhood, and I was happy to know them and call them friends. When I first met them, you guys weren't born yet, and all they talked about was how extra super happy they would be when you came and they would have grandchildren. When you arrived, they were so happy—over the moon happy. Happier than happiness is what you made them.

Your Pops was one of the nicest people I have ever met. If I could tell you one thing about him that I thought was super special, it would be that he always had something nice to say to each person he met (even when they weren't as nice as they could be). By always saying something nice to them, he always made that person feel good. That is a very special gift and one that I know you will have, too. I was his friend on Facebook, and he would always share some story of the good work he would do for the Red Cross, not because he was bragging about himself but because he recognized that some people were hurting and that there were good people out there to help them, and Pops always wanted to share the good in people.

However, his favorite pictures and stories to share on Facebook were about his Abby and John, and those pictures and stories always made his Facebook friends smile. He loves you guys so much. He was so over the moon when he spoke of his Abby and John. He would light up with joy because he loves you so much. If a person ever wanted to see Pops the happiest, all they had to do was ask him about Abby and John. We are happy that Nana still shares pictures of your adventures together.

It's hard for his friends to believe that your Pops went to heaven so early. He is missed by many, many people. I know it's hard for you that he is now in heaven, but you must know that he is always with you and looking out for you. Can you even imagine how big his angel wings must be? Wow, they have to be huge.

He will be there always to look out for you. Of course, he is busy in heaven, too, but if you pay attention, you will get messages from him that will let you know he's around. Abby, I know you will always have the memories of him. John, you may have been too little to remember, but thank goodness for technology. You will have pictures and writings, too, so you will know and remember Pops and what a cool guy he was. Remember all the cool things and aspire always to be like the wonderful person that Pops was and continues to be in heaven.

Kathleen Keleher

Dear Abby and John:

Hello! My name is Sallie. I am so glad that your Nana asked us to share how we knew your Pops. I've known him for a long time, more than twelve years!

Your Pops and I, and about thirty-two of our friends and colleagues belonged to a special group called the Council of Higher Education Management Associations (CHEMA). We all got to see each other at meetings two times a year. I always looked forward to and could count on seeing your Pop's smile welcoming me to those meetings. His smile took up his whole face! He was a smart man and a dedicated leader. I could not wait to catch up with him to find out what he was doing and what he was thinking about. I think we had a mutual admiration society because as soon as we would see each other, we would start talking and many times we kept right on talking through dinner!

Your Pop's was not only a leader in higher education, he was also a leader in association management. He had a long and successful career, and the organizations that he led and worked for were better because of his good works.

I am fortunate to have had your Pop's as a trusted and respected colleague, who became a dear friend. I miss him and especially miss our conversations on Facebook about how much we loved spending time with our grandchildren, trading pictures, and liking each other's posts! Oh, how he loved you so.

Sincerely, Sallie Traxler

Dear John and Abby:

I have known and worked with your Nana for many years. I hold her in very high regard and always looked forward to being with her, so that I could get a booster shot of her energy, positivity and commitment to the higher purpose of better health and health care for all humans. While I never got to meet your Pops, I recall a few conversations with your Nana in which she mentioned her amazing husband. After reading her stories about Pops, I now realize that he was a truly AMAZING human being who touched so many lives. I know you and your Nana loved him with every fiber in your bodies. In my religion, we learn about how humans constantly face a battle between their inclination to do good and their inclination to not do good (like saying bad things about other people, treating people unfairly, not being kind, etc.). For so many people, your Pops was a role model for how to live a life that is filled with the inclination to do good. He was a good man; a human among humans; a man with a huge heart and an ability to give to others all that he had without any expectation that he would get something in return. We don't have enough people like Pops in our world. You are fortunate to have had time with him, to have learned from him, and to have memories of him that will help you navigate the challenges of life. Draw on his memory as a source of inspiration. Don't ever doubt that he is in your heart, mind and soul. He is your secret source of strength. Use this strength from him to help others in need, just like he did day-in and day-out through his entire life.

David Altman

Dear John and Abby:

Your Pops is my superhero, even though I never met him. I know that his love for you goes on forever and ever. Sometimes, things happen that are very hard to understand, like losing your Pops. But I do know one thing: when we remember your Pops, talk about him, and celebrate his birthday, it feels good.

So, even though I never met your Pops, the story of his life makes me want to be the best person I can be. He lived his life for his family, and his greatest joy in life was taking care of you and watching you grow. He also lived his life for people who had emergencies and needed help. This makes him extra special, and I know that you both will grow up knowing how important it is to help others.

My hope for you is that you always remember how very important and special you are to your Pops. We can feel close to people we love by thinking of them often and talking about how important they are to us. Your Pops left you too soon, and that is sad, but remembering him and talking about how much you love him helps a lot.

Looking at pictures of Pops is also a way to remember him, always. I know you have lots of great pictures. Sharing stories and wondering what Pops would think of things happening in your life is another way to feel close to him.

This is my favorite quote from Winnie the Pooh:

"If ever there is tomorrow when we're not together... there is something you must always remember: You are braver than you believe, stronger than you seem, and smarter than you think. But the most important thing is, even if we're apart... I'll always be with you."

Loving your Pops means living a life with meaning and purpose. That is a big idea—your Pops was full of them. Mr. Rogers once said that when things are scary, look for the helpers, there are always helpers. Pops was one of the world's biggest helpers! You come from a family of big helpers! So knowing that can always guide you in life.

Many blessings to both of you, now and forever! Sending thoughts of love, happiness, and beautiful stories about your Pops.

In friendship, Robin Cogan

Reflection

These letters are just a few of my birthday presents today, and I cherish them mightily, as will my grandchildren in years to come. It will be so very important for them to know who their Pops was, what made him tick, and the legacy he left behind. Bob was not famous in the way that we in America might define fame, and he never went after the big bucks, as we in America think of as striking it rich, but he had family, love, faith, and enduring respect—the very things that almost all of us say we want and hope to leave behind.

As I read your letters, a clear theme was how Bob made you feel. I am reminded of Maya Angelou's words: "I've learned that people will forget what you said, people will forget what you did, but people will never forget how you made them feel."

***

ENTRY   2/05/17 7:32 p.m.

"MAN OF CHARACTER"

Bob had his favorite historical role models. One was Abraham Lincoln, who aptly noted: "Character is like a tree, and reputation like a shadow. The shadow is what we think of it; the tree is the real thing." Many of you who knew Bob knew the tree to be strong, steady, and unwavering. I—and many of you— are benefiting from his beautiful shadow and his legacy of integrity, truth, justice, humility, forgiveness, and humor.

You tell me Bob listened to YOU. He made YOU feel secure. He made YOU feel supported and loved, and he made YOU feel funny because he laughed at your jokes, even when they were not really funny, or he had heard them a million times already (Ralph). He was other centered, and other-centered people don't often rise to the proverbial top of what we value in America.

Bob would have always asked about your family. He considered family to be the greatest gift, and he would have connected with you around your family.

He always felt like he was the luckiest chap around, and his optimism was contagious. Matt also said, "Pops didn't sweat the small stuff. He never complained or got upset over immaterial issues. He floated through life with a humble grace that allowed him to roll with the punches and enjoy everything life threw at him. He often prayed for challenges and while he was dealt his fair share, he faced each one with a sense of calm purpose."

Bob valued the truth. When we first met, he wanted to date me, and I was involved with other things like work, school, and career and another relationship that led me to believe that timing was not right for us. So, I lied to Bob. I didn't think it was that big of a deal, but Bob took huge issue with even the smallest of untruths. As much as he wanted to be with me, he said that lying was never acceptable no matter what the circumstances, and he said that he did not want to see me anymore. I was astounded. It woke me up to the kind of man Bob was. Bob was different from other people. Thank God I recognized what a rare gift he was and went to his door one day, knees shaking, to ask for forgiveness. I never lied to him again, and I never will.

Forgiveness and gratitude are enormous life changers and marriage savers. Every marriage has trials. Ours was no different. We handled stress differently, but

Bob ALWAYS saw the bigger picture. Can I emphasize this enough?! He hated confrontation, so he simply apologized when we disagreed. Some would say that always apologizing first is not manly, or that he should have stood his ground and shown Sue her place, but that was never Bob's spirit.

Bob was a faithful man and a master historian. He knew that God wanted us to forgive each other. Bob studied how pettiness in the past resulted in war, famine, needless death and destruction, rape, and broken spirits because humans did not see the bigger picture of how to approach solutions. Humans had to be right. They had to show who was boss—who had the power, the biggest sword and the most intimidating gun. Ungodly competition. Lack of humility. These kinds of things never work in the long run in marriages, on the playground, in the office setting, or in politics. There will be a penalty, he would say.

I received another present today: the card that Bob was going to give me on my birthday. He had not yet signed it, but he bought it and tucked it away. He knew how important cards were to me and took great care in their selection. It made me terribly sad to find it, but also terribly fortunate to have come across it. The card reads:

Why do I love you so much? Because I trust you more than anyone in the world to listen, to help me through, to remind me how to laugh when times are trying. Why do I love you so much? Because you're a part of my favorite memories as well as my most important dreams. Why do I love you so much? Because I can't imagine what life would be like if I didn't have you to love…because I can't imagine what life would be like without love and I can't imagine what love would be like without you.

Blessings for Today: That I learned from a master. I cannot fill his shoes, but I can feel his shadow.

Specific Prayer Requests: That others in this world feel his shadow and learn. That they would understand that there is a penalty for a lack of humility. That Bob's favorite scripture be understood. Micah 6:6–8 says, "With what shall I come before the Lord and bow down before the exalted God? Shall I come before him with burnt offerings, with calves a year old? Will the Lord be pleased with thousands of rams, with ten thousand rivers of olive oil? Shall I offer my firstborn for my transgression, the fruit of my body for the sin of my soul? He has shown you,

O mortal, what is good. And what does the Lord require of you? To act justly and to love mercy and to walk humbly with your God."

Reflection

I think back to the men—no boys—I had met before Bob. Three of them at different times talked of marriage. One I was very excited about, the other two not so much. And when it came to figuring out my path and my future once I met Bob, I still did not immediately jump at marriage. Yes, I moved with him to Nebraska and lived with him. It took me a little while—not too long—but a little while to truly see the kind of person he was and how clearly different he was from the rest. He could not tolerate a person who lied, boasted, treated others unjustly, and had no depth and patience by which to study and solve issues. He would hate the political tenor of this country now. His legacy and his shadow will long remind those who knew and loved him what it means to be a truly decent human being.

***

ENTRY   2/9/2017 at 9:51 p.m.

"QUESTIONS"

Trying to make sense of what happened is a full-time job, and now that I am back at work, it remains a substantial part-time job. Your mind takes you to many places where it has no business taking you. People offer their opinions on why it happened. It was meant to be—No! God decides when to take people, and this was Bob's time—No! Bob's number was up—No! This was done to teach me a lesson. I have actually considered this one. I am certainly learning more lessons now than ever before, but really, this rationale is too punitive. I don't think Bob's accident was meant to punish me or make me feel horrible forever, although it certainly feels this way at times. In the long run, though, I don't think Bob's accident was a cruel plan to reprimand me.

Some say God needed Bob for a higher purpose. I hope this reason is true, since our world needs help. It was an accident, but why did the accident happen? What are their answers to this? Nothing that we can find. No small order or higher-order answers. Some who have lived through the loss of a loved one simply state that there are no answers—at least no earthly answers. There are just questions. I need to get comfortable with the questions and use them as a chance to explore.

"Have patience with everything that remains unsolved in your heart. Try to love the questions themselves, like locked rooms and like books written in a foreign language. Do not now look for the answers. They cannot now be given to you because you could not live them. It is a question of experiencing everything. At present you need to live the question. Perhaps you will gradually, without even noticing it, find yourself experiencing the answer, some distant day."[13]

I have always thought it was more important to ask good questions than to spout off with all the answers. When I was young, I thought that the smartest people were those who had all the answers, and perhaps I was not as smart as some because I lacked all of the answers. But, I have not thought that for a very long time now—way before this insult to my life. I have, in fact, noticed that the smartest people are careful to listen well, seek advice, make sound decisions and continue to solicit feedback. Sometimes smart people do have all the answers, but it comes with experience, from considering previous lessons, and learning from mistakes. If you don't have previous experience and the benefit of input, then asking good questions is the next best thing (or perhaps the best thing).

Bob was extremely smart, yet he always asked questions. Only when he thought he had all of the information straight in his mind would he give you an answer. And sometimes he wouldn't. Sometimes you would have to ask him if you wanted an answer. And sometimes you wouldn't like the answer, so you asked for the answer to be different, and sometimes to keep peace, he changed his answer. You know—"Happy wife, happy life."

Having answers would be easier perhaps, but I don't have any answers at the moment. And even if we had answers, some will always be insufficient—the Holocaust, slavery, war, murders. Some egregious events can be partially explained by politics, bigotry, homophobia, ego/power, religion, mental health issues/general insanity, but context cannot provide an exact answer for loss. Even in a war with thousands murdered, or 9/11, you may understand the horrific context but not the exact reason for your specific loss. Others survived—why didn't my loved one survive? Some people survive cancer—why didn't my loved one survive? Others were in that room and survived—why didn't my loved one survive? Others were on that plane and survived—why didn't my loved one survive? Others—so many others—survive bike accidents. Why didn't my loved one survive?!

I have received some answers—if you can call them answers. They are not direct answers to the bike accident, but they are a result of this tragedy. Some who knew Bob and what he stood for and others who merely have read about him through this blog are stopping to consider their own lives—some for fleeting moments and others for longer. Some are thinking about how they might change their lives, and others have already made changes, including job shifts, prioritizing their marriage, entering marital counseling, starting wills, informing spouses of financial arrangements, filling out end-of-life wishes, expressing gratitude for what you have, savoring moments and relationships, taking stock of family, finding and strengthening faith.

Blessings for Today: Those who have told me how the effects of Bob's accident have created positive change for you. These comments serve as partial answers to the question of WHY?

Specific Prayer Requests: That time will allow me to adequately explore the most important questions, and that in this exploration, I can transform in a positive way with new sensitivities that make me a better person. That I can find an eventual purpose in all of this. That this crazy, unbelievable situation will in some way make sense eventually. Is that even possible?

"He who has a why to live for can bear almost any how." (Friedrich Nietzsche)

2 Corinthians 4:17–18 says, "For our light and momentary troubles are achieving for us an eternal glory that far outweighs them all. So we fix our eyes not on what is seen, but what is unseen, since what is seen is temporary, but what is unseen is eternal." And Ecclesiastes 8:8a says, "As no one has power over the wind to contain it, so no one has power over the time of their death."

The questions— the why of this tragedy—still haunt me. I do have partial answers however. Give back. Make life better for others. Live with purpose. Love. Leave the world a better place.

***

ENTRY   2/18/2017 at 10:25 p.m.

"NEW TRADITIONS NEW MEMORIES...SO THEY SAY"

One of the most important things to do after a great loss is to create new traditions and memories. The budding politician Teddy Roosevelt, for example, was so grief stricken after the death of his wife and mother within hours of each other that he handed his infant daughter over to his elder sister, Anna, and took off for the Dakotas to explore the great hinterlands and try his hand at ranching. The rest, as we know, is history with his record of being one of the greatest conservationists ever, as well as President. No doubt this probably would never have happened without his loss and ensuing journey.

People who have lost great loves, like Roosevelt, and have rallied back are my new role models. In theory, it's not a bad strategy to run off to find your new self, except that an even stronger emotion is the desperate need to remember your loved one. I don't want to ever forget my beautiful Robert Boy! I am firm on this point. I will never, ever be as loved.

I am stubborn in holding on, remembering, rehashing, and revisiting everything. I want to honor the ground where my husband and I walked, the house that we shared, the woods that we hiked, and the songs that we danced to and sang. I am so intent on honoring my husband that even though pursuing new traditions and memories makes sense on paper, I don't want to move on. Sometimes when I do pursue new traditions, I feel guilty. I want to ensure that what we had was solid and will not disappear.

I am torn. I both avoid our places and seek them out. It's hard—so hard—to relive my memories, but it's also comforting. So for now, I do both. I sit in Bob's place on the couch writing this blog and drinking from his cup. Yet, I attend a new exercise class in the morning—one that Bob and I had never been to together. In and out, back and forth.

I keep returning to Risa's advice to "do whatever feels right." Her words are the most comforting and sensible that anyone has uttered to me since the accident, and so far, it is working. I have never much cared too much about what people think of me. I care just enough, and that is a gift. My mother is the same way. I know many people who worry incessantly about what other people think of them, taking up a lot of brain space and perhaps encouraging them to make choices they later regret. It's freeing to me to do what feels right, without worrying about what might be right for another.

In doing what feels right, I am exploring a bit. One of the best gifts for me now is the gift of a new experience. Last week, I went to the Metropolitan Opera House in New York City to see *Carmen*. I used to scoff at hoity toit people who attended the opera regularly. I don't know why I was critical. Bob and I never went. I mostly did not figure I would ever understand what the heck the story was about—and all that singing in foreign languages. Yikes! But when friends invited me, the "do what feels right" mantra kicked in, or at least the "you gotta do something different" notion. A new experience, I thought. Even if I never attended the opera again, I could chalk this up as, "I did something different" and made a new memory. Who would have known that they have electronic translations right at your seat in any language you want, just like the United Nations. I could follow the entire opera, and I realized that it was more akin to a soap opera set to music. I loved it! I found it inspirational. If I were invited again, I would go, especially to the Met.

My experience at the opera reminds me of when George Costanza on Seinfeld had the epiphany that because his life was not going in a positive direction that he must be doing everything wrong. To right those wrongs, he would do everything the opposite of what he would normally do. The opera was the opposite of what I would normally do. The same goes for yoga and meditation. I always said that the expectations to relax during yoga and meditation would make me nervous. But these are different and desperate times, and different and desperate times call for different modalities. I have learned that you can get answers to some of life's most pressing issues by slowing down, being mindful and meditating.

We brought a meditation coach to our Grief Support Group last week, and she led us through a mediation. In the middle of the meditation, we were supposed to welcome a loved one to visit us. The coach said that we could ask our loved one anything we wanted, so I asked Bob what happened on the bike to cause him to have the accident. The coach then asked us to imagine any object at all, and to feel it and smell it, to help us identify the object. I immediately imagined one of Bob's favorite baseball hats that said: "It is what it is." Perhaps, "It is what it is" was how Bob was answering my question to him. I hated that answer—it was cold, final, and lacked compassion, but I think that was his answer.

In any case, with prayer, meditation, yoga, my support system—and yes, even the opera, I will continue to make attempts at being what I am meant to be and do what I am meant to do.

Blessings for Today: That I have people in my life who have committed to doing something "different" with me to help me make new memories. At the same time, I truly appreciate friends and family who sit with me and talk about Bob—the good times, the sweet times, the times I never want to forget. Don't be afraid of talking to me about Bob, please. Don't ignore him.

Specific Prayer Requests: That I never forget. And on occasion, I channel George Costanza and do the opposite to make new and positive memories. Proverbs 10:7 says, "The name of the righteous is used in blessings, but the name of the wicked will rot." Isaiah 43: 18–19 tells us, "Forget the former things; Do not dwell on the past. See, I am doing a new thing! Now it springs up; Do you not perceive it? I am making a way in the wilderness and streams in the wastelands." Finally, Ezekiel 36:26 says, "I will give you a new heart and put a new spirit in you; I will remove from you your heart of stone and give you a heart of flesh."

Reflection

I am still torn between wanting to hold onto the extraordinary memories of Bob and wanting and needing to have some new things in my life. I carry on—and simply by carrying on—I experience new things and make new memories. I don't avoid them. Sometimes I simply hold my nose (so to speak) and jump in.

Other times, I even embrace the new experiences. I have learned to find balance between keeping my memories of Bob and embracing my new life.

***

ENTRY   2/25/2017 at 9:33 p.m.

"WHAT TO SAY AND NOT SAY TO A GRIEVING PERSON"

A few weeks ago a close colleague of mine said that she figured that if she does not know what to say to someone who has lost a loved one, it is simply best to not say anything at all. I bristled at this immediately and (lovingly) told her that almost anything she said to a grieving person would be better than not saying anything. Otherwise, the grieving person simply feels ignored, and I don't think that is ever the intent. In fact, I have suspended judgement for whatever someone might say or not say right or wrong, knowing full well that people don't always know what to say.

Death is not a comfortable subject for the vast majority of people. Even when I worked as a floor nurse, I certainly never fully knew what people were experiencing before Bob's accident, and I am as guilty as everyone else in not always knowing the right thing to say. I feel guilty for times in the past when I wasn't as present as I could have been because I simply did not know what a person's needs were. People who have lost someone feel a universal and immediate gut-punch around the guilt they feel for past words not said or actions not taken with another who is grieving. I have heard this time and again. I was reminded of this recently as I read how Sheryl Sandberg, the chief operating officer of FaceBook, felt guilty after her husband's death for her own past behavior towards grieving people; she simply had no idea what to say or how to respond. It's just the way it is.

Although people grieve uniquely and some phrases hit people very differently, certain phrases may be universally less supportive than others. Some obvious ones might include: "This was his time to go" (depending on a person's age, illness and other circumstances, of course, but it certainly did NOT work in my case); "God never gives us more than we can handle;" "Bob would never want you to be this sad;" "God needs him more than you at this time;" "He's in a better place now;" "This will free you up to do what YOU want to do now;" and "I know just how you feel" (unless you really do). In the beginning, I did not want to hear how strong I was when I could barely stand. As time has passed, I realize NOW that I will be okay (never the same, but okay in the long run). I am okay now if I hear how strong I am.

People should also avoid making certain statements out of feelings of discomfort and their deep desire to try to get "normal" back when the same "normal" is simply not possible. These statements include: "You just need to shake this off and move on" or "Stop wallowing—you have so much more to live for." One of the worst things people can do is to completely avoid the topic and just pretend that the whole thing never happened. I do understand from a psychological perspective the discomfort people feel around death and grief, and, again, their desire to somehow stop my pain and their own. I have tried to suspend judgment, understanding that these statements are well intentioned.

One of the phrases that seems completely innocuous but is a conundrum for newly grieving people is the phrase, "How are you?" Grieving people don't quite know how to answer this question. They are certainly not good or fine, as the question usually hopes to illicit, but to go on and on about how you really feel is simply unacceptable to most people, who are just frankly hoping for a quick okay. A portion of my grief support group was devoted to strategizing how to answer this question. Everyone pretty much has trouble with it, at least during the first several months of grieving (again, all depending on unique circumstances). When people ask me now, I basically tell them that I am hanging in there—a truthful, yet quick way to move past their question. Sometimes I still just ignore the "How are you?" It may seem rude, but it is simply a fact that I cannot answer it at that moment and stay authentic.

I understand that people are looking for signs of healing, but it takes a very long time for grieving people to get their bearing, and their emotions are constant and sometimes cruel. The gamut of feelings—anger, resentment, love, loneliness, depression, gratitude, and of just feeling overwhelmed with tasks—are tossed around my head every day like a fifteen-ingredient salad. I never know how it will be tossed on any particular day, so to really try to answer how I feel and to remain authentic may not be entirely possible. Very close friends and family are interested in the whole story of how you are feeling on that particular hour or day, but many others should be spared (and I think they want to be spared). Grieving is an intense process, and I believe (and have been told) that people who try to breeze through it, many times, do not come out the other side whole.

Other statements might be taken differently depending on a person's personality and stage of grief. Many people told me that they did not contact me because they did not want to invade my privacy or thought it wasn't the right time to reach out. Others said that they did not want to bother me and add to my email burden, or they thought I already had all of the support I needed. One statement that strikes me as unusual (but with also good intentions) is that they did not want to say anything because they did not want to bring up the pain. The pain is always there, and to acknowledge it is always better.

I heard all of these statements and still do, and I felt that whenever anyone reached out, it was the right time with its own unique gift of thoughtfulness (no matter the day or night). It was the right time no matter which memories it brought up. I need all the support I can get and love hearing from people, so please do not worry about intruding on my privacy.

Indeed, the very best thing people could say to me is that they read this blog and mention something they read in it that has helped them. I also like hearing that people pass it on to others who they believe can benefit from my words. To know that I might be helpful in the healing process of another is the best medicine for me.

"I am always here for you" is a statement that I was never quite sure how to incorporate into my life. In theory, this is a great thing to say to a grieving person and I love hearing it, but in actuality, I don't think you would ever want me calling you in despair at 2:00 in the morning, or to pick up some dog food because my dog had not eaten in two days, or to take my mother to the doctor when I am out of town (although The Linkimers and Costas did just this). With people who are very close to me, I was able to come up with some very specific ways that people could help and be there for me, but I was never quite sure how to take it except to accept it lovingly without expectations. More specific offers of help were always the most useful, such as an offer to bring dinner and to ask which night was best for me, or to offer to walk Jake when I was away. No one wants to bother people unnecessarily.

With that said, what indeed is most supportive? Again, everyone's personality, needs, emotions, and own set of circumstances differ, and what works for one may not work for another. Here are mine. You can be assured that some are universal winners, like this first one:

- I am so glad to see you today.
- You look good.
- I think about you all the time.
- I pray for you all the time.
- I wish there was something I could do to take away your pain.
- There isn't a day that goes by that I don't think about you.
- Is Tuesday a good day for me to bring over my chicken casserole?
- We are going to the movies or a play next weekend. Would you like to join us?
- Bob would be so proud of you.
- Bob loved you so much. You were so fortunate to have shared that kind of love.
- I know you feel cheated. He should be here. The rest of us feel the same way and miss him terribly.
- I don't know what to say. I am unsure of the right words, but I want you to know that I care.
- I am going to check in on your mother when you are out of town. I know it concerns you to leave her.
- I know Bob never wanted to leave you, but he sure took care of you ahead of time with his financial preparations. Now that's true love and care.
- I believe that Bob is truly with you now. It's not the same, but you still have a relationship with him, and one day you will be together again.
- Bob would want you (Kim and Mark) to be the very best you can be. He was and always will be proud of you.
- I just love Bob. I'll never forget the way he… (fill in the blank).
- Family always came first to Bob. He was a role model for the rest of us with his giving spirit.
- I hope this day treated you kindly.
- I am so glad that Bob's volunteer and community spirit will live on through the Red Cross award in his name.
- Hugs.

- I love you. No one can replace the love you had with Bob, but I love you as well.
- Listen.
- Humor in small doses.
- And my favorite: You should do what feels right.

Blessings for Today: That there have been so many caring people in my life who have said just the right things at just the right times. If words were not just right, the intentions always were. I make no judgments.

Specific Prayer Requests: That I might have opportunities to help others as you have helped me. Proverbs 25:11–13 reads, "Like apples of gold in settings of silver is a ruling rightly given. Like an earring of gold or an ornament of fine gold is the rebuke of a wise judge to a listening ear. Like a snow-cooled drink at harvest time is a trustworthy messenger to the one who sends him; he refreshes the spirit of his master."

Reflection

It is universally difficult to know what to say and do in the face of a friend or family member's grief. I have lived it and am more aware of what to say and not say, and it is still difficult to approach a profoundly grieving person. As I suspended judgment to people who made insensitive comment, I hope others will pardon me. Yes, it's true: Sometimes there are just no words, but to even saying that is better than silence. In the case of a grieving person, silence is never golden.

***

ENTRY   3/5/2017 at 10:00 p.m.

"PICKING UP WHERE RED CROSS DISASTER TEAM MEMBER BOB LEFT OFF…SORT OF"

Bob always said we had it better than most people, and he meant it. He absolutely believed that we were fortunate and our job was to pay it forward. I was reminded of this today as I served on the front lines—something that feeds my soul, but I hardly ever get to do. In my mantra of, "Do what feels right" in my journey of grief for Bob, it felt right today to drive to a city called Union City (near Manhattan) to volunteer at a Red Cross shelter where thirty families were staying after a devastating fire took down their apartment complex and a beloved community church. A two-year-old boy, Eddie was lost in the fire. It felt good to wear Bob's Red Cross vest and his Red Cross ID card. I could not help but think that he was happy seeing me there.

All it takes is being in a shelter like this with people who have lost everything except the clothes on their back to know that perhaps you really don't have it so bad after all. I was especially happy to be there with people who knew Bob and appreciated the work that he did for the organization. Bob had told me years ago about Karen, the nurse on duty, and we finally met per chance today after several attempts over the years of trying to get together. After all this time, Bob indeed got us together. I found Karen amazing. And, of course, if you knew Bob, then you also knew that he always built me up in the eyes of others, so she too was impressed to meet the wife of Bob Hassmiller, if only from the image he created in her mind.

The theme of loss always reigns supreme at Red Cross shelters. Loss of life, loss of possessions, loss of dignity; having to share the little you have with many others surrounding you in (generally) an open gym, cot-by-cot-by-cot. Red Cross volunteers and staff stand ready to help with the slightest to most monumental need. A poignant story from today shows just how far Red Cross volunteers will go to touch the souls of those who lost so much.

One fourteen-year-old young lady I spoke with today lay hopelessly on the same bench at the same cafeteria room table all day grieving for her dog, cat, and rabbit that were lost in the fire. Listening and affirming was the only therapy we could offer, except for super nurse Karen, that is. While helping some victims board a bus so they could visit their homes to collect whatever possessions might be retrievable, she spotted a red cat. Yes, indeed, it appeared to be the same cat lost by our fourteen-year-old client grieving at the cafeteria table. Karen chased the cat around the neighborhood until she could take a picture to determine if it could be identified as the missing cat. Unfortunately, it was not the girl's cat, but Karen's kindness did not go unnoticed.

Bob would come home with these kinds of stories all the time. He always felt grateful and honored to help people when they were at their lowest, whether it was a place to stay, food to eat, cash to buy a few essentials, and importantly, an arm around their shoulders. There are many single- or multiple-family fires that do not get publicized, but the Red Cross volunteers always stand ready to help. Volunteering with the Red Cross was the foundation of our relationship. I am so proud of the man I married and our affiliation with the Red Cross.

Blessings for Today: That I followed my heart and in turn my heart was nourished. I would love to start exposing my grandchildren to the Red Cross so that the circle of support and gratitude might continue.

Specific Prayer Requests: That the Red Cross will continue to get the kind of financial support it needs so that its volunteers (which make up ninety-five percent of the workforce) can continue to help those in dire need. That those affected by the Union City fire be sustained and find their way back from their losses. And a special prayer for Eddie's family, and whose father is fighting for his life in an intensive care unit after trying to rescue his son. And for the mother, Aaliaya, who must now carry on in the midst of grief, to care for her other two children. Proverbs 3:27 asks us, "Do not withhold good from those to whom it is due, when it is in your power to act." Hebrews 13:16 reiterates, "And do not forget to do good and to share with others, for with such sacrifices God is pleased."

Reflections

Having a larger purpose outside my own world helps. It takes time—at least it should—to resurface and understand what that purpose might be. I have to believe that we are all somehow connected, and there is a larger plan and purpose to our otherwise rudderless lives. Being open to signs, whether they come in words, song, prayer, dreams, an action or some other meaningful symbol can be powerful a reminder of our life's purpose—what we are to do and who and what we are to hold onto during our earthly journey. I believe this.

***

"RESETTING AND RESTORING"

Last week, a trusted soul said to me, "I bet you just wake up some days and think it is all a bad dream." I responded that not one day goes by when I don't wake up and think it is a bad dream. This is simply not believable! Just because 156 days have passed, I do not feel any more closure, have any more answers, or feel any more settled.

I wake up and ask why; I brush my teeth and say I don't understand; I walk the dog and ask how could this happen? I still sometimes ask why during the rest of my day, usually when I think Bob should be with me or I want to tell him something really badly, or ask his advice. Sometimes I ask why he is not with me now when I am in a place where we always went together. The good news is that I am able to participate at meetings, pay bills, fill out applications or simply walk down the hall to the bathroom while I ask these questions. How did this happen? The feelings and questions interspersed with the tasks of living. That's about how it goes.

I can breathe again and eat without getting nauseous, and I don't cry at the slightest memory. I can function quite well, but it certainly does not mean I am forgetting Bob. My dear friend, and integrative health counselor, Alicia told me that I am "resetting" after I exclaimed quite vehemently that I detested the phrase "moving on". Moving on means that I am putting Bob aside, putting Bob behind, and forgetting him. I AM NOT. I love the phrase "resetting". It kind of lets me off the hook for how I am living each day. I am not moving on; I am resetting. The map that I carefully constructed is burned and crumpled away, and the GPS no longer takes me to the destination that I keyed in, so I reset.

And resetting, according to Webster's Dictionary, also means that I am restoring. Restoring means to bring back to a state of health, soundness, or vigor or to reconstruct in the original state, and to reconstruct means to re-create in the mind from given or available information. All of this fits with my reality. I am resetting and restoring.

I started out in life being just me. I can't exactly say that I always understood who I was growing up, but I had a pretty good idea. I certainly knew what I stood for and what I thought was important. But I was much more certain of who I was as Bob's other half. After all, we were together the bulk of my life. Bob was a strong, steady base—always there, always loving, always giving, and always supporting. We made a whole, and our membranes were fairly permeable. Sometimes we would take on each other's characteristics. Our personalities and our politics differed, to be sure, but we were completely simpatico with principles, ideals, beliefs, morals—the core of a person's existence.

In the restoring process, the job is to not lose the original piece—what's at the core—but bring it back to its original value, without harming the structure or its essence. In some cases, restorations can add more value. That's the idea, right? The piece has a history—it has a story or many stories and meaning beyond the piece itself. In restoring, the original shines through, with all the history and stories attached. It makes for a more interesting piece, don't you think? Far better than the notion of "moving on." It takes a lot of energy to properly reset and restore because it is both a physiological and psychological process.

Michelangelo's paintings in the Sistine Chapel have painstakingly been restored a number of times. The process is called sympathetic restoration, which is the act of "restoring where deterioration of one sort or another had obliterated details and caused loss of integrity to the whole," according to Webster. The most recent restoration brought out details and colors that had not been seen for centuries. I can see how sympathetic restoration could occur in humans—perhaps in deteriorating relationships, the details of the unique self are obliterated. But, can it also be that the marriage union I spoke so lovingly about could also possibly obliterate the details of an individual's unique self—its true core? Restoration over time could bring new details to life. I don't know about this. Perhaps.

Authenticity is a core principle in restoration. To keep the object true to its original intent. It must remain authentic, or else it will simply become another replica. I use the word authentic a lot now. I feel deeply that I must tap into what is most important at my core to successfully execute my life. I don't want to be a replica of anything or anybody. My actions and words must be congruent with my beliefs and values. I need to express what those core values are and translate them in my everyday life.

Some people are tuned into their core beliefs and values and understand what is right and wrong, while others never know from one day to the next what they stand for or what they believe in. They are like a boat without a rudder. It's very easy to be unsettled or lost if you don't have a core set of beliefs. My faith has helped me on this journey, and I am not sure how you make this journey without faith. When your whole world has been shaken, you have no choice but to reset, and in that resetting, you start with the core and work outwards. The key is to find and bring to light your values and beliefs and to act on them. This is authenticity.

Blessings for Today: That "resetting and restoring" is my new frame of reference for my life, instead of "shaking it off and moving on." Resetting and restoring helps me to heal in a more positive and freeing way.

Specific Prayer Requests: That I can bring back my core; the integrity of my whole in an even more meaningful way through resetting and restoring. Psalm 23:3 promises, "He refreshes my soul; He guides me along the right paths for His name's sake.

Reflections

The idea of resetting and restoring is much more comforting than moving on. If I had not reached this understanding, then I might still fear that I would not honor or remember what I needed to remember. I was struck with this notion of restoring again recently after I attended a lesson on restoration at the Vermeer Museum in Holland. The restoration expert at the museum said that when you restore a masterpiece by removing what is not supposed to be there and bringing the core alive, its life is extended and made even more beautiful. Exactly.

***

ENTRY   3/19/2017 at 5:20 p.m.

"BUBBLE"

Almost everyone will suffer some kind of grief while living on this earth. I mention this in my blogs as a reminder that I am not alone. In fact, life, as we know it, is a pretty temporary assignment. Grief results from the relationship that one had with the lost entity. It could be a death of a person, a relationship, or even a pet. I wonder what my grief would feel like if I had been older when Bob died. Would it feel the same? I, of course, wanted Bob to live into his nineties—that was my plan. But what if he were ninety-five, and I was in my late eighties? Would I have been satisfied that we had done all we said we were going to do, or would I have still wanted more time with him? Would I have been able to withstand the physicality of grief at a much later age? I won't have the answers of course, to any of these questions, but I still wonder.

My romanticized version of how Bob and I would leave this earth together is played out in *The Notebook,* by Nicolas Sparks,[14] where Noah and Allie simply die in bed in each other's arms at a very old age. The love they shared was simply too strong to keep them apart. I hoped that's how it would be for us. I wonder about all the people in the world who have lost loved ones. Who are they? What do they feel? How do they go on? Having lost a great love makes me sensitive to others who have experienced loss. Does it make a difference if they are lost suddenly, like Bob or a 9/11 victim or through a long-term illness? Does it make a difference if the person is lost as part of a hate crime or through the Holocaust? Or if the person died peacefully, surrounded by loved ones?

I believe that it makes a difference if people have beliefs about what happens to their loved ones when they die. I would think grief would be more acute for someone who believed that the end is merely the end. Both Christians and Muslims, for example, believe there is an afterlife, but there are nuances in beliefs from very strict to more lenient about what happens to people and what it takes for them to get to heaven. According to Seven Ponds, an organization devoted to embracing end-of-life experiences, "many Native American tribes also do not see death as an absolute, but instead they see life as an infinite journey where death is not the end. Death is appreciated as a passage to the next world: the next step in life. Almost all tribes hold this perception of time as being circular. Many tribes believe in reincarnation, and that the soul is an eternal presence that moves from body to body without ever leaving the world. Others believe that when a loved one dies, their soul is transported to the next world where they join their ancestors who passed before them. This different perspective allows the Native

American people to view death not with grief, but with acceptance and happiness. Moving from this world to the next is not something to be mourned, but rather it is something to be celebrated. Death is nothing more than a stepping stone to the next life."[15]

The Jewish religion focuses on the good that we do while we are living and maintains that the good will be rewarded. To life! To life! L'chai-im! Although an afterlife is not completely ruled out in the Jewish religion, there is less emphasis than in Christianity. Buddhists believe that spirits live on and sometimes attach themselves to others. And then there is karma, which, according to Wikipedia, refers to "the spiritual principle of cause and effect where intent and actions of an individual (cause) influence the future of that individual (effect). Karma is closely associated with the idea of rebirth in many schools of Asian religions. In these schools, karma in the present affects one's future in the current life, as well as the nature and quality of future lives— one's samsāra."

And still, even with belief in an afterlife or rebirth, people still grieve—some more, some less, some completely, and some incompletely. I have come to believe that the only wrong way to grieve is to not grieve at all for someone who has been loved deeply or perhaps to set it aside and have it come out in other sometimes unhealthy ways. I don't know how you do that if you have loved deeply. Before Bob, I lost a father and a brother. I was affected for a short time. I took stock, I learned, and I prayed, I missed them, but it was not the same as losing a soulmate. And everyone is different. There are as many differences in grieving as there are in people and who they love.

I just finished *The Nightingale,* a story about two sisters in France and their lives before, during, and after the Nazi occupation.[16] It was tortuous to read about the daily angst of who might be punished, tortured, or taken next and for no reason and what the sisters felt and did to bide their time and brace for the inevitable and unspeakable. I cannot imagine being traumatized each day without relief. With so much daily trauma and loss, does one harden to loss? Does one get used to death? It seemed to me that as the entire experience of criminal occupation and death played out, people were horrified and constantly bracing themselves, but the real grief and trauma (as if you can calculate the atrocities of the time) came if a loved one was taken or killed.

I think—but I don't know for sure—that people, no matter how horrific the circumstances, hold out hope. They think that atrocities and loss may happen to others, but it won't happen to them or a loved one. I always felt sorry for the person or the family who experienced loss—incredibly sorry and horrified in the cases of 9/11, Sandy Hook, or some other of the disasters I have worked—but always relieved it did not happen to me. It could not possibly happen to me, but then it did.

We create a bubble—our protective mechanism to allow us to keep living fully. Living comfortable, safe, and loving lives, with most or all basic needs met (if we are fortunate enough), we act as though grief cannot touch us. We know intellectually that it will; the bubble is teasingly and falsely protective. Such a fragile bubble. Pop! Here one minute and gone the next.

I want to end with the notion of love. Even with this fear of "it" happening to a dear one, death should not keep us from loving. We should never stop loving because we have lost love. There is purpose in grief. For now, I do not think that I could ever love again as a wife to a husband. No one could ever love me the same as Bob did—his love was so thorough and complete. It is too fearful to think about loving anyone else the way I loved Bob, but I can love in other ways. This is all out of my hands, however, and therein lies the journey.

Blessings for Today: The time I am giving myself to fully and completely recover as I restore and reset. The people in my life who I can depend on for love, hope, and faith.

Specific Prayer Requests: That my temporary assignment here on earth might serve to help others along the way. 1 Corinthians 13:13 says, "And now these three remain: faith, hope, love But the greatest of these is love."

Reflection

Keeping the faith, holding on to hope, and loving. Easier said than done, especially in the beginning of such a loss, when my emotions were crowded out by bitterness, fear, anxiety, and utter sadness. Faith, hope, and love are the gifts that we have as human beings. We survive by resetting and restoring and holding onto faith, hope, and love, knowing that in time, with proper attention to caring for our souls, they will fill us up.

***

ENTRY   3/26/2017 at 3:32 p.m.

"TODAY I CLIMBED A MOUNTAIN"

Today I climbed a mountain. Well, technically, it was a butte, but to me it was a mountain. Before the accident, I was up for climbing anything and everything—no matter the height or difficulty. However, with the wind knocked out of me, walking on solid ground at sea level has been just fine, thank you. In the beginning, I could hardly stand, and then I walked and walked some more (thanks to dog, Jake), but until today, I never climbed. I wanted to climb again, but I didn't have the opportunity or strength. As luck would have it, I am staying at the Buttes Marriott in Phoenix, which is adjacent to—well, yes—a butte. A butte is "an isolated hill with steep, often vertical sides and a small, relatively flat top," according to Wikipedia.

I eyed the butte for two days while in meetings, determining if I had the will or strength to climb it. In years past, I would have deemed the butte too easy—a time waster—and sought out bigger mountains nearby. In fact, I could see the Camel Back range in the distance that I had climbed three times. The Camel Back range was something to conquer, and conquer I did. I cannot imagine ever climbing that again, though. But eyeing the butte I wondered if I could even climb it? My muscle mass, lung capacity, and confidence were diminished, but I decided to consider it and eventually talked myself into climbing it.

I donned shorts, a t-shirt, and proper shoes for such an elaborate outing. I took sunglasses, my phone, and just in case I got stranded, a jumbo-size chocolate chip cookie and water. Mind you, in normal times I could have gone up and down that butte in minutes—maybe twenty at the most, but today, who knew? So the cookie and water would sustain me no matter what.

I walked across the street to the butte and saw two teenage girls in short shorts and flip flops walking down the butte. Was it my imagination, or were they skipping down? Well, they were not giving their journey a second thought—that's for sure. I, on the other hand, was over-thinking my trek. I looked to the right, the left, up, and around. There was not another soul in sight, and two thoughts entered my mind. On the plus side, I would not be embarrassed by any younger people wondering why I walked at a snail's pace, but on the minus side, what would I do if I fell and no one found me again?

I began to climb and noticed a sign warning me not to touch the cactus plants and trees. They looked dangerous, and I wondered what I would hold onto during my hike. I never used to fear falling while hiking, except maybe once on the sea cliffs of Kauai—the infamous Napali Coastline, but other than that, not so much. I had the confidence of a sixteen-year-old always because Bob was with me. His long comforting arms guarded me from harm, lifted me when I fell, steadied me when I lost my balance on narrow wobbly paths, and always boosted me to greater heights.

I remembered trekking the Alakai Swamp Trail in Kauai. I did not properly research that trail, which was one of the wettest spots on earth. Translation: We mostly hiked in mud and slid all over the place. Recall the movie *Romancing the Stone* with Michael Douglas and Kathleen Turner. Her character slides down the mountain in a mudslide. That was me, and Bob—my own Michael Douglas—carried me out of a number of mudslides. It was a grand adventure—frustrating at the time, but fun looking back. We recalled this hike on numerous occasions and always with great pleasure. I never felt unsafe, even sliding down a mountain mudslide, as long as Bob was with me. We climbed everything we could, and it was second nature to us.

Realizing that I would not have Bob to hold onto or the cacti if I lost my balance, I decided to eat my cookie and water before I started hiking. After all, I would need both hands. As I climbed, I was struck by how imbalanced I felt—not because the terrain was difficult, but because I did not have Bob's hand to lift me or boost me forward. Could I do this without Bob—my safety net?

I walked slowly, gaining strength and taking in what I saw—mostly lots of cacti, but also vibrant yellow and magenta flowers. I focused on the flowers, reaching figuratively for the ones in front of me. That helped, and then I suddenly imagined that John and Abby were perched on each of my shoulders. If I slipped and killed myself, they would lose both their Pops and Nana. I was especially careful for them—probably too much.

I thought of the quote by author and attorney Susan Estrich, "When a father climbs a dangerous mountain and dies, we mourn. When a mother does, we question her judgment. How could she?"

I stopped just short of the top and wondered if I should continue, the weight of my grandchildren on my back. But I set up the challenge, and I wanted to meet it. Before I continued, I gazed backwards to ensure that I would be able to handle the walk down. I knew that hiking down a mountain, depending on the terrain, could be more dangerous than going up.

I continued hiking and made it to the top without seeing a soul. Spying Camel Back from my perch, I imagined that all the real hikers were there. I was satisfied with my climb up the small butte, however, and I think Bob would have liked what he saw.

Besides Camel Back, I took in the view of the Phoenix airport tower; a steady line of planes waiting to fly in to the city; the University of Phoenix, with all of its classrooms, or so I imagined, brimming with bright, young hopefuls; an over-populated cemetery; and an Arizona Diamondbacks game. It reminded me of the many people experiencing different seasons of their lives. Here one day and gone the next. I thought of all of the people who have trekked this butte before me. What did they see in their time—before the airport and stadium were built and before so many had filled the cemetery?

Coming down was…. Well, let's just say it was best that I was all alone on the butte. It was not a pretty sight. To say that I crawled like a snail would be an understatement. Being a Nana is critically important to me—something that I dreamed about since becoming a mother. So, crawled I did, ridiculously so. If those teenage girls in their short shorts and flip flops came again, my plan was to pretend that I was on my rear meditating. Meditating is big in Arizona, so that's what the plan was—to sit and pretend I was enjoying the view, when in actuality I was planning my next steps. If I could not hold onto a cactus for balance, then sitting and sliding were the next best things.

When I triumphantly reached the bottom, I passed a thirty-something guy on a conference call, who hardly gave a second thought as to how he might reach the top. He was so focused on his call that nothing—not even a climb up a small butte—could break his concentration (or his sweat). I strolled back to the hotel with renewed confidence and energy and asked the bellman if he could suggest a place to walk on such a beautiful day. When he pointed to the butte, I responded, "Oh that—I just climbed it. I'm looking for a longer walk now." It just rolled off my tongue—I had climbed the butte!

And now that I am home, I want to translate the meaning of this adventure for my life. Perhaps if I think I can survive this tragedy by putting one foot in front of the other—perhaps I can make it. I know from experience that small persistent steps—more times than not—get you there. Yes, there are setbacks—different plateaus of the butte, rocks sliding around me, and a lack of something to grasp hold of. But tenacity will get me to the bottom of the mountain again.

Faith is important—faith in my own abilities and in God. Religious leaders will say that faith has the opportunity to grow the most when things are darkest. In other words, when you need it the most. That can sometimes be true. Celebrating accomplishments—something I struggle with—is important. I wanted to blow off climbing the butte like it was nothing. But I knew that it took everything I had at that moment to climb it. It took everything.

Blessings for Today: I did it! With the guidance of my husband and his spiritual helping hand…I did it!

Specific Prayer Requests: That I might find joy and celebrate along the way. Overall, I do not feel joy, although I have fleeting treasured moments, especially with Abby. I did not take Bob's love for granted, but I took joy for granted. I hope I never will again. Remember, Psalms 121:1 says, "I lift up my eyes to the mountains—where does my help come from?" Ecclesiastes 3:1 reads, "There is a time for everything, and a season for every activity under the heavens."

Reflection

I am amazed at the courage it took to climb this rather insignificant butte. I had to overcome deep fears of being alone, hurting myself, and dying (not for my sake but for putting my family through another tragedy). Climbing the butte ended up being a cornerstone in my healing. I overcame my fears by mustering courage, faith, stamina, and persistence—all with the help of a chocolate chip cookie. I think I was also able to see just a touch of humor in my situation. Perhaps not at the time, as I was so intent in just getting up and down, but certainly as I recalled the events.

***

ENTRY   4/9/2017 at 3:37 p.m.

"LIKE ALICE IN WONDERLAND"

"In another moment down went Alice after it, never once considering how in the world she was to get out again." (*Alice in Wonderland*)[17]

Like Alice, I slipped down my own rabbit hole the day of Bob's accident and entered a strange land called grief and all that comes with it. I remember as I entered Griefland (as chaotic as Alice's Wonderland) I immediately wanted to turn the clock back. I would have given anything to turn the clock back to prevent the accident from happening. The "what ifs" that naturally come with this kind of event swirled around my head. I wanted to stop the clock in the hospital like the perpetual tea party with the Mad Hatter and the March Hare, with the clock stopped at 6:00 p.m. It would have been okay with me to stop the clock. Please God, give me more time with this man. Don't let bad and worse continue to happen. Please, let him live. I would still give anything to turn the clock back.

Alice: "How long is forever?"

White Rabbit: "Sometimes, just one second."

Forever—it's what I thought I would have with Bob, and in a second, it was over. I promised to love Bob forever, and then it was over.

There are still many times when I think Bob is waiting for me someplace or hasn't quite arrived—he is off on a disaster call; he will walk in the door at any moment; he did not come with me to Florida this time; he is taking a nap. Sometimes I think I should answer the phone because Bob might need me. As Alice said at the beginning of her Wonderland journey: "Why, sometimes I've believed as many as six impossible things before breakfast." And it's true, I still do. Is it so impossible? Is it?!

Cheshire Cat: "Imagination is the only weapon in the war against reality."

I now want to move time forward as fast as possible. If I cannot turn it back or stop it, then I want it to hurry up and go forward: Faster, I say. Why? Because it is still hard. Perhaps with time the pain will lessen. I am no longer in deep physical pain anymore, but there are times when I feel so sad that I want to turn the clock ahead to feel less sad. This makes sense, right? But it is perplexing. I want the clock to move fast so I can get through lifetime anniversaries and tasks that I must accomplish to keep me and my family afloat. But I still need to hold onto all that was good, beautiful, loving, and funny. I need to be able to function at full capacity (while recognizing that I cannot return to life before the accident). How will this happen? I need to go forward to get out of this pain, .yet go backwards to hold onto my memories. It's a delicate balance of paradoxical wishes.

"Either it brings tears to their eyes, or else—"

"Or else what?" said Alice, for the Knight had made a sudden pause.

"Or else it doesn't, you know."

"It would be so nice if something made sense for a change."

In actuality (and as Alice says), "It's no use going back to yesterday, because I was a different person then." True. True. There is much that I have "gotten through" and much that I have learned—progress I suppose, if you want to call it that. People tell me to be proud of myself. I have completed tasks and trudged through emotionally, and I don't want to undo all that I have learned and the distance I have come emotionally. It has been rather maddening to think of it.

The Mad Hatter: "Have I gone mad? I'm afraid so."

Alice: "You're entirely bonkers. But I will tell you a secret—all the best people are."

Indeed, I was a different person then. Now I have new eyes, new ears, and a new heart—or the pieces that are left, that is. I will never be the same—for better or worse. Maybe some better and some worse. And again, like Alice on her big confusing journey, she wondered, "'Who in the world am I? Ah, that's the great puzzle!" And so I wonder the same. Who am I now? Different, but who, exactly?

Alice: "I'm afraid I can't explain myself, sir. Because I am not myself, you see."

To find out who I am, I must listen, observe, and take in and take stock. What is and is not important? I still have too much of me wound up in the future, however—and although I crave to see the mouse run up and down the clock and wear himself ragged, I need to spend more time in the present.

I finally understand the current focus on being "present oriented" and "mindful." As it turns out, being in the present is the safest and most productive place for me to be right now. Going back in time or jumping forward will not help me as much as getting grounded in the present. Wiser people than me know this well. I am almost REALLY learning and feeling this for the first time. Before, I could tell you exactly where I was going and how I was going to get there—Now I am learning new ways, paths, and directions. I cannot really say where I will end up.

Cat: "Where are you going?"

Alice: "Which way should I go?"

Cat: "That depends on where you are going."

Alice: "I don't know."

Cat: "Then it doesn't matter which way you go."

Alice: "So long as I get SOMEWHERE."

Cat: "Oh, you're sure to do that, if you only walk long enough."

As it turns out, I have been bracing for more loss. My ninety-one-year-old mother has progressive congestive heart failure, and my thirteen-year-old dog, Jake, almost lost his life two weeks ago. Although I know I am not in control of either of those situations, I am mentally preparing to lose two more beloved souls. "I'm not strange, weird, off, nor crazy; my reality is just different from yours." (The Cheshire Cat)

Human beings are not cut out for such deep loss followed by subsequent multiple losses, so friends and colleagues advise me to stay in the present where I can have a deeper appreciation for life. If truth be told, all this bracing is holding me back from the joy I could be having and the memories I could be making. I am seeking to readjust.

"Well!" thought Alice. "After such a fall as this, I shall think nothing of tumbling down stairs! How brave they'll all think me at home! Why, I wouldn't say anything about it, even if I fell off the top of the house! (which was very likely true)."

How does one become more mindful? What does it mean to live in the present? I have learned a few things that I try to incorporate into my life:

- Breathe purposefully. This sounds so Zen—and I am not Zen—but focusing on the gift of life and simple breathing helps me to focus and let go.
- Focus and listen. Don't automatically jump to think of the next thing to say.
- Stand tall. Posture counts.
- Appreciate. Don't gloss over it. Really see, hear, and state what you appreciate. Abby and I always talk about our favorite things. She is my favorite person.
- Forgive.
- Rid inessentials in work and personal life. If it is negatively distracting you OR not moving you forward productively, ditch it.
- Believe that there are solutions. Just believe—period.
- Laugh when possible. At least smile and pretend. Pretending is okay.
- Suspend judgment (very hard for me in today's political climate, but a bit easier with people in general). I believe that most people act on best intentions.
- Try not to procrastinate. It only adds to your worries.
- Slow down and be more deliberate with actions.
- Meditate and pray.

"Alice pictured to herself how this same little sister of hers would, in the after-time, be herself a grown woman; and how she would keep, through all her riper years, the simple and loving heart of her childhood: and how she would gather about her other little children, and make their eyes bright and eager with many a strange tale, perhaps even with the dream of Wonderland of long ago: and how she would feel with all their simple sorrows, and find a pleasure in all their simple joys, remembering her own child-life, and the happy summer days."[17]

Blessings for Today: "You're thinking about something, my dear, and that makes you forget to talk. I can't tell you just now what the moral of that is, but I shall remember it in a bit."

"Perhaps it hasn't one," Alice ventured to remark.

"Tut, tut, child!" said the Duchess. "Everything's got a moral, if only you can find it."[17]

Specific Prayer Requests: To remain in the present. Psalm 46:10a states, "He says, 'Be still and know that I am God'"

Reflection

I am not very good at being in the present, but it is a pretty good place to be. All my wishing and hoping about the past—well, it's just that. The memories are good—I should never forget the wonderful memories and, of course, the lessons, but the wishing, fretting, and hoping to return to the past are simply wasted moments that I can better use to appreciate the present. Easier said than done. Being in the present takes practice, but positive, present-oriented people serve as my role models. The future is tricky as well. My wishes, dreams, and plans were destroyed in an instant. So, yes, I tread lightly and circumspectly, but I walk with intent and hope. Sometimes I take more steps backwards than forward, but that is changing with time.

***

ENTRY   4/16/2017 at 5:10 p.m.

"TURNING UP THE GRATITUDE DIAL"

So, today is Easter and a beautiful day! It's the warmest Easter I can remember (not including my childhood in Florida), and for Christians, it's a day of joy. Joy—hum—still the one emotion that eludes me. Joy to me means a deeper form of happiness. In other words, you cannot get to joy until you thoroughly practice happiness. Happiness is the bridge to joy.

Every time I see one of my counselors she asks me if I feel joy yet. Joy must be some kind of indicator of something to her, but I'm not sure of what. Maybe one day when I tell her I feel "ever so joyful" she can chalk me up as cured and tell me not to come back anymore. She always asks me how I am doing, which is never a simple answer. The last time she asked me, I responded, "Surely you do not expect me to say, 'Oh, just fine thank you.'" Indeed, she said she did not expect that. Then I suggested that she ask me another way. I sent her my blog on "How to talk to a grieving person." I explained in quite some detail how I was currently feeling, and she labeled me as "progressing." I imagine she wrote "progressing" in her notes about me.

A more meaningful experience occurred during a conference I attended a few weeks ago, where Dr. Brené Brown, a research professor at the University of Houston, served as the keynote. Her TEDx talk, "The Power of Vulnerability,"[18] is one of the five most viewed TED talks in the world with over twenty-five million views. She has written several New York Times best sellers, and knowing her topics and how universally relevant they are to everyone, I can see why they sold well.

Brown's talk was about how courage and vulnerability are needed for leadership. She was spectacular. I had never heard of her, but the minute she began speaking, I felt that she was speaking directly to me (and so did the other one thousand people in the audience). That did not stop me from carrying on a one-on-one conversation with her, albeit, under my breath. I never take notes when someone is speaking, as I am drawn to listening only. (Truthfully, much of the time, I don't think there is much to take notes about.) But with Brown, it was different. I borrowed a few sheets of paper from the woman sitting next to me, and even then, it was not enough.

Brown described courage as "telling your story with all your heart." I had never heard courage described that way, but for the first time, it dawned on me why people were saying I was courageous to share my story through this blog. I never did and still don't consider myself courageous—I am just someone who lost the love of her life and am telling others about my experience. Brown then said that courage requires great vulnerability. I knew what she meant—I am certainly practicing vulnerability. I did not intend to practice vulnerability, but I certainly am.

As a pretty private person, sometimes I shuddered thinking about how everyone knew details about my life from Bob's Facebook posts. A few summers ago, I attended Bob's high school reunion. Complete strangers hugged me, asked when

I would be in Florida again, complimented my work at the Robert Wood Johnson Foundation, noted how much Abby was growing—and much more. It was like an out-of-body experience, where all these Martians were spying on me from outer space and they knew me, but I certainly did not know them—and how in the world did they know all this stuff? FACEBOOK! I never understood the Facebook obsession (it's way too personal), but here I am practicing vulnerability that far exceeds what most Facebook users share. So maybe sharing my story takes courage if it is connected to vulnerability.

Brown then said that courage and vulnerability are absolutely required for leadership, and she quoted Theodore (Teddy) Roosevelt to make her point:

"'It is not the critic who counts; not the man who points out how the strong man stumbles, or where the doer of deeds could have done them better. The credit belongs to the man who is actually in the arena, whose face is marred by dust and sweat and blood; who strives valiantly; who errs, who comes short again and again, because there is no effort without error and shortcoming; but who does actually strive to do the deeds; who knows great enthusiasms, the great devotions; who spends himself in a worthy cause; who at the best knows in the end the triumph of high achievement, and who at the worst, if he fails, at least fails while daring greatly, so that his place shall never be with those cold and timid souls who neither know victory nor defeat."[19]

She maintained that "arena moments"—where you show up as your most authentic self—take courage and vulnerability, and they are necessary for both successful living and leadership. I agreed wholeheartedly. Authenticity. I get how important it is to be authentic. You cannot worry much about what others think, and you shouldn't worry as long as you are presenting your authentic self. You have to learn to take off your armor.

Her words made sense as they related to my circumstances. Then she laid it on me—yes, me alone. She said that only when you are truly vulnerable can you feel joy. What? Did I hear her right? How did she know I was having «joy issues»? I followed her points about courage, vulnerability, and being authentic. In my imagination, I yelled back at her, "How much more vulnerable do you want me to get? Are there deeper depths to this grief and vulnerability stint before I can cross that bridge to joy?"

Brown continued that you cannot feel true love or joy without making yourself vulnerable. And again, I wanted further explanation. I don't understand, I told her. She said that when we lose our tolerance for vulnerability, then joy becomes foreboding. She said some people practice tragedy. They worry about something bad or disappointing happening and cannot let themselves feel joy. Like the mother who loves her kids so much but is held back because she feels like something dangerous will happen to them. Between criminal shows on television and the daily news, we are bombarded with tragedies—and we believe that those things can happen to us, she said. And so we "practice tragedy."

Yes, her research fit with my experience of worrying about losing my mother and dog. Brown said that we think we can beat vulnerability to the punch if we protect ourselves emotionally. I thought of my own hesitancy after losing Bob to feel joy and have it ripped back away from me yet again. I experienced the mother of all rips—painfully so—and I don't want to experience that pain ever again.

Humans are not hardwired for bracing or preparing for tragedy, Brown said, and as much as we try to protect ourselves, we will feel pain whether or not we brace for it. We miss out on joy along the way if we put too much emotional energy into bracing.

Brown went on to say that the number one ingredient in feeling joy is "practicing gratitude." That is what meditation or prayer is about—or partially, right? Being grateful and thanking God. Before the accident, I was grateful, but probably not as much as I should have been. My gratitude meter is all out of kilter now—it is not easy to turn up the gratitude dial when you are not feeling grateful. I remind myself that even if I am not grateful about a really big thing, I can be grateful for smaller things. The point is that practicing gratitude brings joy.

So why is this so hard for me? Why?

Blessings for Today: That I have the opportunity to learn joy from some of the best. I made a conscious decision to surround myself with some really joyful people in my life. Even if I cannot be grateful for having Bob taken from me, I can be grateful for many other things. My mother is still with me. When I finish writing, I will take Jake for a walk. I was with my grandchildren today, and Abby told me she loved me.

Specific Prayer Requests: To really acknowledge what I have on more of a daily basis. That a sense of gratitude comes more naturally and more often. James 1:2–3 beg us to, "Consider it pure joy, my brothers and sisters, whenever you face trials of many kinds, because you know that the testing of your faith produces perseverance." And Psalm 126:5 says, "Those who sow with tears will reap with songs of joy." Finally, Proverbs 15:15 says, "All the days of the oppressed are wretched, but the cheerful heart has a continual feast."

Reflection

I see how joy works, but it is elusive. It is easier for me to make a conscious decision to be grateful and really mean it. Expressing gratitude comes easier to some people, and not all situations or people are created equal. Some very wealthy people who have gone to the best colleges and hold the highest positions in this country don't appear to be very grateful. All you have to do is man the local suicide line to observe that the least grateful are not always the most downtrodden, the poorest, or those who have suffered the greatest losses. Many times those who have less exhibit more gratitude and joy. With a conscious effort and practice, people can learn to be truly grateful.

***

ENTRY   4/24/2017 at 8:12 a.m.

"DOING WHAT MATTERS"

If birds of a feather flock together, I am one lucky bird. I hang out with some pretty awesome people—people who give back in meaningful ways and care for

others in their community as naturally as they brush their teeth in the morning. As described in The Wizard of Oz, they are good deed doers.

Fortunately, I don't hang out with people who compare houses, cars, clothing, jewelry, or external appearances, although many of my friends have their own sly way of comparing kids. I understand that, but I don't necessarily go there. I have, unapologetically, however, gone there in describing Bob, and of course, I love to describe how special my grandchildren are. But back to doing what matters.

When tragedy strikes in the form of death, divorce, or serious illness, people often reassess their lives and what's important to them. It's a healthy reaction. Nothing is the same, really. It can't be. Maybe down the road Bob would go before me since he was over seven years older than me and a man (genetics against him, so to speak). But that was only on paper, mind you. I never contemplated Bob leaving when we both still had so much living left. Perhaps it was too scary and way too big to think about. I had my job, grandchildren, and other things to keep me occupied—who has time for "what ifs?"

Sure, I told him that I could never go on without him, but those were words. Heartfelt words—yes—but still just words. You simply cannot imagine what it's like to lose a spouse until it happens, and then it slams you against the wall and beats you bloody until you somehow say out loud that you really believe it. You don't believe it in the beginning, but at some point you say, okay, I guess this is really it, and that's when I began to search for my purpose and determining what really matters.

Fortunately, as I considered how Bob would want me to carry on, I realized that what he would want was completely congruent with how I thought I should carry on. That's what made us so darn compatible. Our ideals, values, morals and wants were aligned. The one big thing we differed on was whether I could make it without him: I said I could not, and he said of course I could.

So, what mattered to us? Family first, of course. I would treasure and spend time with our very tiny family. When they needed me, I would go. I would bring them together and recall the good times (so hard without Bob). I can share some memories with them that include you, of course—our trips with Robin and Ralph and Jean and Greg and our kids. They could recall some good times that we shared, but what about the memories that are only special to Bob and me? Who will care about those memories? Most of my memories include Bob and me. Who will care?

There was the time we got lost in a forest in New Hampshire and starting planning how we would make it through the night. Bob said he would give me his jacket, and I talked about making a bed of leaves for us. We chose the trees that might give us the best shelter. We started searching for food. But then as dusk fell, we found our way out. We were walking in circles the whole time. No one else cares about that story and our elation and sense of accomplishment at finding our way back to civilization.

What about the time that Bob took me on the Tower of Terror at Disney World (a ride that slowly ascends twenty stories and then accelerates towards the ground). I was so scared and could not yell, but I bit Bob's shoulder so hard on the way down that it bled. We laughed about that all the time. Who else would find humor in a bite mark?

Or the time that Jake chased a pack of deer into the woods, and we thought we would never see him again, and we had to practice how we would tell my mother how we lost the dog. But there he was waiting at the car for us after we had hiked in the woods for two hours looking for him. We never forgot that story.

And how we drove off from our wedding with me hanging out the window, veil flying in the breeze, yelling at everyone we passed, "Look at me—look at the bride!" Bob loved it! Whenever I got angry with him, he reminded me how happy I was at our wedding.

And how many times did he ask me to buy a bikini because I was the most beautiful woman in the entire world and I would look good in a bikini? I always yelled back, "Are you crazy? Are you blind? Are you nuts? I would never wear a bikini!" No one else really cares, although I would guess that most people would understand my pushback. Oh, the sheer horror of it!

What else matters? Having a mission-oriented job. Money is necessary, but doing something—really doing something—to help people was very important to us. The nuance for me now is that I need to help in ways that I never thought of before the accident. Because I saw firsthand how few family members were actively involved in their loved one's care, I feel compelled to speak out about the importance of making sure that patients and family members have positive patience experiences—ones in which people believe that the health system is easy to access and navigate; that their needs are being met; and that they are being heard, respected, and able to contribute to decisions related to their own care. I am emphasizing the importance of health professionals exhibiting compassion and incorporating positive patient experiences into their health system's culture as part of the Robert Wood Johnson Foundation's mission to provide everyone in America a fair and just opportunity for health and well-being.

Volunteering with the Red Cross still matters, too. Bob always carried his Red Cross card in his wallet, and it was still there when the nurse at the hospital trauma unit handed me his wallet—a reminder of what was important to us. Rest assured that I will continue our volunteer work. I want to do more to touch and help people on the front lines like Bob did. He was the front-line guy (picture of him at a house fire), and I was the policy person who secretly felt most fulfilled on the front lines. I will cherish meeting the first recipient of the Bob Hassmiller Red Cross Award for Excellence in Disaster Service being awarded this October. The people who receive Bob's award each year will remind me of how important excellence in volunteerism is, and especially, the importance of the Red Cross mission.

Staying as healthy as possible mattered a lot to us. We were not really known for eating as healthy as possible—I was better than Bob in that department and always seemed to find where he stashed the Doritos and Snicker bars. He eventually superseded me with exercise, and that's part of the reason why I take issue with the unfairness of losing him. We loved walking, hiking, dancing, swimming, and biking. I'll be darned if anyone could out-exercise us at our age.

We were always the first ones on the dance floor. Although we took dance lessons, we just found our own way to move to the music. All that mattered was that I could lead while pretending that Bob was—our little secret. I don't suppose people saw me counting in Bob's ear or tugging on his arm, do you? I miss dancing the most.

We both took helping the next generation very seriously. Maybe it was our age, but we also realized that we could give a small boost to some of the many gifted and talented young people to help them transition into adulthood and do important work that would benefit our world. My former pastor who married Bob and me called yesterday and said that he had just heard what happened to Bob. He was heartbroken and crying. He said the most important thing that he remembers about Bob, other than his intelligence and sense of humor, was the way Bob helped his son, Charles. The pastor said that Charles had a very shaky entrance into young adulthood, and Bob showed him time and again what was important in life and how to achieve your dreams.

Finally, I am channeling Bob when I say that my purpose must be to go on and make Bob proud. Bob always said that he was proud of me, and he had faith in me. He believes that I can carry on again, and I must not forget my faith—that faith in God will help me. I need strength to face life without Bob.

Sure, I still think that losing Bob was unfair, but he would say that life is not always fair—that I still must go on and help and influence others for the good. I will do that. I will take to heart the words from *Hamilton's* "The World Was Wide Enough—" a song with the lyrics, "Legacy, what is a legacy? It's planting seeds in a garden that you never get to see."[20] I want our garden from the seeds that Bob and I have planted to be exquisite and a garden that keeps on giving—that's what matters.

Blessings for Today: I am eternally grateful for my health, brain, and life, and that I have the ability and wherewithal to ponder what matters. I want to always act on what matters. In addition to Bob, a number of people I know live what matters to them, and they serve as role models for me.

Specific Prayer Requests: That I remain focused on what really matters in life, and that I stay true to my morals, ideals and faith. That I might be given opportunities to act on what matters. Action counts. Proverbs 3:27 says, "Do not withhold good from those to whom it is due, when it is in your power to act."

Reflection

I am still desperate to never forget the great love of my life, and I always seek tangible ways to remember him by honing in on what brought us together and kept us together all those years: the core value of giving back. Remembering causes me to renew my promise to keep our core value of giving back alive.

***

ENTRY   5/4/2017 at 10:38 a.m.

"PURPLE IS THE NEW PINK"

One of the things that I miss most about my husband's physical departure is our conversations. Even when I traveled, we spoke constantly. When I began traveling two decades ago as part of my work at the Robert Wood Johnson Foundation, we got into the habit of calling each other when it was time for a walk. We talked every day, while we walked, about our current happenings. He was my true friend.

The other night, I dreamt that someone in thin striped hot pink corduroy pants (already a sign that this person was NOT to be trusted) told me that he had taken away Bob as my husband, but that I could still have him as my friend. I yelled, calling him a liar and cheat. I said that when he took Bob away, he took away my friend. The person insisted that I could still have a friend without having a husband, and the yelling continued until I woke up and the dream ended.

I was content with the rhythm of work, travel, friends, love, family—and yes, overcoming the challenges that came our way. My life was fairly predictable. Mark your calendars, and it will unfold as expected. We had many things to look forward to, and we felt joy. My friend and I felt joy. Something that has eluded me now and for the unforeseen future.

Last week I came home from a week-long series of events around the country with a heart that was bursting. I presented in San Diego and New Orleans and saw many colleagues for the first time since the accident. I was warmly embraced by so many. I received a Life Time Achievement award from the Association of

Public Health Nurses, and the monetary contributions from the award will go to the Red Cross. I was struck so many times by the care and concern in action that my colleagues showed.

To top it all off, during a question and answer session after I had given my presentation in Louisiana, a woman who I did not know well named Cheryl, took the microphone and said in front of everyone that she appreciated my being there considering the tragedy. She said how strong I was to be back talking about how nurses can build a Culture of Health in our country. She said that she had been praying for me each and every day since the accident and would continue to do so. She went on to say that she wished me the best and that I should not give up ever because the world needed me. Cheryl handed me a notebook to journal in, a book about never giving up, and a back scratcher—all reminders to be gentle with myself going forward and to never give up. Wow! My heart was very full and happy.

When I returned home, I could not wait to call Kim and Lori to tell them about the kindnesses extended to me. I was overcome with gratitude. I spared no details. Kim cried, as she worries about me all the time, and expressed happiness that others would remind me of what a wonderful man Bob was. We left it at that.

Lori's response after I told her everything was to say, "I hear joy." When I said nothing, she exclaimed, "Did you hear me? I said I hear joy in your voice." I reminded her that joy is a sacred word to me—and struck back that this was not joy that I felt.

Of course, when you have been friends for forty-three years, you pretty much have permission to say what you want, and Lori is allowed to cross intimate boundaries. She said, "You are too busy looking for pink when the new color is purple." When I asked her to explain, she said, joy can come in different colors. I was looking for the old joy that I had, and that color was pink. She told me that I will not experience joy in pink again. However, I could behold new joy. It may not look like or be the color of my old joy, but I could find new joy in purple. She said that I needed to stop looking for pink and start looking for purple. I knew what she meant.

If you find me taking special note of something like the fox mother playing in my backyard with her two babies, or saying no to a work-related event in favor of a walk or being with my grandchildren, then you will know that I am desperately searching for purple.

Blessings for Today: That friends took me hiking in New Mexico and I hung from a tree. To look at the picture, it appears that purple may be on the horizon… at least it was for that moment. That Lori can say anything she darn well pleases to me. That with practiced gratitude and a mind shift, I may be able to see at least some shades of purple.

Specific Prayer Requests: More purple. Although I will never forget the wonders of pink. I am still sorrowful. Proverbs 15:13 tells us, "A happy heart makes the face cheerful, but heartache crushes the spirit." Psalm 33:3 says, "Sing to him a new song; play skillfully, and shout for joy."

Reflection

I cannot say that joy has returned, but I make myself look for it in small ways. I have to call it out and name it, or else it escapes me as yet another normal occurrence. My granddaughter made a joke and laughed so hard at herself that she fell down laughing. This is purple. Someone came up to me after a presentation I gave to say that my words will make a lasting impression on her life. This is purple. A sunset broke through the black clouds. This is purple. If I don't name it, then I will never experience joy again. Purple is the new pink.

***

ENTRY   5/7/2017 at 9:39 p.m.

"THE MIRACLE OF NURSE ABBY"

Over the months Nurse Abby and I kept in touch loosely. She explained how Bob's accident and reading about Bob through the blog always served as a reminder of the importance compassion makes in the lives of her patients. I was struck by the enormity of her words and her actions and the place she held in my heart, so I asked her if she would come to lunch. I wanted to see her, thank her, and

search for more answers. So, today Nurse Abby joined my family for lunch. It also seemed fitting to get together with her during National Nurses Week.

I was nervous to see Nurse Abby. I don't get nervous much, but I think I was unsettled about the connection she held between Bob and me and the meaning I place on that connection. Issa, my hairdresser, said I was crazy to have her over. "Why would you want to pick on a wound that is so desperately trying to heal?" he asked. I told him that I realized that seeing Nurse Abby would cause me to reflect on the past, but I felt strongly that Bob and God had brought her into my life, and I wanted to honor that intention.

At church that morning, a guest pastor spoke about the meaning of the word miracle. He said that we need to be open to miracles happening in our lives— to listen and be alert for how God might be pointing things out or otherwise directing us. He also said there might be miracles in our lives, but unless we are action-oriented about how we respond, we could miss out on the miracle's intended effect. With the pastor's advice tucked away, I hurried home to wait for Nurse Abby with my family. I paced at the front window, and after three false starts of "I think she's here now," she finally arrived.

We gathered around her to convey how special a day this was for us. We wanted to express our gratitude to her and probe how Bob impacted her and ask why she reached out to me in the first place. She saw many patients and families during her shifts. What made her do this? What did she know about Bob that we did not know, but would want to know?

My little granddaughter Abby was thrilled to have a bigger girl with long hair just like hers with the same name in my home. Abby showed Nurse Abby pictures of her Pops.

What struck me first was Nurse Abby's confidence and intelligence. I pictured her, as she described her job as a nurse anesthetist, as imminently qualified to be at the bedside where the most harrowing events unfold. I saw her cool and assured attitude come through. I could picture Bob feeling safe in her care. Nurse Abby described Bob as calm and peaceful, which immediately made him stand out in a very different way as a trauma victim. She said that Bob described what happened to him and everything he felt and could not feel. Nurse Abby was the last person to hear Bob speak.

She could not explain the pull she felt to contact me, other than that Bob reminded her of her own fit father who liked to stay active. She described how she spoke to Bob to reassure him. She said she visited Bob at 2:00 a.m. (long after I had been taken home) to check in on him and to convey that she had met me in the conference room and that family and friends were taking care of me. She wanted to make sure Bob knew this because she knew this mattered to him, and he blinked hard to let Nurse Abby know that he understood. She said his eyes were telling and she could detect a smile in them.

After Nurse Abby found out that we had transferred Bob to another hospital, her gnawing feeling began again, and she felt she must reach out to me to tell me more. She searched my name on the Internet and found me and this blog. She didn't know I was a nurse—she thought I was just a loving wife.

Nurse Abby said that many nurses probably get that gnawing feeling to reach out to family members on occasion, but for a number of reasons they don't. She acted on what she knew (just like the pastor spoke about at church this morning) and contacted me. She felt that she had to act, and she did. She said our circumstances prompted her to make changes in her life with her own marriage, and she did. Because Nurse Abby acted, a number of emotional band aids began to cover some of the many wounds in our hearts. I believe that as Nurse Abby watched the video slide show that we presented at Bob's memorial service and the tears welled up in her eyes, she too felt that this meeting and our lives were destined to connect.

So, I hold onto the miracle of this strong human connection that one nurse made with one patient and his family. Nurse Abby and I talked about the importance of making human connections in real time in the clinical setting. We talked about the current stresses on nurses and the pull of their computers and the boxes they must check to legally get through their shifts and how distracting technology and paperwork can be in forming a healing human connection. Yet, nurses still have that opportunity and the choice whether or not to make a human connection is theirs. If they do, then it will make all the difference in the world.

Blessings for Today: Meeting Nurse Abby today and being so grateful for what she shared with us—Bob's words, her words to Bob, and her own growth as a nurse and human being. I am grateful for her ongoing care for us, and we for her. We will remain connected.

Specific Prayer Requests: For those who need healing—that they will have someone in their lives who will make an empathic connection. That Nurse Abby and I will jointly find ways to share our story. For nurses—that they spark the human connection that is so vital in healing. Famed author C.S. Lewis wrote, "Miracles are a retelling in small letters of the very same story, which is written across the whole world in letters too large for some of us to see."

Reflection

Nurse Abby is a miracle—a surprising and welcome event unexplained by scientific laws and therefore considered an event brought forth by a divine agency. There is no other way to explain her presence in Bob's and my life. I hold firmly to the notion that Bob brought me this gift, and it remains a comforting thought that I hold dear. I hold Nurse Abby up as the ideal of what a nurse can and should be—efficient, smart, effective, and compassionate. I am blessed to still have her in my life, as we continue to bring our story of this miracle connection and the message of compassion to large nursing audiences nationwide. We include Nurse Kathy as well. She too, is an exemplar of extraordinary nursing care, both proficient and compassionate.

***

ENTRY   5/13/2017 at 10:20 p.m.

"HOW I BECAME A MOTHER"

More than anything in the whole world, I wanted to be a mother. Yes, I wanted to be married, but I have to admit that I was probably one of those women who would have bypassed a man (if the right one had not come along), to fulfill the dream of becoming a mother. In fact, I am sure of it. But when I met Bob I knew that in short order, God willing, I would take on the role of motherhood.

However, the doctor told us the year we were married that we could not have children. A big reason for living—to love another more than yourself, to instill lessons, to experience joy, hugs, and kisses more than you ever imagined. No one could take this dream away from me. How could they?

It was a very hard time that tested our relationship, but Bob never lost hope or his sense of humor. In the midst of my depression, tears, and obsession about motherhood, he promised to fulfill my dream—no matter what!

In vitro fertilization had been invented a few years earlier and was not nearly the common procedure it is today. However, Bob relayed his own dream of one day adopting a child. After being in Vietnam and seeing so many orphaned children, he hoped to one day adopt. Bob opened my eyes to new possibilities. With his optimism and both of our hearts full of love, we explored adoption.

In early January of 1982, we applied to the largest adoption agency in the Midwest, Child Saving Institute. We lived in Lincoln, Nebraska. We told no one, except for each of our two best friends at the time, Jane and Dave and Linda and David, who served as our references. We didn't think it was anyone's business, and besides, we did not want to answer the barrage of personal questions that we knew would come with divulging our decision to adopt. We also did not want our hopes to get dashed with family and friends constantly asking if we had heard yet from the agency.

The agency told us it would take between two and five years before we heard back from them. We continued on with our careers while secretly and desperately waiting with silence in our hearts.

A few months after we applied, the adoption agency asked if they could perform an experiment with us. The video camcorder was just being introduced, and they wanted to film Bob and me as we explained why we were pursuing adoption. At the time, birth mothers usually chose adoptive parents after reading through applications in a book (birth fathers usually were not involved). The applications generally showed pictures of the prospective couple and described them, their home life, careers, hopes and dreams for a child, and much more. Birth mothers would have the opportunity to watch our video instead of reading through our written application.

Unfair advantage? Perhaps. I prefer to think of it as being meant to be. The agency held off on videotaping others until they saw how our experience went. They said we came across well. It was evident that we loved each other from the way we held hands while describing our dream of holding an infant in our arms.

I described how much I loved watching the kids at our church sing a special Mother's Day song to the mothers in the congregation. With tears, I said how much it would mean to me to hear my own child sing that song one day. Bob described how he would guide the child with morals and integrity and provide a sound education. Who knows what the clincher was, but within a few months (as opposed to two to five years!), on July 1, 1982, we received a call that would forever change our lives.

Tomorrow we were to pick up a newborn daughter. I was to be a mother!

After a rather sleepless night of wondering how we were to care for a newborn with zero preparation in the house, we journeyed to Omaha. I wanted to name our daughter Kimberly Ruth, and Bob wanted to name her Rachel. We know who won that one. What made the day we met our daughter even more special was how exhilarated Bob was for me. He was happy to become a father, but he was equally happy to finally see me so happy and fulfilled. When the caseworker brought out Kimmy, Bob told her, "Give her to Susie—this is her dream, and this will be her love."

They left us alone to bond. It took me—well, is there anything less than a second? Several minutes later, I offered Kimmy to Bob. He said that he was enjoying watching the two of us and knew his turn would come soon enough.

We brought two-day-old Kimberly Ruth Hassmiller to her forever home. Nearly three years later, on April 22, 1985, Mark Robert Hassmiller became a son to us and a brother to Kimmy. I could not imagine loving any children more than I loved Kimmy and Mark.

For the next thirty-four years, Bob celebrated the gift of motherhood on Mother's Day. Don't get me wrong—he loved Father's Day, but he cherished seeing the woman he loved be reminded every year of how her dream of becoming a mother was fulfilled. Every year, Bob presented me with a beautiful card and bouquet of flowers. He also never forgot flowers and a card for my mother, who has lived with us for around thirty years.

This year, I have my children, but it is not the same without Bob wishing me a Happy Mother's Day and telling me what a great mother I have been. He knew better than anyone what being a mother meant to me.

I did not think this Mother's Day would be hard, because after all, it is my day. It is hard though—very hard. Bob was the only witness to my becoming a mother. He saw the tears, the first touch, and the love I felt for Kim and for Mark. He also witnessed the challenging times when I might have questioned my motherhood—but he never wavered in his firm commitment that I was the best he had ever seen. I waivered at times, but he never did.

So, on this Mother's Day, I will get out the card that he gave me last year. In that card, he reminded me of the unique love that we shared—that I was his best friend, as well as the best wife and mother in the whole world. I think he would consider it still valid.

I also think that he would like me to have flowers, so I will buy some tomorrow and pretend that he left them out for me. Shhh—don't tell—it's a surprise. I will also get my mother her usual flowers.

Blessings for Today: That I am a mother. That my Kimmy is a mother. That my mother is here today, at ninety-one, to celebrate with us. And that Bob thinks we are all the best mothers ever!

Specific Prayer Requests: That I might continue to understand the needs and desires of my children and to continue to fulfill my responsibilities as a mother. Some of this is easy, and some is hard. That my children remain upstanding citizens of our nation and that they stand on their own and give back to others. Proverbs 31:28 says, "Her children arise and call her blessed; her husband also, and he praises her."

Reflection

I ache knowing that the person who was there rooting for me most on my first Mother's Day and every one thereafter is no longer here. No one was ever happier for me, and no one really knew and felt the full extent that the blessings of children brought to my life. I now call upon Bob and his best friend, God, for their guidance as I continue to parent two adult children.

***

ENTRY   6/3/2017 at 10:17 a.m.

"FIRSTS"

This year is like starting over in most respects—it is a year of firsts. I was married for a longer time in my life than I was single, so this is a year of firsts without my best friend. In addition to my ordinary life of work and carrying on, I have nervously (and with sadness) anticipated the first of any upcoming event that I will mark without Bob. I prepare for it as best as I can and am as protective of my heart as I can be.

What does it mean to be protective? It means that sadness and hurt will reawaken in me as an event draws near, and I simply accept these feelings and let them settle in. I have no choice. I also spend time remembering and reflecting what it was like the last time Bob and I experienced the event together. I feel glimpses of the joy we shared, and I try to harness that joy to protect me. I am fully aware that as I protect myself, I must let just enough of the past joy in to bolster my stamina—a strange balancing act, of which I am still standing wobbly on one foot. Importantly, I call upon friends and family to help me. They are a big part of my protection strategy. Some anticipate my pain, but mostly around big events or holidays.

Firsts come in categories divided by tasks and events. Everything in the task category is either hard, anxiety provoking, depressing, anger evoking or just plain annoying. Once I figure out how to complete the task and muddle my way through it, I feel relief. Tasks range from handling my finances to figuring out repairs to being my mother's primary caregiver. The endless task list fills up the time that I used to spend on more productive and enjoyable efforts.

The only thing that differentiates the task category from the event category is the meaning that I place on certain events and the intensity of emotions that surround these events. I often feel anxiety, sadness, and depression, but I can half smile and feel grateful when I reflect on past events and holidays and recall the happiness and joy I felt. I reconnect slightly with that joy—enough to keep me standing. More joy will come later, I know. It takes time. Don't force this on me now.

Some event firsts are big, like the holidays, including Mother's Day and my birthday, but some firsts are ordinary. I continually miss Bob during the ordinary times—the ones that we never really pay attention to except when they are gone. These are the times that most of us surely take for granted. The first time waking up without him, walking my dog without him, going grocery shopping without him, watching the grandchildren without him, and coming home from work and not having him to call to tell him I would be home in a few minutes. I called him anyways, and when I heard his voice on the answering machine, I berated him for not picking up and being at the other end when I needed him the most. Why are you not here? I asked him. What happened? I want to tell Bob what it is like without him, but I can't.

The first time I watched the sun rise at our lake without him and the first time I watched the sun set on our beach in Naples, I realized that I will experience these very ordinary events alone again and again. I check off the boxes for all of the hundreds of firsts—check, check, check. Sadness and relief.

Firsts are a big topic of conversation in my grief support group—made up of extraordinary people who I only occasionally get to meet with now due to my work schedule. We help each other with firsts. The hardest firsts are wedding anniversaries and the anniversaries of the day our spouses left us. I dread these days the most—more than any other holiday. I feel speechless and crumbled to tears just to think of their meaning and the void I feel. I cry tears of joy for what I had and tears of utter sadness for the void—devastating sadness. Monday is an anniversary for one of our members, so we will go to dinner to lend support and listen to what it's like and hear what a wonderful person Joe was. We take stock of and respect our firsts.

Bob always said that I was the happiest he had ever seen me on our wedding day, July 4. He used to point to a picture in our living room of us on our wedding day. I am flashing the biggest smile ever just in case anyone needed proof. When I was angry at him, he reminded me of that day and showed me the picture. He always told everyone that he lost his independence on July 4th and shared the story of how I dressed him and what I made him do!

Six months prior to our big day, I saw a man on the front of Bride Magazine who was dressed in white pants; a red and white pin-striped shirt; a red, white and blue bow tie; a bright red jacket; and a straw hat. Bob said he would not be caught dead wearing something akin to the Good Humor Man, but he appeared on that day the spitting image of the man on the cover of Bride Magazine—mind you, just to prove to the world that he had truly in this one act, given himself over to me.

Now I am flying home from the International Council of Nurses Congress in Barcelona—a trip Bob was supposed to join me on. We made plans—as we loved to do—to sightsee, to round out our time in Spain. I traveled by myself—another first—an overseas trip without him. I didn't have anyone to help me to line up people to check on my mother and walk the dog. I paid the bills on time, took out the garbage, converted the money, scanned my passport, and constructed an itinerary. I sat by myself on the airplane and didn't hold anyone's hand. When the customs agents asked if I was traveling alone, I looked around and said, "Yes I am."

I also must remember my dear friend Lori's words that purple is the new pink. I saw my first Flamenco dance, and it was unbelievably beautiful. I visited Montserrat and felt the spirituality of the abbey and the hike up the mountain. When I told Jean, my friend who met me in Barcelona, that Bob would have loved being at Montserrat, she said, "Then by all means, enjoy it for Bob as well." She always knows what to say.

Blessings for Today: Having been married to a man who loved me so much and who thought I was changing the world. He was proud of me, and I will keep trying to do good to honor his spirit. I am grateful to Jean for having such a generous heart and caring for me in Barcelona. For finding (and buying) a cross at the Montserrat Abbey made of purple mosaic to remind me that purple is the new pink. For Mark and Amanda, Mark's girlfriend, for checking in on my mother to make sure she was safe and for not letting my flowers die while I was away. I have a big issue with things dying.

Specific Prayer Requests: That I continue to take the time I need to reflect on my life and learn, live, and love as a result of these reflections. Isaiah 43:19 reads, "See, I am doing something new! Now it springs up; do you not perceive it? I am making a way in the wilderness and streams in the wasteland."

Grieving is a process. You hurt deeply as you mark events, both small and large, that come and go. In the beginning, I only felt pain, but as the same events come around again, the sharp edges soften. Light seeps in. Gratefulness comes easier to some than others, but with practice, a broken heart can mend. The scars are always there, though. My heart was shattered, but now it beats again and holds treasured memories.

***

ENTRY   6/22/2017 at 9:53 a.m.

"PRAYING FOR CHALLENGES"

Bob was infamous in our family for praying for challenges. We did not always pray before eating, but Bob usually prayed on special occasions, before Abby went to bed, or with our kids when they were growing up. Inevitably, he offered thanks for blessings and then thanked God for our challenges and those that were still to come.

Kim, Mark, and I always held our breath when Bob prayed, waiting and knowing that he would offer a special thank you for our challenges and hardships. We never got it, but Bob was not deterred. Our typical response was to roll our eyes, snicker, or just let Bob have his peace with his words and his God.

I asked him once why he always thanked God for challenges and hardships when I just wanted to make them all disappear—and as quickly as possible! Bob always said that our greatest growth occurred during our trials—as long as we remained open to lessons. Sometimes we would not know immediately what the lessons were, but eventually we would if we were attuned to them.

Successful individuals have also voiced gratitude for their hardships. In his 2005 Stanford commencement address, Steve Jobs said, "I didn't see it then, but it turned out that getting fired from Apple was the best thing that could have ever happened to me. The heaviness of being successful was replaced by the lightness of being a beginner again, less sure about everything. It freed me to enter one of the most creative periods of my life."21 Oprah Winfrey is another example. As she so often stated on television, she went on to help countless millions through lessons learned from her own tribulations of abuse, rejection, and economic hardship.

The more Bob prayed, the more it seemed that his prayers were answered: Our blessings were interspersed with challenges—and pain. Annoying! Mark, Kim, and I wondered if our challenges would decrease if Bob stopped thanking God for our hardships. We never found out, however, because Bob never stopped. He lived every day grateful for what he had—pain and no pain.

Abby was too young to see the dynamic tension in these prayers and just accepted them as part of her bedtime ritual. "Good night, sleep tight, don't let the bed bugs bite, have sweet sweet dreams, and remember that we love you, Abigail Grace Oley, so very, very, very, very, very, very much. Amen! And by the way, Dear God, thank you for the challenges we are facing in our lives—and help us to deal with and learn from all of them."

Bob also appreciated challenges that arose as part of his work as the CEO of two national associations. After a short period of grumbling, he reminded me (as a way of bolstering his own beliefs I suppose), that anyone could be a good or adequate leader when there was smooth sailing. The real test for great leaders was in developing strategies and tactics to navigate the ship during storms and rocky patches. Bob wanted to be a noteworthy, if not a great leader, and learning from challenges would help him to be that and more

Bob took his mantra from some of the best leaders in the world who experienced significant hardship, including Nelson Mandela, Martin Luther King, and Franklin and Eleanor Roosevelt. Even Theodore Roosevelt, who was also no stranger to adversity, said: "Nothing in the world is worth having or worth doing unless it means effort, pain, difficulty.... I have never in my life envied a human being who led an easy life. I have envied a great many people who led difficult lives and led them well."

I, on the other hand, never saw the logic in asking for challenges. What's so wrong with an easy life? Why ask for more challenges when the lot we had was perfectly adequate? Aren't there great leaders who have not been inundated with trials and tribulations? What I did not FULLY appreciate about experiencing hardship is the growth and learning that result from the experience. Bob did not relish the challenges either, but he appreciated the growth that resulted. The two were inextricably connected, and he accepted that.

So, where am I now with all of this growth from challenges and pain business? I get it. I don't like it. I hate it. And I certainly am not in the frame of mind to thank God for all that has happened to Bob, nor do I think I ever will be. BUT I have learned more about life, other people, myself, and my spirit than ever before. I would not wish the sudden loss of a soulmate on anyone, but I dare say that I have experienced an awakening that cannot be quelled. For one, I have seen a good and beautiful side of humanity and heard stories and learned lessons that I never knew existed.

Blessings for Today: I am NOT going to thank God for what happened. I AM grateful, however, for the many people who have come into my life to share kindness and their own stories and lessons. I am also grateful for the opportunity to take some of these lessons and act on them. I am an action-oriented person, and I know myself enough to know that enacting these lessons (the ones I am able to discern and understand—there are many that I don't) will bring me some semblance of peace.

Specific Prayer Requests: That I am able to find as much meaning as possible in this tragedy and apply the lessons I have learned to help others. I understand that much will be left as unraveled threads, but help me to take what I can of the tapestry to have faith and bring meaning to the lives of others. Romans 5: 3–4 states, "Not only so, but we also glory in our sufferings, because we know that suffering produces perseverance; perseverance, character; and character, hope."

Reflection

Bob's gratitude for his challenges is perhaps his greatest legacy. He helped me to unravel the secrets of a life well lived. No life will ever be without challenges, but a person's response to those challenges prods growth. Clearly, those who walk this earthly journey with some semblance of joy are the ones who have figured this out. It is one thing to agree in theory with the premise of being grateful for challenges, but it takes a special person to truly practice this and believe down to her very soul that not only does a better person lie within, but one enshrouded with hope.

***

ENTRY   7/4/2017 at 10:22 p.m.

"JULY 3–4, 2017"

My first wedding anniversary without Bob has arrived. Months ago, I invited Karen and Kristen, my sister-in-law and niece who cared for me while Bob was in the ICU, to visit with their families. Kristen arrived the evening of July 2nd with her husband Stephen and their three kids, ages six, eight, and ten. Karen came on July 3rd.

Other than the times that I thought of Bob, the weekend was magical. We spent July 3rd at the Jersey Shore. Could I describe it any better than to say that we ate ice cream twice? I went in and out—happy to be with family—but sad that Bob was not here to enjoy it with us. Leaving the shore, I got an additional treat when Kim decided that Abby should spend the night with me. Kim knows my heart and tries to protect it when she can. While I drove home from the shore, Abby and Felix, Kristen's six-year-old son, chatted in the back seat. Abby told six-year-old Felix about her Pops.

Abby: My Pops hurt himself when he fell off of his bike. I miss my Pops very much.

Felix: Is your Pops still alive?

Abby: No, he is in heaven, and he takes care of me.

Felix: I once had a great uncle who also died after he fell off of his bicycle. His name was Uncle Bob.

Abby: My Pops' name was Bob, too.

Felix: Oh, they were both named Bob. HUM...

When we arrived home, I tucked Abby in and sang her, "You Can Close Your Eyes" by James Taylor—a song that Bob and I sang to Kim and Mark when they were children and later to Abby.

I sang, "The sun is slowly sinking down, and the moon is surely rising, so this ole world must still be spinning round, and I still love you. So, close your eyes, you can close your eyes. It's all right…Well it won't be long before another day, we gonna have a good time, and no one's gonna take that time away. You can stay as long as you like."[22]

I tell her as I do every day that God and Pops love her so much, and they will always take care of her. Amen.

That night, I didn't sleep well. I dreamt that I was cheating on Bob with another man, but that other man was Bob. He played my husband and my lover. I tried to explain to both men that I loved them both, but I was frustrated because I could not explain my feelings adequately to either of them, and the situation seemed hopeless. I woke up frustrated and could not explain the dream other than that it dealt with loss. Abby woke up and climbed into bed with me to hug me. She saved me for the moment.

As we left the bedroom for breakfast, Abby looked at a photo of Bob and told me that she was going to say good morning to Pops and that I should as well. I glanced at Abby and the photo of Bob and started to cry. When I told Abby that I missed Pops, she said that it was okay because I could look at all of the photos of him. She pointed each one out to me, as if to say that yes, he was missed, but not for a lack of pictures. The moment passed, and we walked the dogs.

Later that day, I hosted friends and family, who I chose specifically to bolster the infrastructure, so to speak. There was utter chaos with Kim, Matt, Abby, and John; Kristen and her family; Karen; Mark and Amanda and her two-year-old twins; my neighbors, Robin and Ralph; my mother; and two dogs. There was plenty of food, activities, care, and love.

Even with the company, my mind drifted in and out to our wedding. I had three people in our wedding party, and Bob had two. It was already going to cost them a lot to come to Nebraska, so we told them to wear anything red, white or blue that they already owned. I had a dream (or was it a nightmare?) a week before the wedding that everyone wore mismatched clothing. I left that as the dream, but otherwise, I really did not sweat much about it. There was no big fuss of the kind of weddings you see today, or at least the kind my daughter had! We had our church and pastor, and we rented out the ballroom at the local Hilton. I sent out invitations that announced, "On July 4th I Will Marry My Best Friend". Everyone just crashed at my house. There weren't any wedding buses to take people around. There were no wedding directors and no drama, except that I had to keep my mother and father apart—the result of a very messy divorce.

Our wedding was small. Most of our friends were now in Nebraska. Karen came with her kids, Kristen and Bobby (ages six and two, who were our flower girl and ring bearer), and her new husband Ray, and his kids Sara and Christa. I was happy to see them.

I remember the heat the morning of our wedding. The weather cooled when a small tornado and hail storm swept through our neighborhood. I packed my bag for church, wedding dress in tow. Bob was to wear his special 4th of July "costume" as he called it.

When I arrived at the church, I saw for the first time what everyone in our wedding party was wearing. There was no rhyme or reason—but the colors were mostly red, white and or blue, just like all the flowers. It was perfect.

Bob looked dashing in his "costume." I wore my gown, along with a white floppy hat from Kmart with a hastily sewed on veil. I would not have worn the hat, except that I decided to get a permanent a few days before the wedding to put some body in my otherwise completely straight and thin hair. So what if it looked like I had been ever-so-mildly electrocuted and my hair was standing on end? My hair could not get in the way of a perfect wedding between two best friends.

During the ceremony, we lit the Unity Candle to signify that we were one now. We were supposed to blow out our individual candles after lighting the Unity Candle, but I left mine lit. Bob laughed at the strong and independent woman he had married, and he told the story again and again when he described how he lost his independence on the fourth of July.

After we said our vows and came out of the church to swirling sparklers, we ate a buffet dinner and danced. Our neighbor dressed as Uncle Sam and danced with all the ladies who were without partners. We went home and shot off fireworks in our driveway—a perfect end to the festivities. Our wedding began the best thirty-seven years of my life and cemented July 4th as our favorite holiday.

———————————

I pulled Kim aside and told her that I am having fun (after all, we are dodging water balloons and squirt guns from many children), but I am lonely amidst the chaos. Bob would have wanted to be here. He never wanted to leave, but there you have it, another box to check—July 4, 2017.

Kim handed me an anniversary card from Bob, just like I gave her a Mother's Day and a Valentine's Day card from Bob. She said that the card she chose was the one that he would have picked out for me. It read:

For the Love of My Life, My Wife

You Are My Friend, and you've shown that friendship by your patience, support, and understanding; I trust you more than anyone else in the world.

You Are My Love…I still feel so much desire for you every time I hold you in my arms. You keep the romance in my life.

You Are My Wife…and no man could ask for a better partner. No matter what happens, I know you'll be beside me. You are, and always will be, the love of my life.

Love, Bob Hassmiller

Blessings for Today: I have plenty, especially my family. I am grateful as this ole world keeps spinning round that I still love and there is still love and no one's gonna take that away. Happy Anniversary, my dear love.

Specific Prayer Requests: I just heard that someone new will be joining our grief support group next week. I pray for this person, and I pray that the support group will provide the strength this person needs to get through a profound and painful loss. 1 Corinthians 13:7 says, "(Love) always protects, always trusts, always hopes, always perseveres."

Reflection

The fourth of July was a day of rebirth for me. It was the beginning of a love that I had never before known; the start of a family that would shape my life forever; and laughter that filled my life—from the costume Bob wore to the red, white, and blue underwear (complete with a liberty bell) that he gave me as a wedding present. I miss Bob so much, but in the end, as James Taylor sang, no one's gonna take this time away. This ole world keeps spinnin' round, and I still love Bob. I still love you, my dear Robert Boy.

***

ENTRY   7/20/2017 at 8:40 p.m.

"FINDING BOB"

I love New York City—all the good, the bad, and the ugly (and for the record, I think it is almost all good). I just spent four days in the Hamptons and New York City with Lori, who is visiting from Florida. We struggled initially to find our way from our hotel on the Upper East Side to the Lower East side, where we wanted to visit the Tenement Museum at 97 Orchard Street. Bob would have known the way. He always somehow knew the way. In Vietnam, he was a platoon sergeant and responsible for leading his men to safety.

I never doubted that he would always lead me to safety, except for that one time in Virginia—long before GPS—when I was sure I was right. We traveled in circles, and out of sheer frustration, I demanded that he stop the car because I could walk faster than he could get us to our destination. Well, actually there was more than one time that we got into it over directions, but in the end, GPS saved us. It's funny how men will never ask a person for directions, but they love their GPS. In any case, GPS got Lori and me to 97 Orchard Street.

We heard fascinating stories of hardship at the Tenement Museum, including many stories of deep hardship and grief. Over 7,000 immigrants inhabited the dwellings at 97 Orchard Street over a number of decades, starting at the peak of the Civil War. For example, John Schneider suddenly lost his beloved wife Caroline. Married for twenty-two years, John and Caroline owned and operated a saloon in the basement of 97 Orchard Street. Among the first German immigrants, John and Caroline worked side by side, all roles clearly defined. She cooked and schmoozed, while he tended bar and managed the finances until one day Caroline became ill and died—just like that.

Our tour guide read us the obituary that John wrote about Caroline. He ended his note, "In deep mourning, John." A broken man, he tried to go on with the help of his close-knit neighborhood, but he couldn't. Nothing worked, so he sold the saloon and moved elsewhere to be become a cobbler. I get it.

John Schneider wasn't alone in his sorrow and grief. Fannie Gumpertz thought her life could get no worse than during the financial Panic of 1873 when 18,000 businesses failed over two years, and unemployment exceeded fourteen percent.

Her husband, Joel, lost his job and disappeared suddenly. The breadwinner for herself and their four children, Joel never came back.

A tailor by training, Fannie picked up the pieces to learn the tailor trade. Joel was later recorded as deceased in Cincinnati, never having remarried. The archivists/historians surmised that Joel might have left so that Fannie could take advantage of the meager widow's pension the New York City government offered at the time, which was much more than he could provide to their family. All fascinating stories of how people loved, loss, and lived again.

After the Tenement Museum, we wanted to go to midtown. I was reluctant to take the subway because I didn't want to figure out how to transfer lines (as simple as it might sound to you or a New Yorker). I have been to New York over one-hundred times, and I can only count three times that I have taken the subway. When Bob was alive, I never really had to think about getting around. I get mad at Bob now at times for leaving me and forcing me to figure out things that I don't want to figure out—like how to get around on the subway. Figuring out the subway is not on my priority list at the moment so we walk.

After four days in New York Lori left on a plane for home. I studied a map at my hotel on the Upper East Side to plot out my walking path to midtown to take the train home. I wrote down the directions carefully. I walked, pondering my solitude, and wished, as always, that I could be walking and holding the hand of my Robert Boy.

I find Bob most frequently when I am alone and visiting the places we used to go. I don't purposefully seek the places we went together—it's just that it's hard to go anyplace where he was not because we were together so much. Bob and I visited New York at least a few times a year. We used to see the sights on foot or from the perch of our bikes.

Some years ago, we rode down to the George Washington Bridge on the Riverview Trail and discovered a little known red lighthouse. Built in 1889, it once stood tall and proud on the banks of the Hudson, but it has since been swallowed up by the giant cement and steel monsters that have now have become affectionately known as the New York City skyline. The lighthouse became obsolete in 1931 when the George Washington Bridge was built, but thank goodness, since 2002, it has been a historic landmark. There is even a book about it, *The Little Red Lighthouse and the Great Gray Bridge.*[23] We visited the lighthouse every year.

Several years ago, we discovered a small but vibrant flower garden at 91st Street. We loved to revisit it each year to take an annual picture. The garden sits in the middle of concrete and adorned with a simple sign: "Started by Garden People." Thank goodness for Garden People. The garden always reminded us that you could find beauty in the most unusual of places.

We loved to explore, and many places were special to us: the Wailana Coffee House in Honolulu, which offered a delicious and inexpensive full breakfast; the horse park in Allentown; and the small condo that Kim and Matt own at the Jersey Shore, where Abby loves her ice cream. We also appreciated the mundane, including the grocery store, my allergy doctor's office, our neighborhood swimming pool, and the post office.

It is a mixed blessing—the great memories of my Robert Boy and remembering where and how we spent our time, and the hurt from knowing that there will be no further memories. It is no wonder that some people who have lost loved ones pick up and leave their surroundings all together. I get it. It helps to be with people to create new memories, experiences, thoughts, and challenges. Even though I like making new memories, I also resent it. It is hard to be alone, but sometimes I crave solitude to better feel Bob's presence. I need both.

I turned right, looking for 7th Avenue, but I made a wrong turn onto 5th Avenue instead. I was about to turn around to get on track when I remembered a very important building that Bob and I sought out every year on 5th Avenue. (No, it was NOT Saks Fifth Avenue.) We always visited a large gray building with steeples soaring to the sky. I saw St. Patrick's Cathedral in the distance and hastened my pace, no longer annoyed for making a wrong turn. It was meant to be—I needed to be at St. Patrick's Cathedral.

As I entered, a mass was in process. I am not Catholic and don't know all the rhymes and rhythms that make up the language between the priest and his congregation, but I respected the rituals, and more important, I felt certain that my Robert Boy was with me.

The priest described how Moses led the Jews to the Promised Land. I thought of Fannie and Joel and John and Caroline and all the other immigrants at 97

Orchard Street whose stories I heard. I thought about their journey to America, their own promised land.

I briefly wondered if St. Patrick's, built in 1878, might have been a home for the residents of 97 Orchard Street—at least the Italians and Irish—but I knew better. The tenement occupants lived on the Lower East Side, and this church would not have been their home. I thought about the disparities in our own country and recognize that in some ways, not much has changed for poor immigrants.

I thought of the lost ships seeking light on the Hudson and finding the little red lighthouse to guide them. I prayed for myself and my family and all who were trying to find their way in this world, including all current immigrants and their hardships—I know there are many.

Blessings for Today: That Lori traveled from Florida to be with me and said something that Bob would have said: "Just pick out whatever you want to do for the time we have together. I am here just to be with you." Also, I'm grateful that I felt my Robert Boy's presence at St. Patrick's Cathedral.

Specific Prayer Requests: That I might find my way in the world, and that I might find meaning and purpose for myself and for those who follow. Genesis 13:15 states, "All the land that you see I will give it to you and to your offspring forever." Psalm 119:105 says, "Your word is a lamp for my feet, a light on my path."

Reflection

Life is a mystery. It seems so random how long we are here, who we are with, and what we do with our days. Nautical analogies come in handy. For many of us, our days are like smooth sailing. Yes, the tides routinely go in and out. Some days the waves are more challenging than others, but we prepare ourselves with all the nautical tools that we have at our disposal, chart our course, and sail ahead. Storms inevitably come, however. We know this, and we think we might even be able to handle the big ones, but you really don't know until you're in it. We draw upon our own navigational skills to avoid falling overboard, but sometimes we still fall in the water. Resiliency, which includes your faith and the help of friends and family, serves as your life preserver. You try to swim as best as your can, but you are weak and exhausted. Finally, you see the little red lighthouse with its bright light, and instinctively, you know that if you swim towards the light, you will reach the shore. Somehow—some way—you will make it.

***

ENTRY   8/5/2017 at 11:37 a.m.

"IT IS WHAT IT IS"

The captain piloting my United flight today just announced that a World War II veteran and his bride of seventy-two years are on our flight. The captain thanks the man for his service, congratulates him on his long marriage, and asks the rest of the passengers to applaud them. I am both envious and happy for them. As they hold hands, I cannot help but think that could have been Bob and me.

I looked for Bob in the airport security line the other day and for a moment thought that he was using the bathroom. Then I remembered, and Bob's infamous words popped into my head: "It is what it is."

Bob used the phrase to explain both important and unimportant things. He responded, "It is what it is" when I told him that our town planned road construction during rush hour. He said it when the weather forecast called for rain during Kim's outdoor wedding. (The rain held off.)

We both said it when my mother chose to do exactly what she wanted in life without feeling like she had to answer to anyone.

"Sue," Bob asked. "Can't you do something about your mother leaving the lights and television on all the time?"

"Robert," I responded. "It is what it is. I can try to get her to turn off the lights when they are not in use, but that's how she likes it, and motivating, reminding or yelling at her has never worked. It is what it is."

Ah—the trials and tribulations of living with members of the greatest generation.

No matter the annoyance—a late plane, brown grass, Jake slowing down, sour milk, or yet another single-family fire to attend to in the middle of the night that week—Bob's response was the same: "It is what it is."

But, sometimes, there are just no answers as to why something is the way it is.

I wonder often about why Bob's bicycle accident happened and how much of it was my fault. The morning of the accident, I told him that I needed to be picked up at my meeting much earlier than we initially planned. He may have been biking too fast in order to get home to get in his car to pick me up. I am consumed with guilt. Bob never wanted to be late for me. Every minute counted because we always had so much to look forward to.

Perhaps the bike shop where he had recently taken in his bike for a tune up did not do a good job. I asked Nurse Abby if Bob had said anything about the accident when he came into the trauma unit, but she said he did not remember it. The man who found Bob also said that Bob did not remember what happened. (A friend of mine talked to this man for me and thanked him for getting Bob help).

Then there are cyclists who whiz along the highway without helmets, lights, or florescent shirts. They blare music into their ear buds and completely fail to pay attention to their surroundings—and yet they remain unscathed. Why?

Even though there aren't any answers, I don't want to accept, "It is what it is." Accepting that phrase in this case means that I am content with the outcome; believe that circumstances will never change the outcome no matter how hard I try; or that I am simply ready to move on to other matters. I am not ready to move on.

There must be some reason and answer. I still search for the meaning in Bob's accident, although not as vehemently as before. People experience horrendous events—wars, the Holocaust, street violence, September 11th, school shootings, devastating illnesses, living with Alzheimer's, and all the natural disasters.

Can we explain tragedy by saying, "It is what it is?" No, I cannot accept that. Lessons must be learned from these atrocities, including how to avert future tragedies. We must do better in cases where we can do better. *Yet, at some point, we all die. That is the way it is. I do accept death, at least in theory.*

Many people have lost great loves, and I understand the grief that they feel. I remember the wrenching physical pain I was in, which has now transferred to mental pain. *Some people never make it out of the phase of physical pain. People who have experienced loss tell me their stories and describe the acute pain that they feel for years on end. Everyone's time table is different and should be respected as such.*

I grieve for others I don't even know—for their past and present pain. I wonder how they managed—and are managing. Many people who have responded to this blog tell me that the words I write help them. Their words always help me, by reinforcing that all humans grieve.

Pastor Dan said that we will never have the answers to some of life's most pressing questions, including this one. He believes that answers will come in the afterlife, and that comforts me.

I accept that Bob is no longer here, but I don't accept why he is no longer here. Can we just leave it at that for now?

Blessings for Today: I acknowledge that many things in life have no ready answers, and that grieving is part of living. Instead of stating, "It is what it is," I will say with conviction that good will result from my loss.

Specific Prayer Requests: That I have the patience, fortitude, and courage to seek understanding and know where I might be of most help in service to those whose paths I have the privilege of crossing. Remember, Jeremiah 29:11 states, "For I know the plans I have for you, declares the Lord, plans to prosper you and not to harm you, plans to give you hope and a future." Also, 1 Peter 4:10 says, "Each of you should use whatever gift you have received to serve others, faithful stewards of God's grace in its various forms." I love this from William Shakespeare: "The meaning of life is to find your gift. The purpose of life is to give it away."

Reflection

It is our responsibility as humans to find answers and solutions to the most pressing of challenges—to help and to be helped. For this one great mystery—the death of a beloved—the answer will come later I am told. I hold onto that notion.

***

ENTRY   8/13/2017 at 5:27 p.m.

"THE HUMAN CONNECTION"

One day after my mother told me about a number of things that needed to be done in the house (that were more important to her than me), I burst out, "I am taking a walk. I am on a mission to save my soul. Enough with home maintenance!"

It's hard to understand such an extreme feeling unless you have experienced the depths of grief. You do what you can to put the pieces back together, and home maintenance is not ever on the top of the list—except for the time when the toilets stopped working. Otherwise, you do what it takes to save your soul.

For thirty-seven years, I never doubted that I was loved and that I was the most important person in the world to one person in particular. That is pretty powerful. I held that position of power and privilege, and I was able to use Bob's love as my base to work and connect to the rest of the world. Indeed, the rest of my world was icing on the cake. I got to have Bob and all the rest? What a great deal!

Bob's love and support were like living in Antarctica during winter. (Isn't it always winter there?) I could explore even in a cold and unforgiving environment, and I could always return to our base camp for warmth, comfort, food, and empathy from someone who understood my plight. I knew that everything would be okay. It's so easy to take a great home base for granted. Losing the base camp was earth shattering. I needed to figure out how to explore and survive in ways that I never imagined nor anticipated. And so, the journey began to save my soul.

I am fortunate in that I was able to draw upon the wisdom of others who found their way back after their base camp exploded—guides, if you will. Our human and spiritual connections provide us with an overall sense of well-being on this earth.

Being socially connected does not mean that you have to be with another human 24/7, but that you could meet up with someone for lunch or a walk if you wanted. It means that someone else values you. Human connections help to build your base camp.

That was the beauty of having Bob as a husband. I never had to wonder, whether we were together or apart. Losing him left a tremendous void and I wondered who would replace this deep and abiding connection. I felt alarmed as I realized no one could. I wondered if anyone could possibly ever love me again the way that Bob did. For thirty-seven years I was the most important person in someone's life and he in mine. Gone.

Brené Brown defines the human connection as "the energy that exists between people when they feel seen, heard, and valued; when they can give and receive without judgment; and when they derive sustenance and strength from the relationship." Research underscores how critical human connections are to an increased state of health and well-being. People want to know they are not alone.

This was evident in the American psychologist's Harry Harlow's study of rhesus monkeys during the 1950s. Social connectedness showed a clear link to healthy growth and development, and in some cases, survival itself.[24] I studied Harlow's work before I started my master's thesis in the early 1980s on human infant attachment. I was interested in studying human infant attachment because of Kim's adoption and my desire to give her everything that she needed to thrive in this world. I wanted to reassure myself that the human connection—and not giving birth in and of itself—was really the most important. In a blinded study, rated by another, my video recordings of mothers and babies showed the importance of touch, eye contact, speaking and a general sense of warmth to both a mother's and child's sense of belonging and attachment.

The Robert Wood Johnson Foundation recognizes the importance of social support and connectedness in its mission to provide everyone a fair and just opportunity for health and well-being. RWJF states that "we need people in our lives that make us feel supported and accepted. Strong, meaningful social support—from a partner, friends, or family—leads to healthier, more resilient individuals and communities."[25] According to RWJF, Americans are not doing as well as we could be in fostering human connections: only half of us feel any sense of belongingness and connection, and people who are White or Asian, have a college degree, and make over $100,000 fare better than those who are Black or Latino, lack a college degree, and make less than $100,000. RWJF-sponsored research has also shown that living in walkable and safe neighborhoods and belonging to a faith community are big predictors of social connectedness. I get both.

One quarter of respondents in another survey said that they have no one with whom they can talk about their personal troubles and triumphs. If family members are not counted, the number doubles to more than half of Americans who have no one outside their immediate family with whom they can share confidences. The authors conducted 1,500 face-to-face interviews for the study, which was supported by the National Science Foundation.[26]

And then there's this blog. One remarkable, yet unintended consequence of writing this blog has been the number of people who have shared their stories with me. The stories range from people who have lost a spouse, a parent, or a child; to those who are grieving a struggling marriage or experiencing the pain of divorce. Others have lost nothing to this point, yet realize that they will someday. One woman told me she is saving every blog for when loss happens to her.

It's comforting to know that we are not alone in our tribulations. I treasure the stories that others share with me, and I am glad that my story has helped others. It has nourished and even helped to save my soul.

Blessings for Today: That I am figuring out how to rebuild a base camp, even with some irreplaceable pieces missing. That there are extraordinary, emotionally intelligent, kind, and giving people in the world, who have heard my stories and shared their own—the human connection.

Specific Prayer Requests: That I might continue to find the resources to build my base camp. To keep my balance. To build my faith. That I might continue to give back to those who have given to me. Pastor Dan said today, "Faith does not deny fear. Faith looks past it." Ecclesiastes 4:9–12 says, "Two are better than one, because they have a good return for their labor: If either of them falls down, one can help the other up. But pity anyone who falls and has no one to help them up. Also, if two lie down together, they will keep warm. But how can one keep warm alone? Though one may be overpowered, two can defend themselves. A cord of three strands is not quickly broken."

Reflection

It is amazing and daunting how many people have their own hidden stories of pain and loneliness from a variety of causes. Many people tell me that witnessing my journey brings them hope. When they have hope, I do as well.

***

ENTRY   8/22/2017 at 2:46 p.m.

"HAPPY BIRTHDAY"

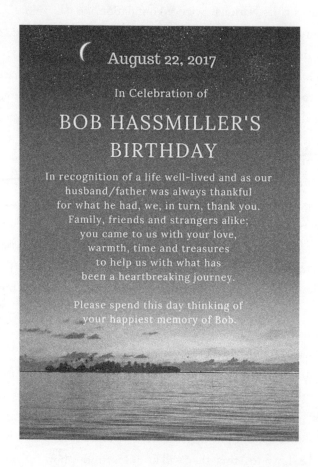

> (August 22, 2017
>
> In Celebration of
>
> ## BOB HASSMILLER'S BIRTHDAY
>
> In recognition of a life well-lived and as our
> husband/father was always thankful
> for what he had, we, in turn, thank you.
> Family, friends and strangers alike;
> you came to us with your love,
> warmth, time and treasures
> to help us with what has
> been a heartbreaking journey.
>
> Please spend this day thinking of
> your happiest memory of Bob.

***

ENTRY   9/3/2017 at 6:26 p.m.

"FIGURING IT OUT"

There is a lot to figure out on so many levels. Some people call it getting used to a new normal, but I hate that phrase. I hate most words that remind me of what happened, so I don't use them. Others use them. I balk at some (mostly in silence), and accept others. Saying after "the accident" or throughout "this trag-edy" is about how far I go.

I initially panicked about figuring out bills, documents, and wills and such. So far, though, I have received only two late notices—okay three, but the third one doesn't count. The third notice was from my high-priced lawyer (as I call her), who has gotten so many multiple, multiple thousands of dollars out of me so far that it is simply infuriating. She has a more than ample cushion, so this is my way of letting her know that I am in no hurry to feed that meter. For now, she is paid up.

Nothing has been turned off yet. It wasn't so hard once Matt set up scheduled e-payments. I still need to learn more about what is coming in and what is going out, but the robot (for the most part) is doing its job for now. We always made a habit of living below our means, and I am following that philosophy.

While the finances were hard, they weren't even the first thing that I needed to figure out. I needed to manage the pain—wondering if I could, and at times, even should, go on. Once I made up my mind to keep going, I needed to figure out how to breathe and eat. I figured out the breathing on my own, and lots of other people helped with the eating.

I always fell back on the admonition to "follow my heart." Things generally worked out (and still work out) when I follow my heart. I am doing missionary work, but instead of saving other souls, I am saving my own. I have found ways to protect myself from the many bombardments in life— personal and family issues, work, politics, and the state of the world.

For four or more months I never turned on a television, and then eased in with Chip and Joanna on HGTV. I trusted them. There were no surprises—only comfort, love, and happiness. They could fix up a bad house in Waco with lots of hard work and love and make everyone happy. Their marriage was reminis-cent of mine. Chip always reminded people that "if the Mama ain't happy, then ain't nobody happy." That was Bob's philosophy exactly. One time, Chip said to Joanna, "Who won in life? Me. Because I got to marry you." Yup—that line came right out of the television, and I knew it was Bob telling me yet again, through some kind of sign, that he still feels that way and always will.

Anyways, back to figuring things out. I needed to figure things out for my mother. I panicked about my mother, and I still worry about her. Who will take care of her when I am at work and traveling? I have been working on her care since before the accident and keep at it every day. I am her only caregiver, and being a caregiver is not an easy job, even it if it is your only job—and it is not my only job.

She should be in assisted living but she wants to live with me. Assisted living would be a much better and safer atmosphere for her, but she has abandonment issues from when she was a young girl. She grew up poor, and her family was separated after she lost her father at the age of nine and the Depression hit. I hired an aid for her, but only for two mornings a week. She is on Medicaid and eligible for more time, but my house is not on a bus line, and I have had trouble hiring someone to care for her part time. So, it falls to me, Mark and occasionally neighbors. Piecemeal.

Someone (probably Lori, as she is allowed to say anything to me) said, "So what's the worst that could happen with your mother? She will die whether or not you are home." The words were kind of calloused, but I have come to accept that if she dies and I am not here, then so be it—that is her decision. There may come a time when I may have to decide for my mother that she is safer in long-term care, but for now, she has decided to live with me with this piecemeal arrangement.

I also needed to figure out if I would ever go back to my work, as much as I loved it. I felt great trepidation. How could I simply pick up where I left off? It was impossible. The Robert Wood Johnson Foundation's mission to build a Culture of Health used to be important to me, but community gardens, jumping jacks and keeping everyone in America healthy were not where my heart was. How could I remain authentic in my circumstances and be the motivator for a life filled with health and wellness when I did not feel healthy or well? Did they not realize that some people died?!

I found my way, slowly but surely. With the help of my colleagues, I reached the understanding that building a Culture of Health also means ensuring a sense of well-being in people even as they approach death or in the middle of some hor-rific chronic disease scenarios. That spoke to me—I could authentically connect around ensuring a state of well-being in individuals and communities.

Not everyone is going to be healthy—not everyone is going to walk out of a hospital bed again to exercise and plant healthy gardens. But while people are in a hospital bed, their well-being and dignity matters, and health systems need to give them and their families the dignity and the power and COMPASSION to be involved and truly engaged as partners in their own care. I am proud to talk about building a Culture of Health, as long as the definition extends to well-being.

I am still figuring out life outside of work. With my job, I know my box—my responsibilities and what needs to be done. Outside of work, I don't want the box that I have been squeezed into—I don't want to make my way as a person who has not chosen to "consciously uncouple" as the new buzzwords have come to describe.

I found out the hard way early on that some travel tours only accept couples—a harsh reality that I may never engage in some activities again. My family and my close friends still include me, but the space that occupied the yin to my yang, the joke to my laughter, and the blame for our tardiness no longer exists. We all feel it—everyone feels that awkward space and is trying to figure it out.

I have figured out the people with whom I am most comfortable. To save my soul, I must be with people who understand, acknowledge, and who can cry, pray, and laugh with me.

Finally, I am still trying to figure out what happened—the big spiritual question. Of course, we have been over this question many times. I still think my Robert Boy is just someplace else, and I will look for him (although not as much as before). Today, I went into a store we frequented together and looked behind me to see if he was there.

A friend of mine who lost her husband around the same time as me said that she keeps a few pieces of clothing in the closest in case her husband returns. Irrational, yes, but grief causes your mind and heart to play tricks, so you hedge your bets. What's the harm?

So far, figuring things out has mostly meant facing things I either don't want to do (or thought I could not do) with whatever I have to give at the moment. Faith helps, as do the very special people in my grief support group and others who choose to journey with me, even for an hour.

I will never completely figure things out. It is a process and a journey. And in the end, it is really not ours to completely figure out.

British author M.A. Kelty said, "Watch your way then, as a cautious traveler; and don't be gazing at that mountain or river in the distance, and saying, 'How shall I ever get over them?' but keep to the present little inch that is before you, and accomplish that in the little moment that belongs to it. The mountain and the river can only be passed in the same way; and, when you come to them, you will come to the light and strength that belong to them."

Blessings for Today: To have some extraordinary people along the way who have provided their time, compassion and counsel as to what is important in life. To know that I have been loved, and to not have to figure that part out.

Specific Prayer Requests: To truly believe what I just saw on a church sign in Washington D.C. this week: For me to continue to be thoughtful about what it will take to save my soul, and to not worry about figuring out every little thing. Also, prayers for all the people who have lost much in the disasters affecting our country. Matthew 17:20 says, "….Because you have so little faith. Truly I tell you, if you have faith as small as a mustard seed, you can say to this mountain, 'Move from here to there,' and it will move. Nothing will be impossible for you."

Reflection

I walked by a church a few weeks ago in Washington D.C. with a sign stating, "God is laughing because you just told him your plan." I laughed back and thought, "Yes, I know exactly what you mean."

***

ENTRY   9/19/2017 at 6:52 a.m.

"RELIVING IT"

More than anything else this year, I have dreaded the one-year anniversary of when it all happened. Quite honestly, this will not be the first time I will have relived this nightmare. How could it be? I have replayed this war-torn tape over and over again throughout the year, much of the time without structure or time. Individual events scrambled wildly, popping in and out of my mind and heart at predictable and unpredictable times. But the actual dates bring a dreaded structure to the events as they unfolded last year. Since I am an organized and somewhat methodical person, the dates—September 25–October 4—replay in lockstep one day and event at a time.

I am also reliving the days leading up to the accident: the last time we walked; the last time we talked; our last text (BFF forever); the last time we spent with Abby together; the last picture Bob sent me dated September 21, 2016, of him, Abby, and Mark eating pancakes at Perkins; our excitement about the Clara Barton Study Tour; and the health system board retreat I was attending when I got the call. I am planning to go to the retreat again this year, but thankfully it is in a different city.

Triggers. Everything is a trigger now. The dark draws nigh. The weather turns cooler, the fall decorations appear, and everything lines up as it did last year at this time, when my life was happy and exciting. It is all just one big trigger. The countdown begins: five, four, three, two, one. The call came—the beginning of the end. The beginning of my "resetting" as I now call my new life—a reorientation and a restoration that will take many years, I am told, to process. I have come a long way already.

Since my wedding anniversary, I have tried to figure out how to brace myself. I looked at my calendar to see where I would be for each of days from September 25–October 4 to plan the reliving. Odd, but it is how this thing goes. The day it happened, our last day together, and every day in between. What should I do? I became obsessed with three things: protecting, preparing, and commemorating.

What steps could I take to protect myself from stressors when I already felt unbalanced? This has felt like an amputation. I know about phantom pain syndrome, from being a nurse. It occurs when someone who has lost a limb feels a sensation or pain related to his or her missing limb. I am experiencing phantom person syndrome—adjusting to a person who is no longer there.

Preparing is intricately linked to protecting. I studied my calendar to determine what was scheduled and made readjustments to eliminate certain obligations that I felt that I could not handle. I told a few pertinent people that I was unsure whether I would attend their meeting; stay the entire time; speak publicly; or cry. Please don't have expectations of me, I told them.

Three special friends have agreed to spend time with me over a few particular days. One friend tells me that they are the "Sue Squad." I laugh. My friends are an awe-inspiring gift of humanity. I am blessed to be able to draw in special people and family at this time to protect me.

I also scheduled time with those who have lost spouses to commune with kindred hearts. I want to fill this week with heartfelt and spiritual friends who lift me up and have always taken the time to acknowledge Bob's absence. Acknowledging Bob is important, just as it was when he was alive.

Abby lifts me up the most. Just three and three-fourths (as she likes to say), but with the soul of someone much older, she has always said the right words at just the right time. Her love, warmth and intermittent acknowledgment of her Pops is hugely reaffirming to me.

One time when we stood at a flagpole attached to a 9/11 memorial, I explained to Abby that flags sometimes fly at half-mast when an important person has died. She could not then understand why every flag she saw from that time on was not at half-mast to commemorate her Pops. Yesterday we heard her telling Siri, the "ask me anything" voice device on Apple phones, the story of how her Pops fell off his bike and how very sad she was. When Siri did not respond, Abby, said, "Siri, don't you think this is sad that Pops fell off his bike?" Siri affirmed that it sounded sad, but otherwise was at a loss for words. I too have toyed with the idea of asking Siri what happened, so understood the logic here.

Abby also recalls the good times. When she heard sirens the other day, a noise that makes me cringe, she told me that the sounds reminded her of how Pops always volunteered for the Red Cross and how he responded alongside the firetrucks to help people who needed it most. Abby told us all during lunch today to wave at the sky because Pops was waving to us—a happy thought indeed.

Despite my efforts to prepare and protect myself, I know enough now to allow the one-year anniversary to unfold. I will not block my pain, busy myself with work, and simply say "it is what it is." I have come to learn that grieving—although different for each person—works best if it is simply allowed to happen without ignoring, blocking, deferring or dismissing. Just let it be.

I am also making time to commemorate the extraordinary husband, father, friend, and colleague that Bob was. I was blessed to have him on loan for thirty-seven years. Sometimes I resent that so much of my time is taken with things other than thoughts of my Robert Boy. On this week, I will reflect on this loss, but in the context of the good and extraordinary that Bob brought to my life.

I asked a few people who have lost a very special soul how they marked their own personal anniversary. The responses included planting flowers, visiting the gravesite, rummaging through pictures, and hiking. Nothing hit me until the latest hurricanes struck and ravished lives. I don't know what exactly I will do, but it will have to do with the Red Cross.

So, now I will settle in for this ride—the scariest one at the amusement park, or rather, the second scariest one. I already rode the scariest one. I will take my turn. I will experience these ten days with all of my senses and let the wind blow as it might. Others will be on the ride, but the seats are for singles only. I have waited in line for quite some time now. I've talked to others coming off the ride and those going on. Some say the ride gets worse as the years go on. For now, I am focused on this ride only. One day at a time in a lifetime filled with missing my Robert Boy—but I believe that Bob will be with me.

Blessings for Today: Some people say that no one truly understands grief until they have also lost a beloved spouse. Some people, though, have a special gift for empathy, and I am blessed that many empathetic people have touched my life. Loved ones came to my side to help, regardless of their own family and work circumstances: Karen and Kristen, Janie, Lori, Robin, and Jean. Many neighbors, friends, and colleagues have helped me along the way by sharing consistent words of encouragement and wisdom, including my grief support group and Colleen, my administrative assistant. Your words have sustained me. I'm also grateful to my three special nurses: Abby, Kathy and Beth Ann, and to my beloved children: Kim, Mark, and Matt. Even though this period has been devastating, it has also been the most spiritually uplifting.

Specific Prayer Request: I am fearful and anxious about reliving this horror—but I will relive it as a healthy means of reflecting upon what I have lost, gained, and what might be yet to come. I need help with the "yet to come" part. Proverbs 4:23 states, "Above all else, guard your heart, for everything you do flows from it." And Jeremiah

29:11 again says, "For I know the plans that I have for you, declares the Lord, plans for to prosper you and not to harm you, plans to give you hope and a future."

Reflection

I was angry shortly after the accident when a counselor said that she was treating me for post-traumatic stress disorder (PTSD). One of my major symptoms was the constant reliving of the trauma-filled events. I fought the notion that I could have PTSD; after all, I had not experienced years of abuse or lived in constant danger in a war-torn country. The counselor told me that no matter the event or series of events, the physical and emotional symptoms display similarly. I could not dispute my symptoms, and with that acceptance and with the support of friends and family, I began to heal. Part of healing is accepting the entire grief process—letting it have its way, with patience and kindness.

***

ENTRY   10/29/2017 at 8:29 a.m.

"LEGACY AND THE BOB HASSMILLER AWARD"

John F. Kennedy's famous words ring true. "Some men show courage throughout the whole of their lives. Others sail with the wind until the decisive moment when their conscience and events propel them into the center of the storm. If you want to leave a lasting legacy, you need to act with courage to reach out to those in need."

This past Wednesday night, exactly one year to the month that I lost Bob, the American Red Cross recognized David Williams of Alaska as the first recipient of the Bob Hassmiller Award for Excellence in Disaster Service. It was an extraordinary honor for my children and me to attend the ceremony and to give witness to the torch being passed. Mr. Williams was chosen as a man who resembled Bob's spirit and dedication to the organization. Two people on the award's committee knew Bob and assured me that his spirit was alive during the decision-making process. One told me she felt that Bob voiced his opinion that Mr. Williams should be selected.

True to form, the award recipient struggled with being named the national winner. "After so many disasters this year and so many heroes working the front lines," he said, "I can imagine that others might be so much more worthy." It was a line taken from the Bob Hassmiller playbook. "But you were chosen to continue to be the leader that you are and to raise up new leaders who will be just as giving and dedicated to helping others," I said. "This is your charge and legacy." He felt he could live with my request. That's how you have to talk to these kind of people.

In my public words to the audience once Mr. Williams was named, I used one of my favorite quotes from the musical Hamilton that I frequently use in my presentations: "Legacy is planting seeds in a garden you will never get to see." I told the audience that planting seeds is something that Bob did, Mr. Williams is doing, and the Red Cross has always done. The gardening has been particularly active this year, and many lives will be changed forever. We rarely see the effects of all of the seeds that we sow. We simply believe that giving to others is required for humanitarian principles to burn bright. It is the Red Cross' legacy.

Every person leaves a legacy—our footprint and proof that for a brief moment we lived on this earth. Some legacies are forgotten once the casket closes, while others live on in infamy. But we all have one—attend a funeral, and you will hear what that person's legacy is.

Several years ago, my husband and I filled out the "Five Wishes" document, which is part of an advance directive and also includes questions of how you want to be remembered. (Everyone should fill this document out and discuss it with their loved ones.) Bob said that he wanted to be remembered for acting on his beliefs; for always supporting and recognizing others; and as someone who loved and laughed a lot, adored his wife and family, and whose heart was filled with gratefulness and little regret. Bob's words spoke volumes to me when he first wrote it, when I re-read them when Bob was in the hospital, and especially now. It is noteworthy that he did not include anything about possessions or work-related accomplishments, even though he penned these words at the height of his career.

I suspect that Mr. Williams would write the same kind of paragraph in his own Living Wishes document.

Finally, I am reminded of the verse that we found triple-highlighted in the family Bible by Bob the day after he left us—and the one that became the theme of his memorial service—Micah 6:8. "H has shown you, O mortal, what is good. And what does the Lord require of you? To act justly and to love mercy and to walk humbly with your God." A window to a soul gone too soon.

Blessings for Today: That I had the unbelievable honor to be associated with a man who cared deeply about leaving the right kind of legacy, and that I am associated with two organizations that care deeply about leaving the right kind of legacy: the Red Cross and the Robert Wood Johnson Foundation.

Specific Prayer Requests: That I pay attention to and be purposeful in leaving the right kind of legacy for the right kind of reasons. 2 Corinthians 8:7 says, "But since you excel in everything—in faith, in speech, in knowledge, in complete earnestness and in the love we have kindled in you—see that you excel in this grace of living."

Reflection

I am reminded how short a time we are on this earth. It is a temporary journey on the way to an everlasting home. I have questioned the purpose of our time here on earth, if we are here for such a short time. What is our purpose? The answer is to leave a positive legacy for others to build on.

***

ENTRY   12/31/2017 at 10:19 p.m.

"THE POWER OF TOUCH AND COMPASSION"

Twenty-two years ago, a neonatal intensive care nurse by the name of Gayle Kasparian was caring for premature infants Kyrie and Brielle. While Kyrie was thriving, Brielle was on the brink of death and nothing short of a miracle could bring her back. Gayle blatantly ignored the protocol at the time and brought the sisters—one healthy and one dying—into the same incubator and saved Brielle's life. It turned out that touch could do what machines and science could not. Now the sisters are thriving young adults. Gayle was lauded at the time as a nurse who brought attention to the powers of touch and compassion.

I have pondered many lessons since my Robert Boy's accident just over fifteen months ago. Perhaps one of the most important to me—as a nurse and certainly as a family member—has been the power of touch and compassion. I always say that my dear Robert Boy received very good clinical care, but I wish there had been a bit more touch and compassion. Too much of the clinicians' focus was on the numbers, algorithms, computers, and machines—and making sure all the tasks were accomplished and the machines were purring along. Too many times, the providers discussed Bob's care among themselves and their computers outside of his door, without so much a look in his direction.

So much technology, so little touch.

I know ICUs are designed to save lives and, for the most part, they succeed. No one would want to forgo the power, knowledge and technology necessary to save lives. I would not want any less from the experts and their machines, believe me! But in our zealousness to save lives, we cannot forget touch and compassion.

A number of years ago, I brought Bob to the emergency room. After four hours at the hospital and being checked by several providers, Bob was discharged and sent home. During the car ride home, he said, "You know, not one person who came into my ER room ever touched me." I was happy that Bob was coming home with me, so I acknowledged that his observation seemed to be true and did not ponder his comment further until we were in the ICU the last time.

Bob would completely understand my desire to advocate for the importance of touch and compassion, and I believe he is smiling when I speak or write on the subject. Although most of the people in the audience are receptive to my message, a few have pushed back, saying that they don't have time to be compassionate. As a result, I began to incorporate into my speeches and articles how nurses Abby and Kathy provided compassionate care to Bob and me.

It amazes me that health systems do not stress touch and compassion more, given the pressure they face to improve publicly reported patient satisfaction scores or face financial penalties. (Everyone can AND SHOULD look up their local hospital's scores by going to: www.medicare.gov/hospitalcompare.) Hospitals also receive star ratings for their scores on a number of variables, including patient satisfaction. A higher number of stars presumably indicate better care.

Hospitals are going to extraordinary lengths to ensure patients are satisfied. Many offer valet and free parking, in-house concierge services, improved food service, and tastefully decorated private rooms. Depending on the person and his or her circumstances, many of these things, taken in whole, matter. But as a nurse and family member, my focus is on distinguishing great care from good care.

Great care means a provider who is mindfully present and engaged, and through body language, shows care and concern and follows through in a timely manner. Part of exhibiting mindfulness and showing concern includes making eye contact (put the computer to the side!), intently listening with reflection, and using touch and body language to lessen the intimidation that many patients and family members feel when they engage with clinicians. In other words, clinicians should sit face to face and engage the patient and/or family member in meaningful dialogue around their needs and desires—and what is important to them.

In her book, *The Antidote to Suffering: How Compassionate Connected Care Can Improve Safety, Quality, and Experience,* Christina Dempsey, the chief nursing officer of Press Ganey, interviews hundreds of people about their views of compassionate care and identifies six themes.[27] The themes include the ability to acknowledge suffering, presenting body language that shows care (including touch), providing patient's autonomy and dignity, and ensuring care coordination by always being there for patients. We all have a right to exceptional clinical care and Compassionate Connected Care.

In addition, the Touch Research Institute at the University of Miami states that, "Touch itself appears to stimulate our bodies to react in very specific ways. The right kind can lower blood pressure, heart rate, and cortisol levels, stimulate the hippocampus (an area of the brain that is central to memory), and drive the release of a host of hormones and neuropeptides that have been linked to positive and uplifting emotions. The physical effects of touch are far-reaching."[28]

Both Abby and Kathy went above and beyond to show compassion and share their touch. I nominated them for the prestigious National DAISY Award, which recognizes nurses for extraordinary skillful, and compassionate care. They touched our lives forever.

Blessings for Today: Out of tragedy comes lessons. Out of lessons comes teachings. Out of teachings comes actions. Out of actions comes amendments. Out of amendments comes healing. Let it be so.

Specific Prayer Requests: That compassion and touch be a mainstay at institutions of healing. Technology cannot replace compassion and touch. So be it if protocol must be broken. Colossians 3:12 says, "Therefore, as God's chosen people, holy and dearly loved, clothe yourselves with compassion, kindness, humility, gentleness and patience." And Daniel 10:18 states, "Again the one who looked like a man touched me and gave me strength."

***

ENTRY   1/28/2018 at 9:01 p.m.

"THE JOURNEY CONTINUES"

A few weeks ago, a wonderful colleague told me that she was so glad that I made it through the door to the other side. I knew what she meant and appreciated how she acknowledged my healing, but a part of me bristled.

I did not want to hurt her feelings, but I gently told her that I did not consider myself on the other side of a door. Rather, I am on a journey that continues and evolves. It's not as though I walked through some door one day, and my grief ended, gone with the click of the lock. I know she did not mean it this way, but it was a wake-up call for me and countless others who travel this winding path of grief. We walk through many doors—not just one.

Should anyone need a reminder of the journeys we are all on as human beings, go on Facebook on Mother's Day to see posts from children who miss their mothers very much. The more we love someone and the deeper the connection, the more we acutely and chronically miss our loved one. There is no other side.

Yes, we continue to live our lives and figure out the reset buttons. That's what I like to call what we grieving people do—we try to rearrange, reorganize and reset our lives. Some people aren't able to make the adjustments-tend to tasks, accomplish their goals, care for and love others. At least, never in quite the same way.

EPILOGUE

"My Igikai"

I have been asked many times if I will write any more blogs. I felt that I would know when the blogs should end, and I stayed true to listening to my heart. One year of grieving publicly was what I had to give. Any other blog posts that I would write would contain the same content as my last entry, "The Journey Continues."

The blogs gave me a safe outlet to release my feelings. Initially, they were intended to keep in touch with friends and family. I had so much grief built up that I thought I would die from it all, and writing helped. As time went on, family and friends gave me an unanticipated gift when they told me that my blogs were aiding others. A minister and several psychologists told me that they shared my blogs in their grief counseling sessions. Other people who were grieving told me that my words expressed their feelings. Doctors and nurses apologized to me for not being as compassionate as they could be. Both women and men experienced a wakeup call for their own marriages and hastily got into counseling after years of neglect. Other people told me that they and their partner had created a will and advance directives. Others said they were grateful for insights into what a grieving person actually feels, and that they were better prepared to understand their own grieving friends and family members, and share comforting words with them. Some said that they were saving the blogs for the day when they might really need them. Many people also told me that my words gave them the courage and hope to face their own challenges and urged me to publish this blog so that others could benefit.

You have come to know me well in that time in space as I endured the greatest tragedy imaginable. Nearly three years have now passed, and I finally was able to re-read my blogs. As painful as they were to read, I have found that some of my hopes, desires, and prayers have been answered, including my greatest desire to still feel Bob's presence.

The memorialized events have come and gone again—birthdays, anniversaries, holidays, first kiss, and last kiss. John is now three, and Abby is five and almost six. I am still upset that John especially will never know Bob. However, John has referred to Bob seemingly out of the blue. Besides the time he told Kim that Bob was sitting in the chair next to them, he told Kim once when they were at my house that "Pops is with Nana right now." When Kim asked him specifically where Pops was, John said, "He is above Nana. It's where I see him a lot." Believe what you want, but a two-year-old only expresses what he sees and feels. Maybe John knows Bob more than we all know—a thought that I would like to hang onto.

Abby continues to light up my world. In the beginning, she stayed with me many nights and asked why Pops was gone. As time has passed, she has returned to her joyful self. Obviously it was much harder for me, but during the times I felt particularly sad, I followed her lead and words—and was all the better for it. For example, Abby told me last year that "when the night is dark and the stars are bright, Pops has turned on the stars switch. And when he does, I know he is telling me he is with me. I was his fairy princess, you know, and those stars are just for me."

My ninety-three-year-old mother recently passed away at home after these unsettled years of immense guilt that God did not take her before Bob. The guilt and anger was something we both had to grapple with. Losing my dog, Jake, which preceded my mother's passing, took its own toll. He was her best buddy and a welcome and loving distraction for me. Sometime in between Jake leaving us and my mother leaving me, she told me, for the first time in her life, that she loved me. We always knew that we loved each other and showed it in innumerable ways, however, it was simply not the family culture for my mother and father to make that statement in my growing up years and it simply stuck. Bob disrupted that culture when he came into our family, however. He told everyone he loved them all the time through his hugs and words—a cycle broken. It would be odd to my children and grandchildren not to verbally express love through that phase now many times a day.

Kim and Matt and my grandchildren have moved to North Carolina for a higher quality of life. They have a new house and a new life, both with new and wonderful jobs and could not be happier. Kim still grieves deeply for her Daddy and keeps his spirit alive with Abby and John. North Carolina, not too far from Kim, is where my beloved niece Kristen and her family also live. Eventually, I will join them all permanently so I can be part of that daily happiness. At some point, I would love Mark to join me. Bob would love that we will be all together!

Mark, although still deeply grieving for his Grandma, is now working as a carpenter's assistant and loving it! The way that he answered a simple employment ad without ever having a lick of experience with carpentry took a great deal of courage. But the real miracle occurred when Pete, his boss, and a master carpenter, hired Mark when nothing logically should have dictated so. When Mark asked him early on why he hired him and why he has kept him when so many more experienced people applied, Pete said it was a combination of his great attitude, dependability, and willingness to learn. Otherwise, Pete said, he really had no idea what led him to hire Mark in the first place. He simply felt led to do so. Of course, I believe this to be divine intervention. It's the only answer I have. He is also volunteering regularly for the Red Cross.

I continue to love my job and speak and write frequently about how nurses can work alongside others to give everyone in America a fair and just opportunity for health and well-being. Every chance I get, I share Bob's and my story and stress the importance of clinicians providing compassionate care and truly prioritizing consumer engagement. I have published articles about Bob's and my experience on the New England Journal of Medicine Catalyst website, the American Journal of Nursing, the Journal of Nursing Administration, and Nurse.com, among others. I include our story in school of nursing commencement addresses that I give each year as well.

My mission to better instill compassion in the care experience has given me my Ikigai—a Japanese word for "reason for being." The reason for waking up in the morning. Each individual's Ikigai is personal and specific to his or her values and beliefs. It is the common ground that takes into account what you love and care about, what the world needs, and how you can earn a living. Speaking and writing about my experience has become part of my Ikigai. My husband's death did not happen in vain, and my mission is to change the care experience for others and to convey to nurses how they can be the best they can be when they take the time to truly connect with patients and their families. I always note the challenges that nurses face in providing compassionate care in a rushed and chaotic environment that is task and technology driven.

I have been humbled and grateful to have been invited into the lives of others who are walking this devastating grief journey. My prayer that I could somehow pay forward the love, compassion, understanding and guidance afforded to me has been answered. In the depths of their sorrow, the most common question grief-stricken people ask me is whether it will ever get better. Will they be able to breathe again? I assure them it will.

I still look for Bob's love, support, and physical presence in so many aspects of my life, but I call upon him in different ways now. I still hate more than anything that Bob and his amazing sense of humor is not with me. Bob always said, "It is what it is," and so I build a re-envisioned life day by day, resetting as I go along.

In one blog, I conveyed how inadequate I felt in attempting to follow in Bob's footsteps. He was larger than life in so many ways, and he gave back to society the same way he gave to our family. One friend conveyed to me that Bob would never want me to be and do everything that he was. His legacy would live on and continue to touch lives and guide us, but each of us who loved him now had our own opportunities to build our own legacies. Kim and Mark call upon the lessons of their Dad nearly every day, but they realize (still with aching hearts), that they must reach within themselves to provide their own light. With Bob and God at my side and in my heart, I must as well. I am grateful. I end with Matthew 5:

15–16, which says, " Neither do people light a lamp and put it under a bowl. Instead they put it on its stand, and it gives light to everyone in the house.[16] In the same way, let your light shine before others, that they may see your good deeds and glorify your Father in heaven."

ABOUT THE AUTHOR

*S*usan Hassmiller is a nationally recognized nurse leader and expert on
nursing and compassionate patient
care. She serves as the Robert Wood Johnson Foundation Senior Adviser for Nursing
and a Senior-Scholar-in-Residence at the
National Academy of Medicine in Washington D.C., helping to lead a national study on
the Future of Nursing. She is also a volunteer
nurse and board member with the American
Red Cross.

She lives in Princeton New Jersey, but
looks forward to moving to North Carolina
to be closer to her young grandchildren, Abby and John. Ballet recitals and soccer
games are in her future. Emails are always welcome at shassmiller@gmail.com and
twitter @suehassmiller.

www.nursesjourney.com

NOTES

1 Tennyson, Alfred. *"In Memoriam A.H.H."* 1849.

2 "From the Corner Office: Dr. Bob Hassmiller, NACAS." *Association Advisor.* November 26, 2012. http://www.associationadviser.com/index.php/from-the-corner-office-dr-bob-hassmiller-nacas/.

3 "Write This Letter to Your Family Before You're Gone." *The Motley Fool.* September 2016. https://www.fool.com/retirement/letter.aspx

4 "Managing Your Wealth, 12.14," Vimeo video posted by Princeton Community Television, 2014, https://vimeo.com/104637798.

5 "If We Could See Inside Other People's Hearts," YouTube video, 4:35, posted by The Cleveland Clinic. May 6, 2013, https://www.youtube.com/watch?v=IQtOgE2s2xI.

6 Kübler-Ross, Elizabeth. *On Grief and Grieving: Finding the Meaning of Grief Through the Five Stages of Loss.* New York: Scribner, 2014 (reprint).

7 Brooks, David. *The Road to Character.* New York: Random House Trade Publisher, 2016 (reprint).

8 *Peter Pan.* Film. United States: Based on book by J.M Barrie, 1957.

9   Milne, A.A. *The House at Pooh Corner.* New York: Dutton Books, 1988 (reissue).

10 *Forrest Gump.* Film. United States: Directed by Robert Zemeckis. Performances by Tom Hanks, Robin Wright, and Gary Sinise. Paramount Pictures, 1994.

11 *The Princess Bride.* Film. United States: Directed by Rob Reiner. Performances by Cary Elwes, Robin Wright, Mandy Patinkin, and Chris Sarandon. Act III Communications, 1987.

12 Baum, L. Frank (Lyman Frank). *The Wonderful Wizard of Oz.* G. M. Hill Co., 1939.

13 Rilke, Ranier Maria. *Letters to a Young Poet.* New York: W. W. Norton & Company, 1993 (revised).

14 Sparks, Nicholas. *The Notebook.* New York: Grand Central Publishing, 2014 (reissue).

15 "Seven Ponds." Accessed June 21, 2019, http://www.sevenponds.com.

16 Hannah, Kirstin. *The Nightingale: A Novel.* Manhattan: St. Martin's Griffin, 2017.

17 Carroll, Lewis. *Alice's Adventures in Wonderland.* New York: MacMillan, 1865.

18 Brown, Brené. "The Power of Vulnerability," video filmed June 2010 in Houston, Texas by TEDxHouston, 20:13, https://www.ted.com/talks/brene_brown_on_vulnerability.

19 Roosevelt, Theodore. *"Citizenship in a Republic."* Speech at the Sorbonne. Paris, France. April 1910.

20 Lin-Manuel, Miranda. "The World Was Wide Enough," Hamilton: The Broadway Musical, 2015.

21 "Steve Jobs' 2005 Stanford Commencement Address," YouTube video, 15:04, posted by Stanford University. March 7, 2008, https://www.youtube.com/watch?v=UF8uR6Z6KLc.

22 Lyrics.com, STANDS4 LLC, 2019. "You Can Close Your Eyes Lyrics." Accessed June 21, 2019. https://www.lyrics.com/lyric/7572312/James+Taylor.

23 Swift, Hildegarde H. *The Little Red Lighthouse and the Great Gray Bridge.* Boston: Houghton Mifflin Harcourt, 2003.

24 Harlow, H. F. & Zimmermann, R. R. "The Development of Affective Responsiveness in Infant Monkeys." *Proceedings of the American Philosophical Society,* 1958.

25 Robert Wood Johnson Foundation. "About RWJF," Accessed June 21, 2019, https://www.rwjf.org/en/about-rwjf.html.

26 McPherson, Miller, Smith-Lovin, Lynn, and Matthew Brashears, "Models and Marginals: Using Survey Evidence to Study Social Networks." American Sociological Review, August 2009. Accessed June 21, 2019, https://doi.org/10.1177/000312240907400409.

27 Dempsey, Christina. *The Antidote to Suffering: How Compassionate Connected Care Can Improve Safety, Quality, and Experience.* New York: McGraw-Hill Education, 2017.

28 Konnikova, Maria. "The Power of Touch." The New Yorker, March 4, 2015. Accessed June 21, 2019. https://www.newyorker.com/science/maria-konnikova/power-touch.

CPSIA information can be obtained
at www.ICGtesting.com
Printed in the USA
BVHW031057030420
576785BV00001B/25